The
Elements
of
Cooking

**TRANSLATING THE CHEF'S CRAFT
FOR EVERY KITCHEN**

Michael Ruhlman

SCRIBNER
New York   London   Toronto   Sydney

SCRIBNER
A Division of Simon & Schuster, Inc.
1230 Avenue of the Americas
New York, NY 10020

First Scribner hardcover edition November 2007

SCRIBNER and design are trademarks of Macmillan Library Reference USA, Inc.,
used under license by Simon & Schuster, the publisher of this work.

For information about special discounts for bulk purchases,
please contact Simon & Schuster Special Sales at
1-800-456-6798 or business@simonandschuster.com

DESIGNED BY ERICH HOBBING

Text set in Adobe Garamond

Manufactured in the United States of America

1   3   5   7   9   10   8   6   4   2

Library of Congress Control Number: 2007014584

ISBN-13: 978-0-7432-9978-7
ISBN-10: 0-7432-9978-7

To Michael Pardus and Thomas Keller
You are great chefs because you are great teachers

The Elements of Cooking

INTRODUCTION

by Anthony Bourdain

It's useful these days when everyone, it seems, has an opinion about food, to know what the hell you're talking about. And, if planning to actually cook seriously, it's advisable, if not compulsory, to know what it is you're doing. Decoding a menu is hard enough since the explosion of food consciousness—with its plethora of culinary terms (often egregiously misused)—but fully understanding a recipe before attacking one's ingredients with a knife, heat, and good intentions is increasingly a necessity. It's no longer acceptable to dump a handful of vegetables and brown rice into a wok, stir them into mush, then invite your friends over and expect them to be grateful. They now know better.

And if you do somehow manage to properly roast a chicken and serve it with a little sauce, it's nice to be able to discuss how, exactly, you did it. Your chicken did not turn brown in the pan by magic. The various elements of your sauce held together for a reason. Others came before you—ruining plenty of similar chickens and sauces before getting it right. Chances are you have learned, explicitly or intuitively, from their mistakes. The mysterious physical forces of the universe, the history and traditions of the human race, and the basic elements of cuisine combine and come into play every time you pick up a knife and begin to cook. There are fundamentals to consider.

The Elements of Cooking is an opinionated food glossary from a writer and cook who knows better than most what the hell he's talking about. Michael Ruhlman is coauthor of *The French Laundry Cookbook* with chef Thomas Keller and of *A Return To Cooking* with chef Eric Ripert, as well as the writer behind an excellent series of books on the training, seasoning, and very soul of chefs. He understands as few others do the basic nature of not just ingredients, but the intangibles in cooking—as well as the kind of motivation, dedication and particular forms of madness it seems to require. If someone is going to hold your hand in the kitchen, you'd find few better qualified than Ruhlman.

It's all here. In much the same way as Strunk and White's classic, *The*

1

Elements of Style, became an essential reference text on every writer and journalist's desk, *The Elements of Cooking* should sit atop every refrigerator. Every bright-eyed and bushy-tailed culinary student should—and likely will—have a copy, rolled up with their knives.

Eight essays on vital, primary concepts like stock, sauce, salt, eggs, heat, and tools . . . and an absolutely rock solid definition of every term professional chefs should know as a matter of course after years of working in professional kitchens; now you will learn them easily and concisely— without burning yourself, cutting yourself, or having your ass kicked in the process. All you have to do is look them up in this book. Every cook— professional or otherwise—who cares about what they are doing, and why, should own this book. It's that simple.

NOTES ON COOKING:
FROM STOCK TO FINESSE

1. STOCK

In the creation of good food, no preparation comes close to matching the power of fresh stock. It's called *le fond,* "the foundation," in the French kitchen for a reason: stock lays the groundwork and will be the support structure for much of what's to come. Stock is the first lesson taught in the kitchens of the best cooking schools *for a reason.* The finest restaurants in the country are making stock all but continuously; were it not for this fact, they would not be the best restaurants in the country.

Ultimately, well-made stock is the ingredient that definitively separates home cooking from the cooking of a professional. There is no way around this fact. Even if you buy the most expensive prepared stocks and enhance them with your own aromatics, the results will never achieve the clarity and lightness of flavor of dishes made with fresh stock.

However, while it's critical to acknowledge the symbiotic relationship between good stock and a good kitchen, there's nothing unfortunate about the fact that few of us will make stock frequently enough to have it always on hand; making stock every other day isn't practical. Two factors mitigating this situation are first, that stock freezes well and second, that stock can be built into your cooking regimen on a semi-regular basis from leftovers and trimmings. And even if you don't take advantage of the freezer or make it a regular, if occasional, part of your routine, it's important every now and then to know how to make a stock, whether for a soup, a sauce, a cooking liquid, or simply for the pleasure of it.

What follows are, first, the benchmarks of preparing an excellent stock and second, the important attributes of the main stocks: chicken, beef, fish, and vegetable. (Veal, the most versatile of all stocks, will be addressed separately on page 7.)

The basics are few and easy: good fresh ingredients and low heat.

Stocks are a distillation of flavor, an extraction by water of the essence of the ingredients. If those ingredients are old, or if they are pale and weak, those qualities will be reflected in the flavor of your stock. Ask yourself: Do these ingredients look good, would they be tasty if I were to cook and eat them as they are? If so, they're suitable for stock. Meat stocks benefit from a good balance of meat (which provides the flavor) and bones and joints (which provide body).

Low heat. It's not enough to say stocks should never boil—ideally, they shouldn't even simmer. Water 170° to 180°F will extract the essence of an ingredient. Agitation from bubbling water can compromise a stock by stirring up fat and other impurities, thus clouding the liquid and compromising its flavor; cooking the meat and vegetables at a simmer tends to overcook their exterior, which will begin to disintegrate before the stock's done, releasing fragments that will soak up your valuable liquid and be discarded after the straining; simmering for extended periods has an oxidizing effect that tends to brutalize and muddy the flavors. Cooking stock at low temperatures requires a little more time, and there are exceptions to the rule, but the benefits of low-and-slow are distinct.

Clarity can refer to two attributes of a stock. The first is its appearance. Is it translucent or opaque? The clearer it is, in most cases, the better the flavor. When you dip a spoon into a white stock, you should be able to see the spoon below the surface; the clearer your view of the spoon, the clearer the stock. With a spoonful of brown stock, you should be able to see the bottom of the spoon clearly; if you can't, it's because the stock is cloudy. Clarity can also refer to taste—if, in a chicken stock, the flavor of chicken is distinct, and you can detect the tomato, the sweetness of the vegetables, and the complexity of aromatics, such as thyme and peppercorns, and if it feels light on the palate, not heavy or sticky, it has a clear, clean taste.

A related issue, and something to be mindful of, is the cooking of the ingredients before the water is added. Water added to raw onions and heated will have a different flavor from water added to onions that have been sweated, which will taste different from water added to onions that have been browned. Brown meat-based stocks are usually made with bones that have been roasted and give stock the roasted aroma that you smell when you pull the bones from the oven. Generally, cooking your ingredients before adding the water deepens the flavor and will make the stock more complex. This is not always desired—sometimes you want the clean sweetness of carrot and onion rather than the complex nuances of caramelization.

Cooking meat stocks. It's best to begin with cold water over the meat and bones (the vegetables and other aromatics should be added toward the end of cooking), and allow the temperature to rise gradually. When the water reaches its cooking temperature—180°F is optimal—skim the stock. If your ingredients were raw, a lot of coagulated blood and protein will be floating on the surface at this point; this, along with any other floating bits and impurities, should be skimmed and discarded. If your ingredients were cooked (blanched bones for a white stock or roasted for a brown), this protein will have already coagulated and so less material will need to be skimmed, but there may still be residual blood and additional fat. This should be removed early while the stock is so dilute, still mostly water.

Skim frequently using a ladle or a large spoon; generally speaking, you can't skim too much, but you do not want to lose stock unnecessarily.

Aromatic vegetables and herbs are critical. The sweet vegetables onion and carrot are most common, as are celery, bay leaf, thyme, parsley, peppercorn, and garlic; avoid simply using any vegetables at hand—you wouldn't want to use turnip or a green pepper as an aromat. Aromatic vegetables, herbs, and spices should be added toward the end. They release their flavors in an hour or less once the stock, cooled by the added ingredients, returns to its cooking temperature; if you cook vegetables too long, they can disintegrate and compromise the stock. Vegetable stocks need an hour or less to cook.

When the stock is done—generally, 1 to 4 hours for chicken, 4 to 6 hours for beef, 8 to 12 for veal, less than an hour for fish, an hour for vegetable—it should be passed first through a strainer or a chinois, then through cloth to remove as many particles as possible.

The stock should then be used or cooled and stored. The faster a stock cools the better for the stock (as for food that is cooked and cooled). Fat should be allowed to rise to the top and either be skimmed off or allowed to congeal for easy removal. Stocks can be cooled rapidly by putting the pot into an ice bath, though this requires a lot of ice and can be impractical. At home, allow the stock to come to room temperature, then refrigerate it until it's chilled, remove the fat, and cover. Alternatively, if you're using the stock throughout the week at home, a stock can be returned to the pot after straining and stay on the stovetop uncovered; the cooking has killed most microbes that might cause spoilage and the convenience of stock at the ready, stock that can be fortified with trim from sweet vegetables and tasty scraps of meat and bones, is appealing for its usefulness and economy.

Stocks will keep well for several days refrigerated and, well stored, for up to two months frozen (longer than that and they begin to pick up the flavors of other food and develop an "off" flavor of their own).

That's all there is to it—good base ingredients, gentle heat for a time appropriate to those ingredients, good aromatics added at the end, an occasional skimming, a straining, and you're good to go. There's nothing like fresh stock and nothing that makes other food so tasty and nourishing.

The salient points on the common stocks:

Chicken: The most common stock because chicken is inexpensive and available and makes an excellent all-purpose liquid. Chicken bones and meat can be used roasted or raw; the carcass from a roasted chicken will make an excellent stock.

Beef: Because the bones of beef result in an unpleasant bone-gelatin flavor, a heavy proportion of meat is the critical component in a good beef stock. Optimally, meaty bones heavy with connective tissue can be used but ground beef works, too. The bones from land animals bigger than chickens are best cooked before they're used for stock to get rid of impurities (such as blood and fat) before the water is added. Bones can be blanched—that is, brought to a complete boil, then strained and thoroughly rinsed under cold water. They can also be roasted, which has a similar "cleaning" effect but will add a complex roasted flavor to the stock that blanching does not.

Fish: Fish stock, also referred to as *fumet* (a word that implies that white wine has been used and reflects the delicacy of the finished liquid), requires the freshest bones from white-fleshed fish treated gently. Aromatic vegetables are first sweated, then the bones are added and sweated, followed by wine and then water. More than for any other stock, it's critical not to allow it to reach a boil. Fish *fumet* requires less than an hour total cooking time and at its peak should be immediately strained and chilled.

Vegetable: Like fish stock, vegetable stock should be cooked gently and briefly. Chefs vary on how they handle vegetable stock—some like to pulverize the vegetables before they add water for quick extraction, some sweat the bejesus out of them. Vegetable stock couldn't be easier at home—use good sweet vegetables, as well as mushrooms for their meaty, brothy effect, and you can't go wrong. It's volatile, though, so it should be made as it's needed or chilled and frozen.

Veal Stock—a personal reflection
on the home cook's most valuable ingredient

Veal stock is distinguished from all other stocks by its neutrality and its gelatin: the meat and bones don't have a strong flavor of their own, and so magnify the flavors of what they're combined with; as they are the bones from a young animal, they contain abundant collagen, which breaks down into the gelatin that creates excellent body in the finished stock.

From such simple material comes not only one of the most exquisite tools in the kitchen, but something more akin to a natural wonder or a great work of art. Few people put veal stock in the same category as, say, the *Goldberg Variations* or Plato's cave allegory, and this lack of understanding amazes me. There's a reason why veal stock is considered the backbone of the finest culinary tradition of the Western world, what many consider to be, in the hands of the right chef, true artistry.

But it's almost never used in the home kitchen, and this is as unfortunate as it is unnecessary. It's no more difficult to make than chicken stock, it's one of the most powerful tools in professional kitchens, one of the biggest guns in the professional chef's entire arsenal, and it's virtually unknown to the home cook. If there is a single ingredient that could transform a cook's repertoire at home, it's veal stock.

Perhaps one reason for its absence in the home kitchen is that most books geared toward the home cook don't offer veal stock recipes. Or they offer recipes for meat stock, not bothering to distinguish between beef, pork, chicken, and veal. Both *Joy of Cooking* and Craig Claiborne's *The New York Times Cookbook,* excellent all-purpose books, contain veal stock recipes without explaining *why* one would make it, as if it were interchangeable with chicken stock. *The New Good Housekeeping Cookbook* contains no recipe, nor does *The Essentials of Cooking,* by the respected author and teacher James Peterson. I'm not sure why this is. Recipes for chicken stock abound in cookbooks and seem not to need a justification. Veal stock is no more difficult to make than any other stock, it's a hundred if not a thousand times more useful, and it's a rarity.

Veal stock is *the* essential. If you could only have *one* preparation in a book of essentials, veal stock would have to be it. In a book with many essentials, veal stock is the only logical choice for the lead-off preparation.

So our cookbook authors don't talk about it and our cooking shows don't much discuss any kind of stock making whatsoever (in the Food Network's 60,000-recipe database, I found a single recipe for veal stock, from Emeril Lagasse, bless him—a traditional brown veal stock like you'd make in cooking school), and our celebrity chefs, if they include a veal stock recipe, tend to bury it in the back of their big beautiful books.

One has to travel all the way back to 1970 to find a cookbook author properly expounding on the notion of veal stock, the American expatriate Richard Olney, living in France, one of the most influential writers on food of his time: "Veal stock," he writes in *The French Menu Cookbook,* "could be likened to an unfinished portrait, its background laid in, the essential volumes and harmonies defined, before the details of particular features are imposed on the abstract structure . . . [I]t is the perfect vehicle for other flavors, lending body and support without altering or obscuring their primitive qualities."

Madeleine Kamman, the French-born cooking teacher and writer, includes a veal stock recipe in her tome, *The New Making of a Cook,* a revision of her 1971 book, and says that "it is very important to use it exclusively for the making of all sauces, be they classic, neoclassic, or modern . . ."

That veal stock today should be so phenomenally underrepresented in all media directed at the home cook during what's considered to be a "food revolution" in America is ironic.

I should here counterbalance what might seem on the surface a sort of veal stock fanaticism of mine. Most cuisines of the world do not rely on veal stock at all. The whole body of vegetarian cuisine, for example, gets along perfectly without veal stock. Asian meat-based stocks rely largely on chicken and pork. Italian cuisine uses it occasionally but on the whole seems relatively indifferent to it. One of America's most innovative chefs, Jean-Georges Vongerichten, a classically trained Frenchman, became well known in chef circles for eschewing veal-stock-based sauces at his restaurant Vong. Judy Rodgers, the Francophile and French-trained chef at the very American, very eccentric Zuni Cafe in San Francisco, includes no veal stock recipe in her *Zuni Cafe Cookbook,* which hews so strictly to the recipes used at the restaurant, her cooks refer to it continually in their daily work. She says she simply hasn't found a good source for veal near her restaurant and so doesn't use veal stock.

But, of course, Vongerichten and Rodgers can work wonders with plain water. *It's the non-pro who stands to gain the most from veal stock, the home cook.* Taking this one item, veal stock, and adding it to your kitchen is like taking the four-cylinder engine of your Mitsubishi and turbo charging it;

with the addition of a turbo, the engine becomes not only faster but more fuel efficient. Veal stock, same thing—it not only makes your food taste better by miles, it makes you more efficient in your efforts at creating delicious food.

Here's how simple using veal stock is. Dice mushrooms, about a cup's worth, and mince a shallot. Have ready a quarter cup of tasty white wine and a cup of veal stock. Get a sauté pan smoking hot over high heat. Add a coating of oil, which should ripple when it hits the pan and begin to smoke. Toss in your mushrooms, let them cook for a few seconds, then stir—the more browning you get the better the flavor—and cook for a minute or so. Add the shallot and cook, add the white wine and continue cooking till it's almost cooked off, then add the veal stock and bring it to a simmer. Add some salt and pepper, stir or swirl in a couple tablespoons of butter, and you have sauce for four portions of a meaty mild fish, such as halibut or cod, or slices of beef tenderloin. This same sauce would be perfect for sautéed veal (add a squeeze of lemon) or pork medallions (add a tablespoon of mustard). If you've salted and cooked your meat properly, the dish will taste better than the fancypants dishes at your favorite French restaurant—rich and mushroomy and meaty, with great body and, from the butter, smooth texture and lusciousness—because it is fresh and made *à la minute,* and because it came from your kitchen. Deglaze the pan you've roasted a chicken in with veal stock and you will soon have an amazing sauce just as it is, or easily enhanced by adding, say, basil, tomato, and olives, or tarragon and chives.

You can do this with chicken stock—you can do this with water, for that matter—but it's not the same.

There's nothing like veal stock. It's a marvel.

None of this is news to a restaurant chef, and any restaurant chef worth his salt could abandon veal stock and make do because they're chefs and have a great range of tools and techniques at their disposal.

But the home cook, limited by time and money and cooking knowledge, ratchets up his or her talent by a factor of ten by making veal stock. Honest to God, it's like magic, like getting your wings.

Making Veal Stock at Home

It's no different than any other stock except for the cooking time, and so no more work than any other stock: roast bones, cook in water 180°F for 8 to 12 hours, add the aromatics, cook for an hour longer, and strain.

Basic Brown Veal Stock

Yield: About 2 quarts finished veal stock

¼ cup vegetable oil
10 pounds meaty veal bones and joints (knuckles, breast, shank),
*   cut into 3- to 4-inch pieces*
4 large carrots, peeled
4 ribs celery
2 large onions, peeled
5 cloves garlic, peeled
¼ cup tomato paste
2 tablespoons peppercorns, cracked
5 stems thyme
5 stems parsley
2 bay leaves

Preheat your oven to 450°F and lightly oil two large sheet or roasting pans. Place the pans in the oven. When the oven and the pans are hot, remove them, and place the meat and bones on them. Make sure they're spread out so they brown as evenly as possible. Roast them for 30 minutes, then turn them and continue roasting for another 15 minutes or until they're appealingly golden brown and smell delicious.

Place the bones in a stock pot. Pour off the fat from the pans, add a couple of cups of water to the pans, place them over high heat, and scrape the brown bits stuck to the pan. Taste this liquid. Sometimes the juices from the bones can burn and make this deglazing liquid bitter—if it's bitter, don't use it. If it tastes good (its flavor will be much milder than its deep color will indicate), add this liquid to the stock pot, then continue to add enough cold water to cover the bones by a couple of inches, about 10 quarts. Bring the water to a simmer, skimming the surface of any fat and impurities that rise. Place the stock pot in the oven and heat it to between 180° and 200°F. Let the stock cook for at least 8 hours and up to 12 hours.

Meanwhile, clean and roughly chop your vegetables. When the bones have cooked for 8 to 10 hours, remove the stock pot from the oven. Add the remaining ingredients. (For an even deeper, richer stock, roast the vegetables and tomato paste till they are slightly caramelized, and then add them to the stock.) Bring the pot back up to a simmer, skimming as necessary, then return the pot to the oven for another 1 to 1½ hours.

Strain the stock through a colander or strainer as soon as it's out of the oven. Strain the stock a second time through a kitchen cloth. Refrigerate the stock. Remove and discard the congealed fat on top of the stock. Use within a week or freeze as necessary.

Issues of Finesse and Variations by Chefs

Veal stock is not only a revelation in itself; how its fundamental premise is varied by chefs reveals much about the flexibility and possible nuances of the stock itself.

As mentioned earlier, Emeril's is as basic as the one above, the kind you learn in culinary school, and describes Emeril's roots as a Johnson & Wales graduate. He caramelizes the vegetables in the classic manner for a complex deep sweetness.

While Judy Rodgers doesn't make a veal stock at her Zuni Cafe because she hasn't sourced good veal in her area (she prefers to keep her sources close to home), she recalls her first encounters with veal stock fondly. It was in a kitchen in Roanne, which happened to be run by Jean and Pierre Troisgros, among the culinary giants in the gastronomic center of the Western world. The year was 1973, Rodgers was sixteen, and she'd just arrived from St. Louis. It was four in the morning and she was offered a ham sandwich prepared by Jean. "We ate standing in his kitchen," she writes in the introduction to her Zuni cookbook, "which was dark and quiet and gave no hint of its legendary status, except for the rich aroma of a veal stock slowly reducing to demi-glace."

She still had the recipe from her notes, which she took assiduously during her stay with the Troisgros family. "At Troisgros," she says, "veal was the mainstay stock." The Troisgros recipe, written in French in the neat rounded script of the sixteen-year-old apprentice, calls for 20 kilograms, about 45 pounds, of bones and a kilogram of pigskin. Pigskin is high in gelatin and adds great body to the stock. Leeks are also included in the basic recipe but no tomato. Rodgers notes that the bones are not roasted ("*pas grillé, innovation de la maison*" she writes; in a footnote at the bottom she notes that chez Troisgros had always roasted the bones, but by chance didn't once and that the resulting stock had a much more natural taste).

Interestingly, Thomas Keller also does not roast the bones for veal stock. Instead the bones and meat are trimmed of as much fat as possible and brought to a boil, then rinsed and cleaned before being re-covered with water, and brought to a simmer.

Keller's kitchens are famous for doing things the hard way and his veal stock is no different. Like the Troisgros brothers, Keller adds both an additional gelatin source, a calf's foot, and leeks. He does not use celery; he believes it makes the stock bitter. He uses a huge amount of tomato paste, which makes his stock very sweet and gives it a pale brown color even though nothing's been roasted. He first simmers the bones and aromatics for about 6 hours. The stock is then strained and quickly chilled. The bones are once again covered with water, then simmered for another 6 hours, strained, and chilled (sometimes referred to as a remouillage). The two stocks—Veal 1 and Veal 2 they're called at the restaurant—are combined and slowly reduced, 16 to 20 quarts down to about 2 quarts.

Perhaps the oddest ingredient variation is Kamman's addition of a bouillon cube.

"You put a Knorr bouillon cube in your stock?!" I exclaimed when she told me this over the phone.

"Yes! I do!" she said.

"You?!"

"Yes, *me*!" She added with a modesty customary among chefs, "In all honesty, I've never tasted sauces like mine."

She explained that the cubes add salt and MSG to the stock, which gives it a greater depth of taste. This seems odd and unnecessary, but cooks are an eccentric bunch.

No matter your variation, the young gelatin-rich bones, combining with the sweetness of the vegetables, creates one of the most extraordinary elixirs in the kitchen and one of the most versatile tools a cook can put at his or her disposal.

2. SAUCE

We tend to think of sauce as something we pour over something else just before serving it, but practically speaking, sauce is any seasoned fat, acid, cooking liquid, juice, plant puree, or combination thereof, that we add to a main ingredient to enhance it, and it's helpful to the cook to think of it in this fundamental way.

Yes, it's the tomato sauce on the pasta, the *beurre noisette* on the sautéed trout, the ketchup on the hamburger, the chocolate on the profiteroles. But the mayonnaise that enriches and binds a tuna salad is its sauce; a quenelle of olive tapenade on a grilled duck breast can serve as its sauce. The vinaigrette is a salad's customary sauce. Braised items help to create their own sauce. A poached egg can get away without having a sauce because it contains its own, but add a spoonful of *beurre blanc* and it becomes an exquisite dish. In a classic chicken chaud-froid (hot-cold), a cooked sauce is spooned over cooked and chilled chicken so that the sauce completely coats, then solidifies on, the chicken—a fancy way to sauce food. Soup is little more than main ingredients in an abundance of sauce. A crème brûlée is in effect nothing more than a seasoned dessert sauce cooked to set the proteins.

Sauce can transform a dish or a meal from good to great but should never call attention to itself—it's always in the service of something else, and as such constitutes an unusual culinary specialty in its own right. This is why in the French *brigade* system, which divides chefs into various departments, the *saucier* is often the most talented cook in the kitchen, the magician and sorcerer. From the beginning of the meal (mustard with the charcuterie platter) through to dessert (ice cream on pie, or raspberry puree with a chocolate torte), there's almost no dish that doesn't benefit from some form of sauce.

From the cook's standpoint, sauce is an idea and a function, and the best are integral to and inseparable from what they accompany. While they can be categorized in several ways, again, they generally fall into one of three categories: stock based, fat based, and plant based (fruit or vegetable).

Stock Refined

The pinnacle of sauce making is reached in the stock-based sauces, not so much because they taste better than any other sauce, but rather because they require the most effort and are distinguished by numerous elements of finesse. And of the stock-based sauces, the brown sauces are at the top of the heap.

Brown sauces are veal-stock based; any meat-and-bones mixture can be roasted and, with caramelized vegetables, make a fine brown sauce, but in the sauce pantheon, the true brown sauces begin with veal stock.

Veal stock was once turned into *espagnole* sauce; that is, it was thickened with a brown roux, and fortified with more caramelized mirepoix. This could be further refined into a classical demi-glace by being combined with more veal stock and reduced. Both brown sauce, the mother mother sauce, and classical demi-glace can be transformed into myriad sauces *à la minute* because they are rich with neutral meat savoriness and vegetable sweetness, and they have already developed an excellent saucelike consistency to add to whatever juices and aromatic vegetables they will enhance.

If even the most timid cook has some *espagnole* on hand, family and friends may think him a genius *saucier,* because any pan he adds it to seems transformed into a magical pan—with some minced shallot, mustard, fresh herbs, and mushrooms, suddenly the plain roasted chicken, the blasé pork loin, or the boring and expensive filet mignon will take on a deliciousness that astonishes, given the small fulcrum of the veal-stock-based mother sauce (which, truth be told, doesn't taste all that appealing on its own—part of its magic).

Any stock can be fortified and prethickened with a roux this way—when it's a white stock (chicken or fish) it's called a velouté—with excellent results, provided you take time to skim the skin off the surface as it forms and the flour cooks out.

Even milk can be thickened this way to make a sauce called béchamel, a concoction of surprising versatility. Here, milk is like a ready-made stock, easily thickened and seasoned to become the base of any number of great cream sauces for pasta, white meat, fish, and vegetables.

Roux-thickened sauces have gotten a bad rap because of their association with heavy antiquated or badly prepared French food. This is too bad because a roux is potentially the most elegant and refined way of thickening a sauce. Stocks thickened only by reduction can feel gluey, and stocks thickened by a pure-starch slurry, such as with cornstarch, can become diluted by the starch and take on a gelatinized-starch texture. A sauce thickened with a roux, one in which the base sauce has been properly cooked and skimmed, has a rich flavor, luxurious body, and a lightness on the palate.

The only problem with roux-thickened sauces is that they require more work. To make a veal stock one day and then further to make a brown sauce from that stock will take up a big chunk of a second day. Because milk is at the ready, béchamel sauce may be the most practical of the roux-thickened sauces for the home cook. For committed cooks, mother sauces and their derivatives are worth doing, as the process contains many lessons for the cook, not least of which are the pleasures of eating a great sauce. Also, mother sauces freeze well, so a big batch can be divided into small quantities for future use.

Practically speaking, any stock can be reduced, fortified with elements of the meal—additional aromatics, bones and meat trim, herbs, seasonings—

to make fine stock-based sauces. Veal is the easiest and most versatile of all the stocks. It can be served as is or thickened with a slurry (cornstarch and water).

Don't ignore water as the fundamental stock and sauce base. No, it doesn't have any flavor or body of its own, but it picks up flavor very quickly and so last minute pan sauces can be fast and easy even if you don't have stock on hand. Water is certainly superior to canned broths. If you roast a chicken in a pan, for instance, you can put together a delicious sauce while it rests using water to create a basic stock and sauce right there. Remove the chicken to a cutting board, pour off excess fat from the pan and reserve any skin stuck to the pan, the wing tips, and the neck, gizzard, and heart if you have roasted them with the chicken. Set the pan over high heat, add a cup of chopped carrots and onion, and cook briefly. Deglaze the pan with white wine and cook it down till the pan is nearly dry, then cover the vegetables and chicken trim with water and cook over high heat. Season with salt and pepper. You will have a flavorful *jus* in a few minutes that can accompany the chicken.

If you have time, let all the water cook off to brown the sugars released into the water from the vegetables, add more water, and cook this down again.

For a more refined sauce, strain it into a small pan, swirl in some butter, some fresh herbs, or some mustard, to further enhance it.

Would such a sauce be deeper and richer if you used a good chicken or veal stock instead of water? Yes. But can you make a good quick sauce without stock? Absolutely, and it will be far superior to one that you made using a store-bought stock or broth instead of water.

Finally, derivative sauces and meat-based sauces are volatile. There's a reason they're finished *à la minute*. If they're made and held, their flavor becomes dull. They need to be completed just before serving for the freshest and most vibrant flavor. Leftover sauce can be reused after it's been refrigerated, but it needs to be refreshed with additional stock and straining.

Fat's Great Transformation: The Emulsified Sauce

Fat is by far the easiest material to transform into sauce because it's virtually a sauce already—it's rich and luxurious at the outset, and all the cook must do is flavor it and adjust its consistency. Consistency is extremely important in fat-based sauces. Canola oil by itself is not enticing, but whip it into a mayonnaise and the consistency alone is appealing. Flavor, which makes the fat distinctive and satisfying, comes from the usual sources: acid, aromatics, spices, and salt.

It's also the easiest sauce to give to a dish. Butter on chicken or steak is excellent by itself, a good olive oil mixes perfectly with the sweetness and acidity of a tomato from the garden.

Butter offers its own category of sauces in what's called compound butter, that is butter flavored with fresh herbs, aromatics, and acid, and put directly on the food. When butter is heated, the solids separate from the clear fat and brown, the flavor deepening into nuttiness; herbs and acid finish it to make a delicious all-purpose sauce.

But when the cook applies some energy and craft to fat, emulsifying it—transforming it from liquid to thickly creamy—sauces of great distinction result, sauces that may be more satisfying than any other category of sauce.

There are two primary fats used for emulsified sauces: oil and butter. Oil emulsifications are mayonnaise or mayonnaise variants. When the fat is butter, the result is referred to as an emulsified butter sauce, such as hollandaise. Both use egg yolk as the means for emulsifying a lot of fat into a little bit of water. For mayonnaise-style sauces, oil is whipped into raw egg yolk (and a few drops of water and/or citrus juice and seasoning). For emulsified butter sauces, the egg yolk mixture is cooked and the butter (clarified or whole) is then whipped into the egg mixture.

The ratios for both are fairly standard though they can be varied according to your tastes and style. For mayonnaise, use one yolk for each cup of oil. For butter sauces, the classical ratio is three yolks for eight ounces of butter (though the extra eggs are more for texture and richness than for the emulsification).

The principles are mainly the same. For a mayonnaise, the liquid (lemon juice and water) is combined with salt so that the salt melts; this is combined with the yolk, then the oil is whipped in, at first drop by drop as the emulsion is formed, then in a thin steady stream as you whisk continuously. For the butter sauces, a reduction is used to flavor the sauce; a mixture of aromatic herbs, vegetables, spices, salt, and acid (vinegar and/or wine) are cooked and strained; this liquid is combined with the yolks in a pan or a bowl. The yolks are put over heat (typically a hot water bath to avoid overcooking the yolks) and are whipped as they cook. When they are cooked and foamy from whipping, the butter is slowly whipped in. The sauce can be finished with fresh herbs and aromatics.

Emulsified butter sauces and mayonnaises are delicious with all manner of meat, fish, shellfish, vegetables, and eggs. Mayonnaises, such as the garlic–olive oil aïoli, are especially good with meats, shellfish, and vegetables that are served cold.

There's also a kind of eggless emulsified butter sauce that takes advantage of the fact that whole butter is already an emulsification of water, solids, and fat. Aromatic vegetables such as shallots or onions are cooked with wine till the liquid is reduced, then the butter is whipped in piece by piece. These sauces, called *beurre blanc* or *beurre rouge* depending on the wine used, are very easy and quick to make.

Likewise, there is an eggless oil-based sauce, heavily reliant on acid—the emulsified vinaigrette. Salt and mustard season one part vinegar, then three parts oil are mixed in. Because mustard has some emulsifying power, a stable emulsion can be achieved, though one that's considerably looser than a mayonnaise. This is easiest to make using the power of a blender but an emulsified vinaigrette can be made the same way as mayonnaise.

Contemporary Sauces

American cooking has evolved dramatically during the past decade. So has the way we think about food. The definition of sauce is not relegated to those special preparations to spoon over meat and vegetables but instead should be described as a kind of continuum of flavor and texture that can range from solid (a compound butter) to waterlike (a *nage*) depending on the food it's meant to elevate. A puree of tomatoes, cooked, has long been one of the main sauces, considered to be a mother sauce, but any vegetable puree can serve as a sauce.

An asparagus sauce—asparagus cooked, shocked, pureed, then seasoned with salt and lemon and enriched with butter as it's reheated—is every bit as satisfying as a butter sauce on a white fish. It can be highly refined, thinned by straining or served thick and substantial.

What you are doing is simply transforming the consistency of the ingredient to turn it into a sauce. You are cooking the asparagus as you would if you were planning to serve it whole, right down to the salt, butter, and lemon juice. You can do this with any vegetable. Likewise, most fruits can be cooked, pureed, and strained for delicious dessert sauces.

Such preparations can be taken even further—they can be served as soup. In contemporary cooking often the line between soup and sauce is completely blurred. Broths can function as sauces, for meat and fish; vinaigrettes can be used like classical sauces, vegetable juices can be transformed into sauce. The definition of sauce is ever expanding.

As Americans travel more and American restaurant culture grows increasingly diverse, we are becoming familiar with a range of sauces from other cultures—Asian dipping sauces (based on fermented soybeans and fish, which represent a whole new category), South American chimichurri (in effect a vinaigrette-soaked herb sauce), to Mexican moles and Asian curries (often using pureed peppers, seeds, and nuts for flavor and body).

There's no end to the world of sauces but they're very easy to organize in your mind when you're thinking about what sauce to combine with tonight's dish. Indeed, sauce isn't about anything more than flavor and seasoning. When you're adding a sauce to a dish, you're not doing anything more complex than seasoning it. Just as you season a dish with salt, not so that you can taste the salt, but to enhance the dish. Think of sauce as an elaborate form of salt. Which of course is what the word sauce means and derives from. Salt.

3. SALT

I remember clearly the moment I heard it—a bright Saturday afternoon, on the phone, seated at my desk in our old house. The truth of the news struck me like a spike. I was working with Thomas Keller on the proposal for what would become *The French Laundry Cookbook*. Relatively new to the world of professional cooking, I asked, "What's the most important thing for a cook to know in your kitchen?"

He paused, then said, "Seasoning."

"What do you mean, seasoning?"

"Salt and pepper." He paused again. "Salt, really."

"The most important thing for a cook to know is how to salt food?"

"That's right," he said.

The truth of it would only deepen as I continued to explore the craft of cooking. It is true not just for cooks in professional kitchens, but for all cooks in all kitchens, everywhere: learning to salt food properly is the most important skill you can possess.

No surprise, then, that salting food is one of the first things taught in culinary school. When my instructor judged my soup to be flat he told me to take out a ladleful and salt it, then compare the two. This would help me to understand what he called "the effect of salt," he said. You don't want to taste salt in the food—that means it's been oversalted. You want it to taste seasoned—meaning that it has an appropriate depth of flavor and balance, is not pale or insipid. Same with the water you boil pasta in. Before culinary school, I'd salted pasta water by putting a pinch into a giant pot of water. I don't know what I thought that was going to do—if I'd given it even two seconds of consideration, I'd have had to conclude that the salt had absolutely no effect. My instructor explained that our pasta water should taste like properly seasoned soup. This would ensure perfectly seasoned pasta. Or rice, for that matter.

We learned to "season as you go"—that is, salt your food throughout the cooking process because food salted at the beginning of or during the cooking tasted different from food salted just before it was served. The former tasted seasoned; the latter tasted salted.

So even from the outset of learning to cook properly I had discovered that I wasn't doing one of the most routine kitchen acts, salting food correctly. Keller said it was one of the first things they taught new cooks at The French Laundry. I scarcely thought about it—salt had been an *afterthought.* That's what the salt shaker on the table's for, right?

Wrong. How to salt food. It's the most important skill you can have.

After my conversation with Keller nearly ten years ago, I paid a lot of attention to salt and how people used it. I also listened to the ubiquitous health warnings about the overconsumption of salt. I even wound up writing a book largely about salting food, *Charcuterie: The Craft of Salting, Smoking and Curing.*

Judy Rodgers was the first chef I knew to address this matter head-on in her *Zuni Cafe Cookbook.* Common wisdom had always been that if you salted food early, it dried the food out. Looks that way. Salt a steak and a few hours later it's sitting in a puddle of red juices. But in fact the perpetual osmotic effect of salt enhances juiciness by changing the cell structure so that it holds more moisture. Salt also *enhances* the flavor of the meat by thoroughly penetrating it. And it dissolves the sticky protein myosin, so that in ground preparations—hamburger, sausage—the meat holds together.

Rodgers urges cooks to salt food early. The bigger the food is, the more salt it needs, and the more time with the salt that it needs. This is uniformly important with meat, but less so with fish; some fish is delicious after it's been packed in salt (salmon or cod) but some flesh is so delicate the salt can damage it if used too early. And it can even be true of vegetables. Vegetables with large watery cells are enhanced by early salting, such as onions, eggplant, peppers.

Rodgers learned about salt from French mentors for whom salt was not simply a seasoning. To them salt was, she writes, "the thing that keeps you from starving." Indeed, salt's role as humankind's all-purpose preserver of food—allowing for a surplus of food, food that could serve as a basis for an economy, food that could feed crews on ships during extended explorations—makes it one of the most influential substances on earth.

Salt should never be an afterthought.

Salt and your health:

Salt is so critical to our health that we have developed an extraordinary capacity for tasting it—in order to regulate it. When we eat natural foods, that is unprocessed foods or processed foods containing only a few ingredients, we can use as much or as little salt as tastes good to us and do so without health concerns. Salt has become a problem in this country because we rely on heavily processed food (food that comes in boxes and plastic bags), which is infused with salt we don't necessarily detect, and we can easily consume far more than our body needs.

Some people have problems with high blood pressure and hypertension and must restrict salt intake. But generally speaking, salt is not bad for you. If you eat a lot of processed food, salt might be a problem, along with other health concerns. If you are healthy and eat good food, you should feel free to salt food to levels that taste good.

How to salt food:

There are only a few dictates when using salt. Use kosher salt, which is both economical and available everywhere, or sea salt, or another specialty salt if you wish. Never use iodized salt (iodide deficiency is no longer a problem in this country). Salt early in the cooking process, whether seasoning meat or seasoning a soup. Taste your food continually throughout the cooking and season it appropriately as you go.

Salting meat:

Most meat can be salted as soon as you get it, regardless of when you intend to cook it. Salting meat as early as possible not only allows the salt to distribute itself throughout the meat, it keeps the meat fresher. Salt prohibits the growth of microbes responsible for food's going bad.

Ironically, you need to be careful about salting creatures that lived in salt-water. Some fish is so delicate salt crystals will "burn" the flesh rather than distribute itself through it (scallops are a good example; they should be seasoned shortly before cooking).

Salting water:

There are two levels of salted water. Heavily salted water is used for boiling green vegetables and anything else that is not going to absorb a lot of the water. Moderately salted water, water that simply tastes seasoned, is used for rehydrating foods, such as pasta, rice, and legumes. See salted water in the glossary for recommended quantities.

Brines:

Brine—salt dispersed throughout a very dense medium—is an extremely effective salt delivery system, infusing food uniformly, predictably, and quickly. A good ratio for a brine is between six and eight ounces of salt per gallon of water; the stronger it is, the faster it works. The water can also be infused with aromatic vegetables, herbs, and spices; the salt helps to carry this flavor into the meat. Food that has been brined benefits from resting outside the brine before it's cooked so that the salt concentration, heavier at the exterior, equalizes throughout the meat (not dissimilar from allowing meat to rest after it comes out of the oven).

Preserving with salt:

Just about anything can be preserved with salt—meat, fish, vegetables, and fruit—with varying results in terms of quality and culinary uses. Pork is the meat most often preserved because it tastes so good. You *can* preserve beef tenderloin but why would you? Better to preserve a beef brisket (called corned beef, or, if smoked and spiced, pastrami).

Food can be preserved in dry salt. Bacon, salt cod, and duck breast are items typically cured this way. And it can be cured in a brine—Canadian bacon (pork loin), beef brisket, and vegetables. And some food starts out in a dry cure but releases so much liquid, a brine is created—salmon, cabbage (sauerkraut).

Even a sprinkling of salt, as if you were simply seasoning the food, has curing effects. Meat can be dredged in salt and left to cure. As much as a cup of salt per gallon will make a good curing brine. For natural pickles, that is a pickle that creates its own acid through fermentation, a precise 50 grams of salt per liter of water is perfect (a little less than 2 ounces, about a quarter cup of Morton's kosher salt, per quart).

All food behaves a little differently in salt. Ultimately you have to pay attention. Taste. Remember. Salt, taste, remember. Learn your own salt levels in cooking. Put a little soup or stock in a bowl and salt it, then compare the salted against the unsalted. Taste an unsalted tomato, then taste it with salt. Teach yourself about the effects of salt.

4. THE EGG

My reverence for the egg borders on religious devotion. It is the perfect food—an inexpensive package, dense with nutrients and exquisitely flavored, that's both easily and simply prepared but that is also capable of unmatched versatility in the kitchen. Yes, an egg is just an egg, but it is also ingredient, tool, and object, a natural construction of near mystical proportions.

The egg is both nutritious and inexpensive. The egg is delicious served on its own. In combination with other ingredients, it can be even better. It adds flavor and richness to countless preparations, to others, texture and body. The egg is a versatile tool that transforms the consistencies of other ingredients: it can give liquids silkiness, turn oil into a sauce that has the luxurious, dense smoothness of a face cream, make chocolate fluffy and cream molten, turn a batter from liquid into a light solid sponge. It can be used whole or separated; the white and the yolk behave with unique and powerful properties of their own, either raw or cooked, and *when* cooked, cooked to any number of degrees. Even its shell can be used. And as an aesthetic object, considered for its design, the egg is artful and, except for its propensity to roll off counters, efficient.

Eggs are appropriate to serve at any time of day for any meal. They can be the main item or the garnish, they can be served simply, in rustic preparations, but they are equally suited to four-star cuisine. No other ingredient has so many uses and effects. The egg is a wonder.

Mastering the use of eggs is a worthwhile accomplishment for the aspiring cook and a requirement for the aspiring professional. If you could choose just one ingredient to have absolute expertise in, understanding it, knowing all its uses, being able to intuit its vagaries, the egg would be your best choice: perfecting egg technique elevates your abilities as a cook more than perfecting the use of any other single food item.

The Egg Breakdown

Cooked whole, as is:

Commonly, the egg is cooked whole and as such can be a featured item at breakfast, lunch, dinner, or as a midmorning, midafternoon, or midnight repast. The following are notes on the various applications of heat usefully deployed on whole eggs:

Poached: Poaching in water that's just barely at a simmer is arguably the best way to cook an egg whole. The temperature is gentle and so keeps the egg tender. (Do we ever pause to consider how lucky it is that it's the white and not the yolk that sets first? Easy to take for granted, but it would be a different culinary universe if they set at the same time.) The cooking medium doesn't impart its own flavor, nor does the heat brown the protein and thus introduce new flavors, so the flavor of a poached egg is unadulterated, elegant egg.

An egg white has two different consistencies; part of it is loose, watery, and part is dense, viscous. Crack an egg on a plate and you can see the different textures. When you gently ease an egg into hot water, the loose white congeals into useless shreds, while the dense part of the white congeals appealingly around the yolk. Many cookbooks recommend that the water be acidulated to help prevent the flyaway white from forming; I've never been able to see the difference between eggs cooked in vinegar-spiked water and plain water, and the acidic water needs to be rinsed off after cooking, so adding acid to your poaching water is not recommended. Fresh eggs tend to have a greater proportion of the dense white than factory eggs, and this does make a big difference in the size and appearance of your finished poach.

Harold McGee, in noting the egg white disparity, offers this excellent recommendation for making prettier poached eggs (and when done properly, they're very beautiful to look at, which is part of the fun of cooking and serving them). Crack the egg into a ramekin. Pour the egg from the ramekin into a large perforated spoon and briefly allow the loose white to drain off, then return the egg to the ramekin to proceed with the poaching. This greatly reduces the amount of flyaway white.

Poached eggs should be cooked just until the white is set, and no longer, removed with a slotted spoon, allowed to shed the excess water, and served immediately. Alternatively, they may be moved from the pot to an ice bath until thoroughly chilled and can be easily reheated as needed within a day or so (an excellent strategy when serving numerous people).

Fried: Fried eggs are delicious, in part because the high heat partially browns the egg white, which gives it additional flavors. You can alter the flavor of the egg with the fat you use—olive oil, for instance, or whole or clarified butter, rather than neutral vegetable oil.

Cooking fried eggs can be tricky. When you use a plain steel pan, the cooking surface must be immaculate, you must use plenty of oil, and the pan must be very, very hot—fail in any of these requirements and the egg will stick. Nonstick pans are most convenient and allow you to cook the egg at lower temperatures, and they are more easily flipped for over-easy. To avoid flipping but to ensure that the white is set, the pan can be covered and removed from the heat to finish cooking. A well-seasoned cast iron pan is a good choice for frying eggs.

Hard-cooked: Hard-cooked or hard-boiled eggs have numerous culinary uses, whether as a convenient nutritious snack, chopped and tossed with a yolk-emulsified sauce (aka egg salad), or as garnish. There's also the clever deviled egg, a technique that cooks the egg, separates the white and yolk, and then puts the egg back together in more tasty and elegant form.

When hard cooking eggs, it's important to stop their cooking when they are done to prevent the yolk's turning a drab, sulfur-smelling green. The yolk of a properly hard-cooked egg is a uniform, sunny yellow. To achieve this effect, place the eggs you're cooking in a single layer in a pan and cover them with about 2 inches of cold water. Bring the water to a boil, remove from the heat, cover the pot, and set a timer for 12 minutes (some books recommend a shorter time, others a longer time—the time can vary depending on the size of the eggs and the number of the eggs, but 12 minutes is a good starting point; observe your eggs and make adjustments accordingly). Remove to an ice bath and chill thoroughly. Some people like to crack the eggs as they go into the ice bath, which facilitates peeling them and may also reduce the chance of the yolk's discoloring. If you're going to be peeling them right away, this is advisable.

Baked: Eggs can be baked in two satisfying ways, shirred and coddled. These eggs are served as individual items, not as garnish. To make a shirred egg, crack the egg or eggs into a buttered ramekin and cook over medium-low heat until the bottom is set. Finish the egg in a 350°F oven for a few minutes. Customarily a little cream is poured on top (and perhaps some Parmigiano-Reggiano or whole butter) to enrich the dish and mollify the heat.

While some refer to coddling as boiling eggs in their shell for a couple of minutes, a coddled egg can also refer to an egg cooked in a ramekin or container, covered, in a water bath, like a custard. This can then be seasoned with a flavorful fat such as butter or an excellent olive oil.

One specialized whole-egg preparation should be noted—preserved eggs. Eggs can be preserved with salt and with vinegar. Eggs that have been hard-cooked can be pickled in an acidic liquid. And salt-cured eggs are part of some Asian culinary traditions, of which the "thousand-year-old egg" is an example.

It should be noted that in addition to being great items on their own, eggs cooked whole this way are excellent garnishes. Most are familiar with hard-cooked egg chopped or sliced and served in salad. But a fried egg on a salad is excellent; a poached egg on a salad is a classic French custom. A fried egg on a ham and cheese sandwich can't be beat. It's an excellent sandwich ingredient on almost any sandwich, in fact. A whole egg dropped into piping hot soup is almost never a bad idea. A poached egg used as a garnish for steamed asparagus (and a nice *beurre blanc*) would make an elegant appetizer-sized course or light lunch. When in doubt in the kitchen, look to the egg, it will rarely fail you.

Cooking eggs whole but blended, free-form (scrambled eggs) or structured (omelet):

After the chicken breast, scrambled eggs are probably the most overcooked item in America (followed by the pork chop). Properly scrambled eggs are moist, delicate, glistening; they should even have a liquidy element to them, as if they've been lightly sauced.

Begin by combining the eggs completely, whipping with whisk or fork until no clear white can be seen. The egg mixture should be uniform in color and texture.

As a rule, eggs always respond better to gentle heat—high heat makes them rubbery and dry. If you use a nonstick pan, eggs can be scrambled over low heat in butter. The more stirring you do, the finer the curd; curd size is a matter of taste.

If you don't have a nonstick pan, or a well-seasoned iron pan, you may need to use a higher heat to prevent the egg from sticking and browning; if this is the case, you'll need to start them on the high heat, shaking the pan and stirring as soon as the eggs are in the pan, and then finish them off the heat, stirring continuously.

For an omelet, eggs are scrambled—continuously stirred—at the outset to achieve fine curd, allowed to set, then rolled from the pan. A seasoned pan or nonstick pan is helpful; using a clean steel pan is a little more tricky, in which case the same rules apply as for scrambled eggs in a steel pan. Omelets should be a uniform bright pale yellow, not browned, very moist, not dry. Omelets can contain cheese or cooked vegetables, though they shouldn't be overstuffed; when using cooked vegetables, make sure these are very hot so that they may finish cooking the egg after it's rolled. An omelet can be given a lovely sheen by finishing it with a bit of soft whole butter on top.

A thoroughly whisked egg can also be poached to interesting and tasty effect. Simply add it to barely simmering water until it's cooked, then strain it, and season with salt, pepper, and butter.

The egg, separated:

Separated, egg whites and yolks are rarely cooked on their own. Whites are sometimes deep-fried into Styrofoam-like chips, and some people eat omelets made with whites only (why anyone would, I've yet to fathom). Egg whites, sweetened and whipped to peaks, can top a lemon pie (among numerous other dishes); this meringue is typically colored by being browned briefly in the oven but the egg white is raw.

Raw eggs can be used to great effect, in eggnog, for instance—the liquid is enriched with raw yolk, sweet fluffy meringue is folded in. A raw egg can fortify a milkshake with flavor and nutrition. But raw whites are not delicious on their own. Yolks, on the other hand, are; they're delicious as a garnish on just about anything. The yolk is like a ready-made sauce—on a hamburger, grilled steak, or raw tartare.

A note about eating raw eggs. Factory chickens, that is battery chickens caged indoors in the tens of thousands in long coops, can be crawling with salmonella and other bugs, so it's not a good idea to serve these raw or even poached if you need to be careful (if you're serving the very young or very old). It is always advisable to use organic eggs or eggs from pasture-raised chickens when serving them whole with a runny or raw yolk, or when using a raw yolk, as for a mayonnaise. It's worth the extra expense from a health standpoint, flavor standpoint, chicken standpoint, and environmental standpoint.

The egg as tool:

Eggs are so gentle and delicate in flavor that they pair beautifully with countless meats, vegetables, and grains. A custard (milk or cream and egg) alone is wonderful, but a custard can also hold other things, as in a quiche Lorraine, bacon and onion suspended in the smooth concoction that sets delicately when gently cooked; other preparations—frittatas, soufflés, egg salad, French toast, not to mention their many uses as a garnish—describe felicitous ways the egg joins other ingredients.

But perhaps the most important topic in the study of the egg is its use as a tool. It can enrich, thicken, emulsify, leaven, clarify, and even color.

Whipped egg can be brushed on pastries and doughs to create deep and appealing golden brown color under heat. Egg whites when added to a cold cloudy stock will, when that stock is heated, form a net that clarifies the stock as it congeals and rises to the surface. Egg shells have routinely been added to stocks being clarified, though most chefs who use them are rarely aware why this may be more than a chef's myth; in fact, some food science experts believe the alkalinity that shells add to a stock enhances the egg white's capacity to clarify.

Egg yolks will become thick when whipped over gentle heat, and thicken the liquids that contain them, resulting in such preparations as zabaglione and lemon curd, savory sauces, puddings, and custards to be turned into ice cream.

Another egg yolk technique is called a *liaison*—cream and yolk are combined and added, typically, to a stew to enrich it (but it has negligible thickening powers).

The most dramatic uses of the egg as a tool, though, and the yolk and the white perhaps vie for supremacy in their separate effects, are to emulsify and to leaven.

The egg yolk's capacity to turn clear oil into an opaque, solid cream results in some of the most pleasurable sauces known. The yolk is the linchpin of hollandaise, béarnaise, mayonnaise, and aïoli, sauces whose very presence transforms (often upstages) the meat or vegetable it accompanies.

An emulsion happens when oil is mechanically split into infinitesimal orbs that remain separated by continuous sheets of liquid; the lack of movement and the many bonds created make the oil both stiff and opaque. When the orbs break through these sheets and combine into one big mass, collapsing into soup, the sauce is broken. The molecule responsible for keeping these miniscule orbs from coalescing with their brethren is called lecithin, which is half oil soluble and half water soluble; it embeds half of itself into an oil droplet, while the other half remains in the water "phase" of the emulsion, preventing other miniscule orbs from connecting and coalescing and amassing and breaking the sauce.

The result of a properly emulsified sauce is a lesson in the power of texture to convey flavor and pleasure. A good hollandaise, or a fresh mayonnaise, is a thing of beauty. A broken hollandaise is not. A broken mayonnaise cannot be served. The emulsified sauce is first about texture; combined with a great flavor, whether it's simply lemon juice, or garlic and basil, or tarragon, shallot, and vinegar, the pleasure of an emulsified sauce is unmatched by any other sauce, indeed by most foods period.

Traditionally, clarified butter is used for the emulsified butter sauces, and this does result in a very elegant flavor, but whole butter (itself an emulsion) can be used as well. For a neutrally flavored sauce, mayonnaise, which is seasoned with salt and lemon juice, or a fresh vegetable or canola oil should be used. For aïoli, some olive oil. If you want to make an emulsified vinaigrette that is very stable, an egg yolk can be added. The freshness of the fat is critical—if you use old oil or rancid olive oil, the off flavors become magnified. Always use the freshest best-tasting fat possible. And the fat need not be relegated to one of these three, either. The egg yolk can turn any clear fat into an unctuous pleasure. To an egg yolk mixed with a reduction of minced shallot and wine vinegar, for example, one might whisk in clear warm bacon fat for a bacon-shallot emulsion that can be served atop a poached egg.

The consistency of the emulsified sauce—whether a béarnaise sauce or an aïoli—should be as stiff as mayonnaise. Unless you don't want it to be that stiff. It can easily be thinned with water or cream. If you fold whipped cream into an emulsified butter sauce it's referred to as a mousseline.

Egg white's capacity to contain countless miniature air bubbles (a mirror image perhaps of egg yolk's capacity to separate oil in countless miniature droplets) allows it to leaven many preparations, whether raw (as with a mousse), or cooked (everything from soufflés, both savory and sweet, to sponge cakes). This egg-as-leavener has even more uses than the yolk does as an emulsifier, and is more widely used.

*   *   *

The eggless kitchen is difficult to imagine. Eggs are everywhere in cooking, in myriad forms. It's important to acknowledge and understand the powers of the egg. I said above that the egg will rarely fail you; a more complete expression of the same idea is this: you will fail it more often than it fails you, and the more capable you are with the egg, the more capable a cook you will become.

5. HEAT

The ability to control the temperature of food involves a set of kitchen skills and food knowledge that, more than anything else, defines the excellence of the cook. An expertise in temperature control won't turn poor ingredients into good ones, but it will determine much of what follows once the ingredients are in your house. Only the ability to use salt (see page 18) has an impact of a similar magnitude on food.

The notion of temperature control refers not just to *cooking* food—high temperature sautéeing, low-temperature poaching, et cetera—but also to the temperature at which food is stored, what its temperature is when it begins cooking, the temperature of the vessel into which the food is placed, the temperature at which the food is removed from the heat, how long it sits after cooking, and the temperature at which it's served. All are critical components of temperature control.

While cooking is the most varied and complex of the subcategories of temperature control, the before and after phases of it are important to acknowledge. Why do we refrigerate food? It's helpful to think about this question exactly, to know why cold food lasts longer. Some foods and many beverages taste better cold, but most food does not. Almost always the main reason we refrigerate food is because the cold temperature dramatically slows the growth of bacteria that makes food go bad. Why is it better to thaw frozen foods in the refrigerator rather than at room temperature? Because left for hours at room temperature, the exterior of the frozen food will be well above refrigerated temperature while the center is still frozen, a situation that encourages microbial growth; if you thaw food in the refrigerator, all of the food stays below 40°F during the thawing. How critical a health issue is this? Depends on the food and how quickly you need something thawed (to thaw food outside the refrigerator, common restaurant pratice is to thaw it in a container under a thin stream of cold water—water speeds the process but maintains a low temperature). Other foods, such as tomatoes, are compromised by the cold temperatures and should never be put in a refrigerator.

Another critical issue of temperature that doesn't involve the stove is the temperature of the food when it begins to cook. Meats will cook much more evenly if they don't go into the oven or pan straight from the fridge and freezing cold; so for whole cuts of meat that don't require hours and hours of cooking, it's useful to allow them to temper for a time appropriate to their size. The larger the cut of meat, the more important this tempering phase is; a thin cutlet will cook pretty much the same whether it's cold or at room temperature. A boned leg of lamb that goes from the refrigerator into the oven will inevitably be overcooked on the outside, and undercooked at the center; you'll get what's sometimes referred to as the bulls-eye effect—a pink center surrounded by a gray ring.

In other words, if you don't treat the meat appropriately *prior* to cooking it, you doom yourself to imperfection even before you turn on the heat.

At the other end of the spectrum—after the cooking—the way you handle temperature is important to consider. Has the leg of lamb (or the roasted chicken) been allowed to rest so that the temperatures even out and juices distribute themselves within the muscle? Has the green vegetable been shocked in ice water to preserve its fresh flavor and vivid color? Is the plate—on which you're putting the hot food—cold? Are you serving very hot food on a very hot day? These are all issues of temperature that are important to the ultimate effect of the food, from its healthfulness to its appearance to its flavor to the pleasure of eating it.

The most dramatic control of temperature is in the cooking. In culinary schools and culinary school texts, cooking, the application of heat, is broken down into three categories: dry heat, moist heat, and a combination of the two. This is in effect defining cooking relative to an absolute—the boiling point of water. So another way of describing these categories is "above 212 degrees," "below 212 degrees," and a little of both.

The reason for this above- or below-boiling distinction is, first, that food behaves dramatically differently on either side of the divide. Also, the composition of the food determines the type of heat you must use. Foods that are naturally tender and don't require a long time in the heat to break down tough connective tissue typically benefit from high heat, temperatures at which sugars and proteins brown, adding additional flavor and texture. Tough pieces of meat benefit from a long cooking time and so to avoid overcooking them and drying them out you must cook them in a flavorful liquid. Cooking in a liquid ensures a low even temperature, whether the food is submerged in the liquid or a vessel is placed in a hot water bath. Tender items that don't need browning can also be cooked in liquid, which is a very gentle form of heat used for delicate items, such as fish and vegetables and eggs. And sometimes we use both temperature zones, first browning tough meat, veal shank for instance, to develop an appealing color and flavor, and then tenderizing it by long slow simmering in liquid.

Dry-heat cooking, cooking at high temperatures, is divided into two subcategories: with fat (deep-frying, pan-frying, sautéeing) and without fat (roasting, grilling, and broiling), but I don't know that this is a particularly meaningful distinction. What is more important to address is the heat level. Cooking oils will reach about 450°F before they start to smoke and begin to break down and sometimes you want that heat, which will evaporate the surface liquid of food so that sugars and proteins brown and become tasty and crisp. (Remember, if there's liquid in the pan, if the piece of meat is wet, for instance, the water will cool down the fat and no browning will be possible until it's evaporated.) You want to roast a chicken in a very hot oven, to ensure a crisp, golden brown skin. But high heat cooking has little tenderizing effect, so only meats that are tender to begin with should be cooked at this temperature. A thick piece of bacon, on the other hand, which requires time to render its fat and to become tender, should be sautéed over much lower heat. If you want to cook vegetables without browning them, a technique often called "sweating," a low dry-heat temperature is also required. Deep-frying is best done at around 350°F, moderate heat, hot enough to make the outside golden brown and crisp, but not so hot that it will burn the extrerior before the interior is cooked through. So there are many levels of "dry" heat, and which one you choose depends on what needs to happen to the food you're cooking.

Likewise, roasting and grilling can be done in low, moderate, and high temperatures, choices the cook makes based primarily on how large and how tender the item is that's being roasted or grilled and what its final internal temperature will be.

Moist-heat cooking means at or well below water's boiling point. As with dry-heat cooking, there are subcategories that are important to distinguish: deep-poaching, shallow poaching, stewing, steaming, and boiling.

Deep-poaching is a method in which the food being cooked is completely submerged in some kind of stock, often a court bouillon, a quickly made stock flavored with sweet aromatics and acid, and gently cooked. To poach, the water should not be boiling—usually a temperature of around 190°F is optimal—just before the liquid simmers. Salmon is commonly cooked this way, so is beef (as in a *pot au feu*), whole chickens (*poule au pot*), and eggs.

Shallow poaching is a technique often used for flat white fish and its main advantage beyond gentle cooking is that the cooking liquid becomes the sauce.

There will be no browning in these methods, which is fine for delicately flavored meats. You could poach a pork tenderloin, for instance, but you wouldn't, because the meat would be gray and unappetizing and would lack the browning flavors that enhance the mild flavor.

Poaching is performed quickly on tender food. Stewing is in effect long-term poaching. Items that require hours of gentle heat—some tough meats, dried legumes—are stewed in a flavorful liquid until they're tender. This can be done on the stovetop but it's most consistently achieved in a low oven, 300°F or less. Chunks of tough veal that have been blanched are sometimes stewed in beef stock to make what is called a *blanquette de veau*, and tough birds are often stewed. Stewing is a method used for items that are not browned. If the items are browned first, the method is called a braise (in the third category of heat). Also, some chefs distinguish stew from braise by the size the main item is cut into—a pot roast is a braise but if the meat is diced, it becomes a beef stew.

Steaming is a moist-heat method used when you don't want the cooking medium to affect the flavor of what's being cooked, such as with vegetables and fish. Steam is hotter than boiling water, but it's not nearly as dense and so doesn't cook quite as efficiently as boiling water, but this can be an advantage: it's much more gentle than boiling water for especially delicate items (dumplings, for instance); it's excellent for reheating foods; and it will keep food moist without saturating it.

Boiling is used for foods such as vegetables that must be cooked quickly in moist heat (it's distinguished from poaching by the heat level; again, poaching is done below the boiling point). Boiling, the technique, should almost never be used, with the exception of green vegetables and pasta. Very few food items benefit from the agitation of boiling. Boiling will fray tender food, and in stocks, soups, and sauces it will emulsify impurities into the liquid.

The third form of cooking combines both moist heat and dry heat, and most commonly refers to braising. For tough cuts of meat that benefit from browning, we brown first, then cook them gently in stock until they're tender, then use the cooking liquid, defatted, as the sauce or the base for the sauce.

Classic braises include beef *bourguignonne* and osso bucco. Chunks of beef or thick cuts of veal shank are seasoned and floured, then browned in sizzling hot fat till they have a gorgeous aromatic crust. They are then combined with stock, just to cover, brought to a very gentle simmer, and placed in a low oven and cooked till they're fork tender—that is, the meat gives no resistance to the tines of a fork. The meat is then cooled in the cooking liquid so that it reabsorbs some of that liquid; fat that congeals on the surface is removed and the meat and liquid are reheated.

Vegetables can be braised. A bulb of fennel might be halved, floured, and sautéed to give it an appealing color and additional flavors, then cooked until tender in stock. Fish aren't usually braised; braising implies tenderizing by low slow heat. But anything browned first, then finished in liquid, such as a sausage that's finished in sauerkraut or beer, or a chicken breast that's browned and finished in its sauce, can reasonably be called braised.

Braising is the quintessence of efficient cooking. It requires inexpensive cuts of meat; as the stock cooks it, it enriches the stock, which becomes the sauce, and through the craftsmanship of temperature control—high heat to sear and develop flavor, low heat to tenderize—the inexpensive or common piece of meat is made exquisite.

There are, in addition to dry heat, moist heat, and combination cooking methods, a few specialty forms of cooking.

One of those is poaching in fat, and because fat and flavor are all but one and the same, it's a favorite method among chefs. Very dense fat, usually a flavorful animal fat, will also cook foods very slowly and gently, but also contribute great flavor to the food being cooked, whether it's cooked relatively quickly—a white fish such as cod or halibut—or for hour and hours, as with a confit. For confits, meat (usually duck or pork) is first cured for a day with salt and seasoning, then poached in fat until tender, then cooled within that fat. Confit not only results in great flavors and melting textures, it is also a form of preserving the meat—confited meat will keep for months inside the fat. Butter poaching is also a popular form of cooking meat and fish. Fat's density conducts heat efficiently; the poaching temperature ensures gentle cooking.

Cooking with acid is a popular method for some tender fish, fluke or snapper, for instance. Some fish that can be eaten raw are tossed with an acid, typically lime juice, which in a way cooks the exterior of the fish (the proteins denature and the flesh becomes opaque), and flavors it, a technique called seviche.

Another special cooking method, a new development in cooking, really, relative to, say, cooking over open flames or in an enclosed heated box, is called sous vide, French for under vacuum. Food is sealed in a plastic pouch and cooked in low-temperature water (as low as 130°F) for extended periods, sometimes days. Developed in France for commercial food preparation, it has been embraced by restaurant chefs because it provides new flavors and luxurious textures, and is also an efficient form of cooking and holding foods for service in restaurants. But the method can be used in the home as well. Sous vide techniques can mimic the effects of braising but require less stock, can mimic the effects of confiting but require less fat. Lean tender pieces of fish can remain that way cooked sous vide, and many vegetables and fruits can be cooked well using the unique qualities of cooking under vacuum.

And the last specialty "cooking" method, one of the oldest, uses salt and evaporation instead of heat—it's called curing. Some ham and sausages and fish never go above room temperature before they hit the plate, and yet are not only safe to eat, but delicious as well. A ham may be salted for several weeks, then hung to dry—the salt and evaporation makes the interior of the meat inhospitable to microbes that would cause spoilage and also changes the flavor and texture; a sausage may be stuffed and hung to dry while a live bacterial culture within feeds on sugars and generates acid that both protects the sausage from harmful microbes and adds an appealing flavor. The nature of fish is such that salmon can be cured in as little as a day when packed in salt, then rinsed and sliced and eaten.

We categorize qualities and intensities of heat in order to think clearly about food and its cooking. Defining heat this way forces us to think about the composition of food. A chicken breast doesn't have a lot of flavor on its own, so you want to give it as much flavor as possible, first by using high heat (sauté for a golden brown sear, or grill so that it will pick up flavor from the flame and the smoke). A chicken breast is tender to begin with and so high heat is appropriate. For a lamb shank, which is very tough, we need high heat first to create flavor and color and texture, and then we tenderize it with moist (low) heat. This way of thinking about food relative to the form of heat you intend to give it applies at every level of cooking.

6. TOOLS

I'll assume if you're reading this that you already have a good amount of kitchen equipment, but I'd like to imagine the kitchen as a white box with nothing more than a stove, fridge, countertop, and sink—not a single other element used for cooking in it—and then to pose a hypothetical question: if you were asked to outfit the kitchen with as few items as possible, the absolute minimum you could possibly get away with and still be able to cook most things, what would those items be? Answer this well and you've discovered the tools that can be considered the true fundamental cooking tools; and it logically follows that here is where you should put your money and buy the very best quality, forgoing all manner of gadgetry and convenience-making appliances.

And by minimally outfitted, I'm not talking twenty or thirty items or even ten. I'm talking count-them-on-one-hand.

I could outfit a kitchen—a hot kitchen, not a pastry kitchen, because baking requires a broader range of fundamental tools—with five items and do virtually anything I needed. The output would be limited, but on the other hand, there's nothing I wouldn't be able to improvise on (I wouldn't be able to make waffles given my list, for example, but I would be able to make a similar batter preparation if that's what the day called for).

The five items are these, in order of importance, but really, take any one away and you are all but out of commission as a cook.

- Chef's knife
- Large cutting board
- Large sauté pan
- Flat-edged wood spoon
- Large nonreactive heatproof bowl (ideally Pyrex)

Put this hypothetical question to any chef, how to outfit a kitchen with five items or fewer, and their list is going to look pretty much the same.

What does this mean? It means that if you have these items, but they are cheap, flimsy, or compromised in any way, you are crippled. Therefore, these are the items you must have in your kitchen and it only follows that you should be sure to have chosen the *best quality* of each that you can afford. You don't need a seven-piece set of second-tier pans, you need two really good ones.

What I intend to do here is to describe these essentials in terms of the three categories represented by the list above—cutlery, cookware, and utensils—and then broaden out from recommended essential tools for your kitchen to the increasingly less essential tools.

Cutlery

A cook needs two knives made of high-carbon, stainless steel, a chef's knife—a long, broad all-purpose knife, usually about 1¾ inches wide and 8 to 12 inches long—and a paring knife. All other knives are nonessentials. That's not to say other knives don't have their uses, only that a cook should be able to perform all kitchen tasks with a big knife and a little one. A boning knife, a slicing knife with a flexible blade, a serrated knife, these can make various tasks easier, but again, they are not essential. Because a chef's knife and a paring knife are essential, you should own the very best you can afford and you should keep them, as M.F.K. Fisher would say, "sharp as lightning." Therefore, own and know how to use a steel as well, that long bar at the end of a handle that usually comes in the center of your fancy seven-piece deluxe set. This thing does not sharpen a knife; if you drag your knife's edge along it at the proper angle (about 20 degrees), it will straighten and align the microscopic teeth that form a sharp blade. It takes some practice, so do it slowly at first till you feel comfortable. Have your knives professionally sharpened once or even twice a year.

Choose additional knives according to what you do most. A serrated knife is really the only knife you should cut bread with, so a serrated knife can be important. If you fillet a lot of fish, a knife with a thin flexible blade comes in handy. A tournée knife, which has an inverse curve to facilitate controlled cuts, is helpful for shaping vegetables. Utility knives come in various shapes and sizes—some will feel more comfortable and useful to you than others. Determine your knife needs beyond the chef's and paring knives according to what and how you cook. But spend your money on the essentials—there's no good reason to buy a whole set of fancy expensive knives. Those sets are a marketing ploy by knife manufacturers designed to get you to buy more knives than you need.

In addition to knives, you need to have something to cut on: a large wood or hard-rubber cutting board, the bigger and heavier, the better. Under no circumstances use a cutting board that is harder than the edge of your knife, such as, say, an extra piece of your new granite countertop, or even very hard plastic (astonishingly, these are widely available). Wood is the preferred material for its all-round utility, appearance, and feel. Keep your board clean with very hot water and soap and allow it to dry completely and you won't have a problem with bacteria; some people worry about this, and if you are among them, keep a small container of bleach under the sink (manufacturers suggest a ratio of about one ounce bleach to four cups water, mixed fresh each time) and wipe your board down with a solution to ensure that it's sterile after cutting your chicken. Additional cutting boards of varying sizes are convenient, but not essential.

Cookware

The essential pots and pans:

Two heavy-gauge, stainless steel sauté pans, one large, one small, with metal handles. A large, heavy-gauge stainless steel pot that holds between 6 and 8 quarts, and a small one that holds between 1½ and 2 quarts. These should have lids and no plastic parts so that they can be used in the oven.

The heavier the gauge, the more even the heat and, just as important, the less heat you'll lose when you put cold food into it. A cheap pan will lose a lot of heat, so the cold food will stick and not brown properly. It's really hard to sauté well in a cheap pan. Your heavy-gauge steel pans should be your default pans. You should not reach for a nonstick pan first (I'll get to this in a moment), rather you should learn to heat your steel pan properly. Buy professional quality pans, which are widely available. Do not buy pans with plastic handles or handles of any material that can't get really hot; as often as not, you'll want to put your sauté pan in a hot oven.

That's it for pots and pans, those four are all you need forever.

Optional pots and pans:

There is of course a seemingly infinite variety of pots and pans, all kinds of shapes and sizes, and if you do a lot of cooking and need to have a lot of items on the stovetop, you're going to make use of this variety. If you have the four essential pots and pans, you don't need them, but they come in handy, such as a small saucepan for cooking or finishing very small quantities. A medium sauté pan gives you more options depending on what you're cooking—you don't want to cook small items in a large sauté pan. A *sautoir* is a shallow pan with straight sides and a lid and has many uses, from sautéing to braising. A *sauteuse* is the name for what we think of as a traditional sauté pan, one with sloping sides.

Special pots and pans:

Cast iron pans are highly recommended. These are outstanding if you maintain them properly (and maintaining them properly basically means never washing them with soap). They're inexpensive, heavy, will keep a virtually nonstick surface, and can take a serious beating (or even give one!).

Cast iron enamel is also highly recommended, an excellent cooking material and the best choice for many forms of cooking, especially braising. They are very heavy and so stay hot. Their surface allows browning but is virtually nonstick. They can be used on top of or in the oven. And they're attractive. A cast iron enamel Dutch oven—pot and lid—is likewise highly recommended and has many uses.

Nonstick pans: buy a very good one and treat it like royalty. There are few cooking tools more useless than a *cheap* nonstick pan. Furthermore, they tend to scratch easily, and once they're scratched, they aren't nonstick anymore, they're simply cheap. Avoid inexpensive nonstick pans and the people who sell them. Indeed, be wary of all nonstick pans. Even the best should be limited to special uses. When you do need a nonstick pan, you want a good one that has been well maintained. The problem with even the best nonstick pans is that they make it difficult to develop a fond on your food or in your pan, that very tasty browning of proteins.

Nonstick pans should be used not simply when you don't want something to stick (you almost never want food to stick to a cooking surface, but this does not mean you should always use a nonstick pan), but rather when you need to cook something gently; at gentle temperatures, some foods stick in a steel pan. If you want to cook eggs gently, for instance, you need a nonstick pan. Delicate fish in a really hot pan may not stick, but it may overcook; delicate fish in a medium hot steel pan may cook perfectly, but it may also stick, so for this, you choose a nonstick pan.

A very large pot for making big quantities of stock is valuable for those who make stock often.

Copper pots and pans can be good cooking vessels, but they are expensive and require diligent cleaning to maintain their luster.

Steamer inserts can come in handy. Don't buy a double boiler—mixing bowls set over pots of simmering water work just as well. Special cookware devices can be fun but aren't necessary. A wok is a good cooking device. A tagine can be used with good effects (but use the earthenware kind, not the steel imitations).

Additional cookware in a properly outfitted kitchen:

At least one heavy-gauge sheet pan or baking sheet. The heavy gauge will ensure even cooking; the flimsy sheet pans tend to burn food. (Avoid putting a hot sheet pan under cold water to ensure that your sheet maintains a flat surface.)

A good roasting pan comes in handy but a good sheet pan accomplishes most of the same things.

A well-stocked kitchen should have a couple sizes of baking dishes and mixing bowls. Pyrex is an excellent material for these, though not essential.

All other cookware decisions—a marmite, a jelly roll pan, pie plate, bread pan—need to be made by the cook.

Utensils

Beside the stove:

Wood spoons, sturdy tongs, a perforated spoon, a solid spoon, a 2-ounce and a 4- or 8-ounce ladle, a sauce whip and a balloon whip, a nonstick spatula, a metal spatula, a small offset spatula, a fine mesh strainer, a small container of tasting spoons, a pepper mill that grinds finely. And something to grab hot things with. Home cooks typically use pot holders for this, but these thick square mats can feel awkward to me. There's a reason chefs don't use pot holders. Chefs use side towels. I recommend finding high-quality side towels for the home kitchen because of their versatility and ease of use. They can also be tucked into a belt so that they're always with you.

In your drawers and on the shelves:

A digital instant read thermometer, digital scale, digital timer, metal measuring spoons (buy a good set, not a cheap one), measuring cups (both Pyrex liquid measures and dry measures), a rolling pin, a pastry brush, rubber spatula, a vegetable peeler, a set of ramekins (for cooking in and for *mise en place*), a Microplane grater, a waiter's corkscrew (sometimes referred to as a wine key), a grater, plastic storage containers.

Other items that are not strictly necessary but can come in handy and are recommended: a ricer or food mill, Benriner mandoline, mortar and pestle, garlic press, and meat pounder.

Recommended appliances:

A standing mixer, food processor, standing blender, hand blender, coffee mill for grinding spices, microwave oven.

Unnecessary tools, or tools no self-respecting chef would be caught dead with:

As a rule, any tool that has only one use should be avoided: examples include the shrimp deveiner, cherry pitter, hand crank fruit peeler, special slicers for butter, eggs, avocado, mango, et cetera. Also be wary of buying sets of anything; figure what you need, and buy that.

A well-outfitted kitchen is defined by its efficiency and by the quality of those tools that make it efficient. The fanciest kitchens with the most beautiful pots, pans, and appliances I've found to be the least used kitchens and therefore the worst kitchens. I hope the kitchen as status symbol is a short-lived phenomenon.

7. SOURCES AND ACKNOWLEDGMENTS: (FIFTEEN GOOD BOOKS ABOUT FOOD AND COOKING)

Much of the information in this book is a direct result of learning to cook at the CIA and continuing to cook and to hang out in kitchens, simply keeping my net in the water and then writing books about food and cooking later. Most of it is common knowledge to professional cooks and chefs, though many of the opinions and nuances of phrasing are endlessly debatable.

But there were a few books without which I couldn't have written this one, or without which this book would be direly incomplete. What follows is a list of the fifteen books that were literally by my side as I wrote, a description of them, and the reasons why I continue to find them such valuable resources in a world flooded with good books about food and cooking (see bibliography, page 245). I include the list here among the essays,

rather than as an appendix, because it's not only important to describe and credit sources, but because there's much to be learned from my personal list, which is by no means complete or definitive. It's eccentric, and in that eccentricity the good cook might take something useful away from a discussion of what I believe are the basic texts, just as I learn from the eccentricities of others, rather than from the conventional choices and beliefs.

Of the fifteen books stacked and scattered on the desk and the floor to my left, two books were invaluable, the ones I relied on with the most frequency. They were by far the most influential in terms of my completing this book, and without them it would be considerably diminished: The CIA's *The Professional Chef* and Harold McGee's revised and updated *On Food and Cooking: The Science and Lore of the Kitchen* (2004).

I'll begin with McGee's book because it's the most important book about food and cooking ever written, probably in any language, probably that ever will be, at least in my lifetime. It's difficult to imagine a book that could surpass it.

From a purely informational standpoint, *On Food and Cooking* has both astonishing breadth *and* depth. McGee, who was born in 1951 in a Chicago suburb and now lives in Palo Alto, California, describes virtually the whole of the food world, beginning with milk and dairy products, continuing on with eggs, meat, fish, shellfish, edible plants (fruits and vegetables) and plants we use for flavor (herbs, spices, and those for beverages), seeds, two major branches of food preparations—doughs/batters and sauces—then on to sugars and sweets, alcohols, cooking materials and methods, and concluding with a primer in basic chemistry and the fundamental makeup of food. The book is neither perfect nor complete (no book could be), but the authority McGee brings to both the big topics and the most minor details is unparalleled, and the clarity of his prose makes it accessible to all.

Harold McGee was the first writer to tackle questions of food science for the nonscientist. He is the forefather of a whole genre of food-science writing, and remains the ultimate word on all things relating to the reason food behaves as it does. At food conferences he passes through the crowd like the town rabbi.

Much of his influence comes not from his work in the library stacks but from his work as an original and compelling writer—he has a distinctive literary voice and he brings extraordinary balance and wisdom to his work, qualities that allow him to put this wealth of information into perspective. He has degrees in science from California Institute of Technology and in

literature from Yale, and he brings both disciplines to bear on his work. In addition to the facts about cream, for instance, percentages of fat, how the fat is dispersed in globules far larger than those in milk, pasteurization temperatures, and the like, there is also this: "We value cream above all for its feel. Creaminess is a remarkable consistency, perfectly balanced between solidity and fluidity, between persistence and evanescence. It's substantial, yet smooth and seamless. It lingers in the mouth, yet offers no resistance to teeth or tongue, nor becomes mealy or greasy." Sound like a scientist? Poet-scientist, more like. And all this aside, I know him to be a man of great personal generosity and kindness.

In this book few texts other than McGee's are directly cited because so much of what he's done is original. "See McGee" appears numerous times, referring you to this book for complete and detailed information on chemical reactions and diagrams. I also note when I used information from his book that I could find nowhere else as easily—the melting point of collagen in red meat, say—or simply used information that was interesting, such as the fact that a covered pot in a hot oven is about 20°F hotter than an uncovered pot. I've always observed that liquid in a covered pot was hotter, but I'd never gone to the trouble to measure the difference. McGee did. McGee's gone to a lot of trouble. His book is a treasure trove of such details, and I've strived to make clear when and where I've relied on his work alone.

The second of the two books I relied on most heavily for reference is *The Professional Chef,* created by a fleet of chefs, writers, and photographers at the Culinary Institute of America, the country's most influential culinary school, who have amassed, organized, and put into perspective decades of culinary expertise. Part of my affection for this book, or this series of them—I own the fifth (1991), seventh (2002), and eighth (2006) editions, which have shown successive growth, the eighth being longer by 25 percent, at more than 1,200 pages, than the fifth—is that the fifth edition was my first cooking text, my guide through the basics at that school. (I was a journalist there, not a cook, but I did learn to cook, and I was awarded an honorary degree in 2006; so while I'm not affiliated with the institution, I remain very much a part of it.)

I continue to refer to *The Pro Chef* for information about the fundamental preparations and methods upon which all cooking is based, and recommend it to all students of cooking, both vocational and avocational. This is precisely why I find it so valuable. It's all about the fundamentals of cooking, from *mise en place,* to stocks to sauces to soups, to various forms of pro-

tein and vegetable cookery, baking, and pastry. If I want to check the specifics of the foaming method or the ratio for *pâte à choux,* this is the book I turn to first.

I still prefer my fifth edition to the later ones because it hews more directly to the fundamentals, whereas the most recent versions are more stylish, seem to have more recipes, perhaps in an effort to be more attractive to the home cook as well as the culinary student and chef, which I think distracts from attention to the fundamentals; but they've enlarged the books to encompass a culinary landscape that is quickly expanding, with discussions of international cuisines, and American regional cuisine. Their basic stocks—chicken, veal, fish, court bouillon—also now includes *brodo,* Italian for broth, and using poultry and red meat, and dashi, a Japanese stock made from seaweed and bonito flakes, neither of which is even mentioned in my trusty fifth edition, let alone given "fundamental preparation" status.

But again, *The Pro Chef* remains valuable not because it has a recipe for dashi or curried goat with green papaya salsa, but rather for its focus on the fundamental preparations and basic ratios that make up all of cooking regardless of country or region, the essence of cooking.

The CIA has published numerous excellent books, including the pastry counterpart to *The Pro Chef* called *Baking and Pastry: Mastering the Art and Craft,* which is also included in the fifteen by my side.

The culinary fundamentals, without which nothing, according to August Escoffier, *nothing,* mind you, can be accomplished, are endlessly fascinating. These are the books that I returned to again and again for reference and comparison. Escoffier's 1903 *Le Guide Culinaire,* was published in English as *The Complete Guide to the Art of Modern Cookery.* This book is not only a great reference, it's an excellent tool for the young cook; it's valuable to see what's changed and what hasn't and what has returned in terms of technique; it's also a valuable resource in terms of flavor pairings; generally it is a bountiful book of ideas.

My favorite book about fundamental preparations for a broader audience is Jacques Pepin's *La Technique.* Published in 1976, it inspired numerous young cooks who would become renowned chefs. And it's still an enormously valuable tool for the cook, not to mention a fascinating description of classic French dishes, such as ham in aspic and *vol-au-vent à l'ancienne.* That, and its followup, *La Methode,* were both at my side; happily they were republished in paperback in a single volume, *Jacques Pepin's Complete Techniques.*

I didn't use it often here, but Julia Child's *Mastering the Art of French Cooking* was right there, too. I just love to look at it.

From an American point of view, I kept *Joy of Cooking* there, too, the 1997 revision, called *The All New All Purpose Joy of Cooking,* because from a cooking basics perspective, it's the best of the volumes out there, relying on numerous experts in the field who each weigh in on their specialty. (The newest one, 2006, returns casseroles to the index, a telling revision.)

Every now and then, I'd check in with *The New Best Recipe,* by the indefatigable folks at *Cook's Illustrated.* This is a useful basics book because they get down to serious brass tacks with regard to why this basic method (whether a custard or a crust or a sponge cake) worked best and what variations they tried in coming to their conclusions. It's the cookbook I bought for my daughter, then age nine, because I wanted her to have a home-cook-friendly book that also paid attention to and took the trouble to describe the whys of their recipes.

The main culinary reference books I used, in the order of frequency of use, were *Food Lover's Companion,* by Sharon Tyler Herbst, *The Oxford Companion to Food,* by Alan Davidson, and *Larousse Gastronomique.*

Herbst's book is an invaluable dictionary of cooking terms and food items, and was re-published in 2007 as *The New Food Lover's Companion.* I used this book mainly as a backup and double-checking device as opposed to a source of information, but I reached for it continuously throughout each day of writing. I recommend this book not so much for the home cook; while it defines cooking terms, other basic cookbooks do a more complete job, and that's not really its purpose; its intent is to be a general reference, a dictionary providing accurate objective descriptions of all things culinary, from abalone to zwieback, and in this it succeeds beautifully.

Davidson's encyclopedia is an extraordinary work of culinary scholarship. If anything I tried to avoid using this book to check information because every time I opened it, I'd end up reading for a half hour, unable to pull myself from the elegant and fascinating text.

Larousse, of course, is the traditional culinary encyclopedia first published in 1938 (this was part of my parents' culinary library, the entirety of which totaled something like four cookbooks in all). It's a great source for all things classically French.

Eric Ziebold, a Washington, D.C., chef I met when he was a sous at The French Laundry, stumbled across a pocket-sized soft-cover reference called *The A-Z of French Food.* It defines in English hundreds of French cooking and food terms. Eric knew the book would be useful, so he bought several copies for the restaurant, one of which I feel very lucky to have procured.

Marcella Hazan's compilation, *Essentials of Classic Italian Cooking*, was the default reference for all things Italian.

And last, two chef cookbooks I found consistently valuable. First, *The French Laundry Cookbook*. This is a celebrity-chef coffee-table monster, filled with exquisite photography and impossibly involved recipes that nonetheless is a cookbook bestseller. While the bulk of this book is high-end chef recipes for elaborate dishes, it's one of the best books there is on a great restaurant's basics. (I wrote the text.)

And *The Zuni Cafe Cookbook*, which is the distillation of the cooking career of a talented and articulate chef, Judy Rodgers. I've yet to encounter a chef who is more observant about the way food behaves and then able to convey it in words. The book is filled with recipes from the eponymous San Francisco restaurant, but I used it for referencing fundamental cooking techniques and observations about them. Rodgers's convictions about cooking are a delight to read.

And, of course, my paperback copy of Strunk and White's *The Elements of Style*, which I purchased in high school for $2.75, the inspiration for this book and an inspiration generally in my writing life.

8. FINESSE: THE COOK'S FINEST CHALLENGE AND PATH TO THE ULTIMATE REWARDS

Everyone who enters or leaves the kitchen at the Manhattan restaurant Per Se passes by the definition of finesse. It's not just posted or framed on the wall. It's written on the tile—it's part of the wall:

> fi-nesse (fe nes') *n.* refinement and delicacy of performance, execution or artisanship.

The wall of The French Laundry features the same words. It's a reminder from the chef never to lose sight of what is, in his mind, the most important element of cooking. When he signs his book, his customary words are "It's all about finesse."

If my understanding of the fundamentals of cooking began with Michael Pardus in Skill Development I at the Culinary Institute of America, my understanding of the value of perfecting those fundamentals began with Keller at The French Laundry in the summer of 1997. Keller didn't use the word finesse back then but he practiced its ethic. I'm not sure when or where he chanced upon the word and realized that it, more than any other, described his objective in his craft, but it is explicit now in many ways. For those who cook to earn their daily bread, for those who cook in the service of others, for those who have mastered the fundamentals of their craft, finesse becomes the ultimate compulsion.

The idea of finesse is simple, but the practice takes knowledge, thought, care, and stamina. In cooking, the concept rests on a conviction that paying attention to a few small details in any given preparation has an enormous impact on the finished dish and is the final gratification for the cook in his or her pursuit of excellence; the level to which the cook attends to these details describes the finesse of the cook.

Take one of the basic preparations of the kitchen, a proper veal stock. Finesse has nothing to do with gathering the right ingredients; doing that, making sure they're good ingredients, fresh aromats, making sure you have the appropriate amount of meat and bones, et cetera, that's a given. Finesse is understanding what steps in a veal stock's preparation will make it the best rather than good. In the pursuit of finesse, okay is not okay. Indeed, the finesse elements can be defined as the steps that will result in a *superlative* veal stock rather than an excellent one.

The finesse elements in a veal stock are these: preparation of the bones, cooking temperature, adding the aromatic vegetables at the appropriate time, and fat removal. Other steps in the preparation are important—duration of the cooking, straining, reducing it to the proper strength—but they are either ones of personal taste or are part of the obvious fundamentals (as opposed to the perfecting of those fundamentals). Choosing a good mixture of fresh bones with plenty of connective tissue (resulting in gelatin and therefore body in the stock) and plenty of meat (for flavor) is an obvious fundamental. If you don't do that, no amount of finesse can help you. But preparing the bones is not an obvious fundamental.

If you are making a traditional brown stock, you must roast the bones properly—which means putting them in the right-sized pan so that they aren't crowded; if they're crowded, they will steam and you will have a lot of gray coagulated protein forming and no browning, and you will not develop a fond in your pan. Well-roasted bones should be attractively browned and should smell as appealing as a roasted rack of veal. If you are making a white (non-roasted) veal stock, finesse dictates that you wash the bones, removing any fat first, then clean them by bringing them to a boil to get rid of the blood and impurities that would compromise a stock were you simply to remove them by skimming, then strain and rinse them thoroughly.

Temperature: you want to cook your bones at below-simmering temperatures, between 160° and 190°F. Cooking your stock at temperatures that result in bubbling water will churn up fat and impurities and emulsify them into the stock, resulting in a fatty, cloudy stock.

Add the aromatic vegetables at the end; they release all their flavors in a half hour to an hour after the stock has resumed its temperature. If you cook them too long, they begin to disintegrate, compromising the stock and reducing your yield (the particles caught in your strainer are like sponges soaked with valuable stock).

The final finesse element is the removal of fat, also called degreasing. Fat and impurities should be skimmed continually throughout the process of making the stock. After it's strained, fat should once again be removed either by skimming or chilling the stock so that the fat congeals on top and is easily removed. Any fat remaining in the stock will be emulsified into the stock when you reduce it.

These points are what I say are the finesse elements of veal stock (and they more or less apply to all stocks), but I wouldn't say they are the only ones or that they are absolute.

Judy Rodgers, for instance, would say that one of the keys to great stock is to strain the stock as soon as it is cooked perfectly. Don't let the finished stock sit there cooling on the stove because you've got other things to do. "Get it off the bones," Judy says. This makes good intuitive sense.

Finesse has nothing to do with expensive food or haute cuisine preparations. Scrambled eggs have equally critical finesse elements: low heat (so that they will be tender and moist), proper fat (butter). Do you want to make scrambled eggs with *fines herbes* and a little cream? Excellent idea, but that's a matter of taste.

The excellence of a humble custard, whether in a savory quiche or a sweet crème brûlée, is its texture—a voluptuous, silken creaminess. So the finesse elements for a custard are not the ratio of egg to cream or whatever else you might be adding to the custard for flavor, but rather those steps of the preparation that work toward a perfect texture, the first of which is simply to acknowledge what is the primary goal in creating a custard, followed by the application of gentle heat and a careful monitoring of its doneness to achieve that goal.

For sauté, finesse means salting your meat far enough in advance that it melts and does not come off in the pan, heating the pan to the right temperature before you add the meat, and making sure the surface of the meat is free of excess moisture before you lay it in the pan, followed by monitoring the heat.

But finesse has an important secondary meaning, beyond that of perfecting fundamentals: it can also refer to the extra effort that puts something beyond the edge of excellence. In a braise—searing floured meat in hot fat first, then simmering gently in a flavorful liquid—the finesse elements are to get a good sear, a beautiful golden brown crust, and to do this you need the right-sized pan so that the pieces are not crowded, and second, to cook them enough that the meat is fork tender but not so much that they will be dried out. But here, the secondary element of finesse might be to make a flavorful marinade for the meat before searing it.

If you are marinating with wine, the finesse element would be to cook the wine with aromats first to reduce the high concentration of alcohol, to infuse the liquid with the sweetness of the vegetables and herbs, and to intensify the fruit flavor of the wine. Another element of finesse might be clarifying the marinade by cooking it, straining it, and using it as additional flavor in the sauce.

But cooking your wine marinade takes forethought and time, time both to cook and then to chill it before you can use it, and then, later, preparing it afterward, heating it gently so that the proteins coagulate and help to clarify the wine, then straining it and, depending on what you've marinated, using this wine to begin a sauce or adding it to the *cuisson,* the cooking liquid. Do you really need to go to all this trouble?

Of course not. Not if you don't want to. Don't give it another thought.

The Berkeley, California, wine merchant, wine authority, and author, Kermit Lynch, hoping to get a better handle on the word finesse as it applied to wine—for the French use it often, as they do the word *terroir*—wrote to his friend Lulu Peyraud, proprietress of the Provençal vineyard Domaine Tempier. He wrote in his company newsletter, "I had trouble understanding Lulu's response until I realized that she was defining finesse in human rather than wine terms." He quotes her: "Finesse is the opposite of coarseness or crudeness. It is a light touch as opposed to heavy-handedness. It is spirituality, subtlety, and intelligence, from which comes an aptitude for knowledge and deeper understanding. It is also a matter of sensibility, of perceptiveness combined with a great deal of delicacy in regard to emotions and feelings."

I'd like to underscore two observations in Madame Peyraud's elegant description as they relate to cooking. Finesse is the opposite of coarseness. It is close in meaning to its root, fine. You can feel the difference. A sanded, oil-rubbed piece of cherrywood versus a split log; a puree that is grainy on the palate versus one that is perfectly smooth.

But as with everything there are implications in that fineness, both for the person enjoying it and the person who has prepared it. Fineness—refinement and delicacy—has an impact on those who encounter it. No matter the form. I've written about excellence both in the kitchen and outside it. Finesse is an expression of excellence, and whether that finesse is in art, in craft, in business, or in medicine, its effects are parallel. My first experience eating the new American *haute cuisine* at its highest level helped me to see the work of the chef and the world in general more clearly. The surgeon who ensures that his or her stitches, in repairing a baby's heart, are spaced perfectly uniformly so that the stress on the tissues is uniform, is expressing a degree of finesse that has life or death implications. Finesse should not be considered a flourish, an extra final step, but rather something fundamental in our actions.

The second point is that the practice of finesse results in knowledge for the person putting it to use. The exertions required for finesse are not expended but rather transformed; struggling hard to achieve finesse does not leave us spent and empty, it fills us. A builder of wooden boats is a different creature from one who builds fiberglass boats. A surgeon for whom finesse is second nature understands the human body and healing and decay with more depth and clarity than the surgeon who has no sense of finesse. The cook who cares as much about peeling asparagus as he does about making a beautiful finished plate will have a greater understanding of, and appreciation for, the work of the professional kitchen and what it means to serve people than the cook who is only focused on the end result.

If anything, that's what *The Elements of Cooking* is all about: an effort to appreciate the power and importance of finesse.

THE ELEMENTS OF COOKING
A TO Z

A

Acid: Acid's power as a seasoning device is second only to salt. Typically in the form of vinegar or lemon (but often any number of other juices), acid adds brightness and balance to the flavor of a dish. While acid has wide-ranging effects on food (it slows browning in cut apples and artichokes, turns greens brown, intensifies the red in cooked red cabbage, uncoils protein molecules), and on cooking, from eggs to beans to vegetables, its main use for the cook is to enhance flavor. Acid can be perceived at levels so low that we don't necessarily sense sourness. The acidity of a soup, sauce, stew—sweet and savory dishes alike—should always be evaluated and adjusted for seasoning as necessary, and acid is one component of that seasoning. Acid is the definitive component in one of the most versatile sauces, the vinaigrette—whether that vinaigrette is in the form of a salad dressing or a Spanish escabeche. The ability to use acid, is one of the most important skills in the kitchen.

Aerate: To aerate means to incorporate air or a gas into food or liquid (a batter, a puree, a custard, a sauce) with a whisk, with a blender, with steam, or by pouring. Aeration can increase volume and enhance texture. A sabayon is aerated with a whisk to achieve body. The carbon dioxide in soda water will lighten a frying batter. A custard whipped frothy can hold ingredients suspended within it, as with a quiche. Contemporary chefs use techniques of aeration to create foams by mixing or with gas. In pastry, aeration is one of three forms of leavening (along with chemical, via baking powder, and organic, via yeast); when a cake batter is aerated—the whipped egg whites in an angel food cake, for instance—the gas bubbles give the cake a light crumb.

51

Agar: Agar is a carbohydrate derived from seaweed used to gel liquids in both the savory and sweet kitchen. Its distinguishing quality is that, unlike protein-based gelatin (which comes as powder and in clear sheets), agar won't melt after it sets until it's very hot (185°F; see McGee), allowing the cook to serve hot gelatin that maintains its shape.

Aïoli [*ay-O-lee*]: Aïoli is an emulsified sauce—that is, one that combines two liquids that don't combine by themselves—mayonnaise flavored with garlic and often other aromatics, common in Provençal cooking. Use it as you would a mayonnaise, as a dipping sauce for crudités or cold shellfish; for a sandwich; as a sauce for hot or cold meats, fish, and vegetables; as a seasoning and enriching garnish in a soup or stew (compare rouille, for example). Most, but not all, aïolis are emulsified by whisking oil into raw yolk with a few drops of water, acid, and seasonings (the standard ratio for making mayonnaise is one yolk per cup of oil). Originally aïoli was emulsified in a heavy mortar using a pestle, still a superlative, if strenuous, method, and some sources say that egg yolk was not originally included.

À la minute [*ah lah mee-NEWT*]: *À la minute* denotes right before serving and implies a quick preparation. The term is often used with sauces as well as for small cuts of meat that must be served as soon as they're cooked. An *à la minute* sauce is usually one that's made in the pan the item was cooked in, often using stock or a demi-glace as the base. Butter is often mounted into sauces *à la minute*. Sauces tend to be freshest and cleanest when they're finished *à la minute* (see the essay Sauces, page 12).

Albumen and albumin: Albumen is the white of an egg, which is composed of several proteins. (Albumin is a group of proteins found in a variety of substances in blood, egg, muscle, milk, and vegetables.) Albumen is a nutritious and versatile substance. It can be whipped into meringue, used as a leavener for cakes and breads, added to stocks to clarify the liquid (see consommé), and it helps custards to set up. (For more on its extraordinary powers, see the essay Egg, page 22.)

Alcohol (cooking with): We use alcohol, an excellent cooking tool, for its flavor and sometimes for its impact on a dish's aroma. Wine is reduced to a virtual concentrate and mounted with butter for a classic French sauce (*beurre blanc* and *beurre rouge*), chicken is braised in wine, beef is braised in wine or beer (be careful with beer; if too much is used or it reduces too much, the sauce can be bitter), and distilled spirits are often added to sauces for their intense flavor and aroma. Risotto, a grain-based dish, is typically started with wine. Raw alcohols in the form of wine or champagne can be added to fruits and other dessert preparations. Alcohol can also enhance presentation when it is flamed. Wines are often used in marinades; while most methods suggest using raw alcohol, the effectiveness and flavor of a marinade is improved substantially by cooking it first to reduce the amount of alcohol and to enhance the flavor (it's difficult if not impossible to cook all the alcohol out of wine, beer, or spirits). Alcohol does not tenderize meat but in a matter of speaking "cooks" the exterior of the meat by denaturing (changing the shape of) the protein on the surface of the meat. As a rule of thumb, only use in your food alcohol that you would drink with pleasure. You get back what you put in.

Al dente [*ahl-DEN-tay*]: Al dente means food that has some bite to it. The term usually refers to pasta and risotto, but it's also an important term with regard to vegetables. Vegetables cooked al dente still have some resistance or crunch. While some people prefer to cook vegetables al dente, al dente should not be considered fully cooked. A fully cooked vegetable has no resistance to the teeth.

Alginate: Alginate, like agar, is derived from seaweed, and is often in the form of sodium alginate. It thickens liquids and gels in the presence of calcium. If sodium alginate is added to a juice, for instance, that juice, when added to a solution containing calcium, will gel on the outside to create a little ball of juice, a self-encapsulated liquid (a common technique defining avant garde cuisine).

All day: line-cook slang for total orders pending. If two steaks are being fired—that is, in the process of being cooked—and orders for three more have just come in, joining four other steaks ordered but not fired, that's nine steaks "all day." The word can be extended to mean total—"How many covers did you do all day?" or "I peeled ten potatoes for the dauphinoise and five for the gaufrettes, so fifteen all day."

All-purpose flour: See flour.

Allumette [*ahl-yu-MET*]: an elegant vegetable cut named for its shape, "matchstick," officially ⅛ inch square and about 2 inches long, often used to refer to potato—*pommes allumettes.*

Almond: The almond is a nut of great versatility in both the savory and the sweet kitchen. It gives a nutty crunch as a garnish to vegetables and fish and can be crushed and used as a coating. Almonds are used more abundantly in the sweet kitchen, sliced or slivered, or ground to a powder, or ground and mixed with sugar to form a paste. Almonds are sometimes sold young, when they are called green almonds, before the nut has hardened and is soft and juicy.

Amandine [*AH-mon-deen*]: Amandine, a classic French sauce of almonds sautéed in butter until both are browned, is valuable for its simplicity and versatility. The sauce is often finished with lemon juice and parsley. Green beans and fish, such as trout, are often served "amandine."

Ambient or room temperature: Pay attention to the temperature in your kitchen; your environment will affect your food. Carryover cooking may be enhanced in a hot kitchen, and sausage or other forcemeats may be more likely to break. The ambient temperature can affect the mixing and fermentation of a dough. A cold kitchen can be beneficial when working with soft fats, such as butter, and may retard carryover cooking.

American regional cuisine: Dishes and methods indigenous to specific parts of the United States—the chowders of New England, the jamabalaya of Louisiana, Kentucky burgoos, salmon preparations of the Pacific northwest—reflect specific landscapes, climates, cultures, and history, and remain a vibrant part of current culinary practice in restaurants. American cuisine, like our population, has a vagabond nature, spreading from region to region. Though ingredients once available regionally are now commonly available everywhere in the country—poblano peppers in Wisconsin, Maine lobsters in Kansas—regional cuisine continues to be a meaningful term for home cooks because of its reliance on letting the season dictate what should be cooked, which often happens to be the products grown or produced nearby. Thinking regionally is also a valuable strategy in deciding what to cook at home. Because so many ingredients are available throughout the country, it's possible, and good, to cook with an eye on specific regional cuisines. Now an idea so common as to seem obvious, the impulse to explore regional cooking was once less so. Paul Prudhomme opened K-Paul's in New Orleans in 1979, earned national acclaim, and made blackened fish, a local dish, a touchstone of regional fare. But not until the early 1980s did restaurants begin to explore it. The American Bounty Restaurant at the Culinary Institute of America, which opened in 1982, and An American Place, which opened in 1983 in Manhattan, were two other important restaurants to devote themselves to preparations that were distinctly American.

Amuse bouche [*AH-muse boosh*]: *Amuse bouche,* sometimes abbreviated as *amuse,* is the term for a complimentary canapé-sized item sent out by the chef to begin a meal, also called *amuse gueule.* This restaurant custom, intended to lift the spirits and surprise hungry diners even before the meal begins, can have a similar, beneficent impact at a dinner party.

Anchovy: Though sometimes available in the United States fresh, anchovies are typically cured in salt and packed in oil. Anchovies, with their strong salty flavor, are used primarily for their seasoning effect, chopped or mashed in vinaigrettes or tapenades, for instance, or even used whole. Quality ranges considerably; the worst come in a brine or packed in oil (often rancid); the best anchovies tend to be packed in salt, are worth seeking out, and can be delicious by themselves. Salt-packed anchovies should be soaked in milk and rinsed to remove the salt. Anchovies are a useful ingredient—often overlooked in the home kitchen—for seasoning, because of their umami effect, enhancing a sauce without being recognizable itself. If you have access to fresh anchovies, they are easily cured at home: clean them, pack them in salt, and store them in the refrigerator; they'll be ready to eat after a few days and will keep in salt for months.

Anglaise sauce: See crème anglaise.

Antioxidant: Oxidation of the components that compose our bodies, our cells, is one of the main forms of damage our bodies endure as we live and age. Molecules that prevent such oxidation (of our DNA, of blood cells, of our body tissues) are called antioxidants. Vegetables and fruits are loaded with them. Chocolate, coffee, tea, and seeds can be a good source of antioxidants as well. In kitchens, the term is loosely used to refer to acids and other ingredients that prevent the surfaces of cut fruit and vegetables from browning, such as lemon juice on apple.

Appareil [*AH-pah-ray*]: An *appareil* is a preparation or a mixture, a general term usually indicating that the preparation will become part of a larger dish—a filling or a batter for example. A mushroom duxelles, for instance, that will be the filling for a ravioli or used to stuff a pork chop, can be referred to as an *appareil duxelles,* sweetened flavored whipped cream as an *appareil* chantilly, or one might say in the kitchen, "I've done the *appareil* for the cheese soufflés," which would refer to the béchamel base.

Apple: When using apples for cooking, most chefs choose tart crunchy apples, such as Granny Smiths, because they tend to hold up better after being cooked, retain their texture, and don't become mealy and mushy. Because their tartness also allows the cook to add more of the complexity of cooked sugar without the dish becoming too sweet, they give the cook more control.

Aquaculture: Aquaculture refers to the farming of fish. It's been going on for millennia, but only since the 1960s has it grown into an international industry. Like any industry it has pros and cons. It may be a source of abundant fish in an era plagued by the overfishing of our oceans. But aquaculture can result also in environmental pollution and contaminated fish. Often farmed fish is less flavorful and less firm than its wild counterpart. Despite its drawbacks, the industry is young and remains a promising one with enormous potential advantages.

Aroma: Aroma is an important component of our sense of taste, so the aroma of a finished dish is an important part of that dish. But aroma is also a kind of tool or device in cooking; more precisely, using your sense of smell, being aware of aromas in the kitchen, is part of cooking. If you are roasting bones to make stock, those bones will be cooked long enough when they have a deep rich roasted aroma; when they smell like a perfect roasted chicken or rack of veal, they're done. You will over time begin to associate nuances of specific aromas—whether you're baking cookies or toasting nuts or roasting a bird—with the doneness of a dish, whether it's a specific aroma or the duration of an aroma. Your sense of smell helps you to be a better cook. Aroma is also a source of pleasure not to be ignored but to be considered and enjoyed—the aroma of floured meat browning crisp in hot fat, the aroma of short ribs braising for hours.

Aromatics (aromats): Abbreviated in kitchens (and sometimes throughout this text) as aromats, aromatics refers to aromatic vegetables and herbs, commonly onions, carrots, and celery (see mirepoix), thyme, parsley, bay leaves, garlic, and peppercorns (see *sachet d'épices*), or lemongrass, ginger, and scallions in Eastern cuisine. Aromats may include anything added to a stock or a stew to enhance its flavor (though not everything is aromatic or should be used as an aromat—bell peppers, turnips, and zucchini are not aromats). We associate aromats with sweet and floral flavors, and they're usually removed from the finished preparation once they've imparted their flavors. Abundant use of aromats makes an enormous difference in the end result and their importance would be difficult to overstate. Their use is not relegated to stocks and stews; sauté mushrooms in oil in a hot pan, then try sautéing mushrooms in oil in a hot pan to which a few stems of thyme and garlic cloves have been added and you will taste the impact of aromats.

Arrowroot: Arrowroot is a pure starch made from a tropical tuber used primarily to thicken sauces (see lié and slurry). Cornstarch is an acceptable and less expensive substitute (though its thickening power is not quite as strong and it tends to break down more quickly when kept hot for extended periods).

Ascorbic Acid: Ascorbic acid is another term for vitamin C. It's an antioxidant, good for our bodies, and can help prevent fruits and vegetables from browning.

Aspic: Aspic is clear, gelled stock, commonly used in *haute cuisine.* It can be diced or chopped and used as a savory garnish. It is a kind of tool that holds ingredients in place within a mold—diced vegetables (vegetable terrine), an egg (*oeuf en gelée*), pork (headcheese). In a *pâté en croute,* it fills in the space between the cooked *pâté* and the crust. Food dipped in aspic will take on a lacquered finish for a fancy presentation. Certain meat stocks, especially those that have included a calf's foot or pigskin, will contain enough gelatin to set completely when chilled. Other stocks such as those made from fish or vegetables require the addition of gelatin. Aspics can be delicate, such that they hold their shape but are very tender, on the verge of collapse. Or, if they must hold ingredients together in a terrine, they can be made firmer, into what's sometimes referred to as a sliceable aspic. Any clear liquid—consommé, the clear strained juice of tomatoes, called tomato water, or clarified vegetable stock—can be transformed into aspic. A general rule for a liquid containing no natural gelatin is to add, for a delicate aspic, 1 teaspoon of powdered gelatin per cup of liquid and for a sliceable aspic, 1 tablespoon of powdered gelatin. If you're unsure about the strength of a meat-stock aspic, pour a couple tablespoons onto a plate and chill it quickly in the refrigerator to evaluate its strength.

Avant garde cuisine, or cooking: a style of cooking popularized in the early years of the twenty-first century by Spanish chef Ferran Adrià, characterized by classical pairings that are deconstructed, the use of foams, alginate, agar, gelatin, sous vide, and unconventional serving methods. Sometimes referred to as molecular gastronomy.

B

Bacon: The depth of flavor and crisp chewiness make cured, smoked pork belly not simply an American staple food but one of the most powerful ingredients in the kitchen. It will season, enrich, and deepen the flavor of countless dishes in any category—salad, vegetable, pasta, rice, meat, fish, and even sweet preparations. It's difficult to overstate the versatility and power of this ingredient.

In France cured pork belly is called *lard* and is not smoked, nor is it typically smoked in Italy, where it's cured with savory aromatics, rolled, and called pancetta. The best bacon in the United States is dry-cured with salt, sodium nitrite, sugar, and seasonings, then smoked over hardwood or fruitwood.

Commercial bacon is made by injecting the belly with brine, which saturates the meat and cures it very quickly; the flavor and texture is not the same as traditionally cured bacon. Traditional dry-cured bacon tends to be richer in flavor, saltier, less watery, and more densely textured. Commercial bacon, because of its high water content, cooks well in a microwave; it's very tender and thus good on tomato and lettuce sandwiches. Both forms of bacon have their place in the kitchen, but it's important to distinguish between the two.

Bacon can be bought in a slab, which allows you to cut it in the dimensions appropriate to the dish you're making—lardons for a frisée salad, chunks for a beef and wine stew, or roasted or grilled whole and served sliced.

Pork belly is very easy to cure at home and results in excellent bacon.

Good bacon should almost always be cooked slowly over low heat to tenderize the tough belly meat and render its copious fat (as with rendering, it can be started in a small amount of water). To cook larger quantities of bacon strips, lay them out on a sheet pan and roast them in a hot oven; for uniform, flat strips, lay a Silpat or second sheet pan on top of them.

Because of its high fat content, bacon freezes well.

Bacteria: Most bacteria is harmless, and some enhance our food by generating acid (bread, pickles, and yogurts, for instance). Some bacteria we rely on for our health; our digestive tracts are filled with them. Other bacteria can make us sick and in some cases kill us. Bacteria, good and bad, often flourish at room and warm temperatures. A small colony, dormant on a chilled chicken breast, will multiply rapidly at room temperature. We must assume that bacteria is plentiful on our food and treat specific foods accordingly. By keeping foods cold and cleaning work surfaces well, we reduce the opportunity for bacteria to multiply to harmful levels. The most bacteria-ridden spot in our kitchen tends to be the sponge, that moist, room temperature cleaning tool. Sponges should be cleaned regularly by boiling, washing in a bleach solution, or microwaving damp.

The bacteria that cause the most trouble in our food at home are salmonella, the deadly form of *E. coli,* and the bacterium that causes botulism poisoning.

The dangerous form of *E. coli,* present in the digestive tract and on the skin of cows, is problematic when it's ground into hamburger. It's important to remember that *E. coli* does not infest the interior of a muscle. This is why you can eat a steak, cooked bloody rare over a hot fire, and not risk *E. coli* poisoning, but you can get *E. coli* poisoning from a bloody rare hamburger cooked over a hot fire. It's prudent to cook hamburgers to an internal temperature of 155°F for children, who are especially vulnerable to the bacteria.

Salmonella and *E. coli* can contaminate fruits and vegetables, so it's prudent for food safety reasons (and matters of taste as well) to wash any fruit or vegetable that will be served raw, even if you're peeling it, and to refrigerate it or serve it shortly thereafter.

The bacterium that causes botulism, *Clostridium botulinum,* is anaerobic and can only grow in a low-acid, oxygen-free, warm environment, such as in the jar of garlic in olive oil on your pantry shelf, the beans you canned last summer, or inside an improperly cured sausage left at room temperature. It can be prevented by rigorous sterilization procedures (in home preserves) and with sodium nitrite or sodium nitrate, which prevents the bacteria's growth, in smoked and dry-cured sausages. An acidic environment also discourages the growth of the bacteria; beneficial bacteria in dry-cured sausages generate such acid. Nor will the bacteria grow significantly in refrigerator temperatures (below 38°F).

For more information on the nature of specific bacteria go to http://www.cdc.gov/ncidod/dbmd/diseaseinfo.

Bain-marie [*BEHN-mah-ree*]: A *bain-marie* is a hot water bath. *Bains-marie* are used in restaurants to keep sauces and other preparations warm during service. Items that must cook gently, such as custards and *pâtés en terrine,* are cooked in the oven in a water bath, a *bain-marie;* the water maintains a low temperature around the vessel. For items that must be melted gently and evenly, such as chocolate, a *bain-marie* is often used. A double-boiler is in effect a *bain-marie* and likewise used for gentle cooking. The inserts or vessels that go into the hot water are often also loosely referred to as *bains-marie* or simply Americanized as bains.

Baking powder: Baking powder is a chemical leavener, composed of baking soda (a base) and an acid that, when combined with a liquid, releases bubbles of carbon dioxide and is used to leaven batters and non-elastic doughs that cannot contain bubbles for long periods (as bread dough can). Baking powder also releases gas when it's hot, that is, while cooking, thus the term "double-acting" baking powder. Baking powder can contribute a chemical taste to the finished food; to avoid this, measure baking powder carefully. Chemical leaveners can sometimes be replaced by natural leaveners, such as egg whites.

Baking sheet: See sheet pan.

Baking soda: Sodium bicarbonate is a chemical leavener, which reacts with the acid in a batter or non-elastic dough to release gas quickly—so you need to use it in conjunction with some form of acid. It's what makes buttermilk pancakes fluffy rather than flat and dense. Unreacted baking soda can contribute a soapy, chemical taste to the finished food if there's not enough acid to neutralize it; measure baking soda carefully. Chemical leaveners can sometimes be replaced by natural leaveners, such as egg whites. Baking soda has secondary effects on flour proteins, weakening the gluten structure, enhancing Maillard reactions, and lowering caramelization temperatures.

Balsamic vinegar: Balsamic vinegar is a seasoning device, a condiment, a sauce element (usually when reduced), and, in the case of the best balsamics, an excellent *digestif.* Balsamic is traditionally made from the unfermented juice of wine grapes—most commonly Trebbiano—which is cooked, fermented, and aged in barrels, resulting in a very special vinegar that's sweet and acidic and complex in flavor. There are good balsamics and cheap ones (often the latter have other wine vinegars and sugar added to them), and you should distinguish between them when cooking. All true balsamics come from Italy, most famously from Modena, a province of Emilia-Romagna, and will say so on the bottle; they may also note how long they've been aged. Taste is always the best way to judge quality, and this must be experienced and learned. A good balsamic is an important pantry item that can elevate a dish—whether a simple salad, grilled vegetables, a sauce, a cheese course—from good to great. Balsamic is often reduced to a thick, sweet, complex syrup.

Bard: To bard means to cover a piece of meat with a layer of fat while it roasts, usually pork fat. Barding is used with a leaner cut of meat whose surface might dry out during a long roast, not unlike wrapping lean meat in caul fat for roasting. While adding more fat to a dish, or using fat as part of the cooking medium, is rarely a bad idea, barding, like larding, is no longer a common technique. It's especially useful for wild game that tends to be naturally lean.

Baste: Basting food with the hot fat in the pan improves flavor and color and texture, whether you're spooning, brushing, or squirting cooking fat and meat juices over a roasting chicken or browned butter over roasting cauliflower. The important ideas underlying basting are these: the fat in the pan will be very hot and can help to render the skin of a bird or help to crisp fish skin being sautéed on the stovetop and give more color to vegetables, and will also help the food to cook evenly. Also, when basting roasted meats, the concentrated meat juices and solids in the fat will coat the exterior meat, enhancing flavor; this is particularly true when butter is part of the fat. The butter solids, which are especially flavorful when they're browned, adhere to the surface of the meat or roasting vegetables. Basting pan-roasted meat this way, meats more lean and tender than roasts—that is, adding some butter to the pan and using this as a baste—is an especially effective technique.

Baton: a type of vegetable cut meaning stick, also called by its French name, *bâtonnet,* typically used with hard root vegetables. A baton is a straightforward rectangle, typically 2 inches long and about ¼ inch thick.

Batter: A loose mixture of flour and liquid, a batter often contains egg, fat, a leavener, and additional starch and/or seasonings, that result in cakes, pancakes and waffles, blinis, popovers, gougères and éclairs (see *pâte à choux*), fritters, as well as coatings for vegetables, meat, and fish for deep-frying (see tempura). Batters can be sweet or savory, very loose, as in a crepe batter, or thicker, as with a pound cake batter. Usually, a batter is distinguished from a dough by its containing more liquid than flour, and its varieties are determined by that ratio, as well as the varying amounts of fat, eggs or egg whites, and sugar, and the way they are mixed (ingredients for loose batters for, say, popovers, are mixed all together; for an angel food cake, flour is folded into a meringue, then baked directly; for a *pâte à choux,* flour and water are cooked, then eggs are mixed in; ingredients for tempuras are mixed just before using and some include soda water for additional lightness).

Bavarian cream: vanilla sauce (crème anglaise) to which gelatin and lightly whipped cream (and sometimes egg whites) are added; the gelatin sets it, and the cream lightens it. Bavarian cream can be served as a dessert on its own, almost like a pudding or a mousse, or as the filling for a more elaborate dish, in pastries or cakes; the mixture can be flavored in any number of ways—aromats, extracts, liquours. Bavarian cream is a preparation that does not appear in many current cookbooks covering basic preparations, which is curious because it's lighter than a panna cotta, pot de crème, or crème brûlée, is easily made ahead of time, and is well suited to the home kitchen.

Bay leaf: Mediterranean bay leaf is a versatile aromat, standard in seasoning stocks and stew, and a component of a standard *sachet d'épices* (a variety of aromats enclosed in cheesecloth), adding a depth of flavor with its "woody, floral, eucalyptus, and clove notes," writes McGee. California bay is a different plant and noticeably stronger than the bay laurel; California bay is very strong, sometimes astringent, and is often sold as "fresh bay leaf." Bay leaves are available fresh and dried; again, the fresh ones tend to be stronger than the dried. Pay attention to their color (they should have a deep color, not faded) and their fragrance—like all dried herbs and spices they lose their flavor over time.

Bean curd: See tofu.

Beans (dried): Dried beans—black, white, mung, black-eyed peas, split peas, lentils—are a nutritious versatile component of your pantry, whether they're grocery store beans or heirloom beans (now available via the Internet). Some beans don't need to be soaked (black-eyed peas, lentils, mung) but the bigger harder beans should be, 4 to 6 hours or overnight; no beans have to be soaked, they'll eventually cook through, but the more gradual their rehydration the better. The key to cooking beans well is cooking them gently so that they remain intact, not boiling them hard so that they break apart. Beans need to be gently hydrated and gently cooked. They absorb the flavors of the cooking liquid, so adding lots of aromatic vegetables and herbs, and seasoning the water with an acid and salt, improves the result, depending on how you want to use them (taste the water—that's how your beans will be seasoned). Start beans in cold water. Some chefs recommend blanching the beans first, then rinsing them before cooking them to remove some of the carbohydrates that result in flatulence (but you lose nutrients as well). Most chefs recommend adding salt to the water midway through cooking, that is, after they're hydrated but before they're cooked; some believe that salt can interfere with the rehydration process, others say salt toughens the beans. A good way to ensure gentle heat is to begin the beans on the stovetop and transfer them, covered with a lid or with parchment paper, to a 275°F oven until they are tender, tasting for seasoning as you go.

After beans are cooked, they can be pureed for a soup or a dip, served hot, served cold with a vinaigrette, or even deep-fried till crunchy. Soaked, uncooked beans can also be deep-fried, salted, and eaten as a snack or used as a crunchy garnish.

Beans (fresh): All kinds of fresh beans are available today in grocery stores and farmers' markets. No matter what kind you're using—green, yellow, pole, fava, lima, soy—they can all be cooked in numerous ways. Most commonly they're plunged into hard-boiling, heavily salted water (see blanch), then seasoned and eaten immediately or shocked in ice water, drained, and refrigerated until ready to eat, whether cold with a vinaigrette or reheated with salt and butter. Beans can be blanched, shocked, and refrigerated for up to a day before serving. If an acid such as a vinaigrette or lemon juice is part of the seasoning for any green bean, it should be added just before serving to prevent the beans' color from becoming dull. Fresh beans can also be oiled and roasted, grilled, sautéed, or deep-fried, with excellent and differing results.

Beard (on mussels): See debeard.

Béchamel: See also mother sauces. Béchamel is an all-purpose white sauce made by thickening milk with a roux and cooking it gently with aromatics.

The béchamel is often maligned as emblematic of heavy, old-fashioned, French food, but carefully prepared, the béchamel is not only delicate and refined, but also inexpensive (milk, flour, aromats), quick, and far easier to make than the stock-based mother sauces or reduction sauces. It can be used as an ingredient in a dish, say a lasagna or a creamy pasta or gratin, or other ingredients can be added to it to further refine it into any number of derivative sauces (cheese can be added to make a Mornay sauce, crayfish stock to make a Nantua sauce, or cooked onions for a soubise). The basic method is to sweat minced onion in butter, add the flour (1 to 2 tablespoons of flour per cup of milk), cook the flour with the onion and butter till it loses its raw aroma, then add the milk and aromats (a grating of nutmeg, a bay leaf perhaps—*oignon piqué* is also a classic seasoning), and cook it for about 45 minutes, skimming the surface regularly until the granular flour texture and raw taste is cooked out, then strain and use or refrigerate it.

Beef: This text advocates using meat from livestock that has been naturally raised, not fed growth hormones, antibiotics, or meat by-products. Such beef is available over the Internet but also increasingly, and less expensively, at grocery stores throughout the country.

Thinking about beef generally, we break its meat into three categories, the tender muscles that are delicious when quickly sautéed, pan-roasted, broiled, or grilled (tenderloin and loin, for instance, from which we get filet mignon and strip steaks); tough, well-marbled muscles such as the brisket and the shank, cuts best braised to break down the connective tissue (or ground, to mechanically tenderize it); and the large heavily used muscles that are neither exquisitely tender nor well marbled nor especially flavorful, such as the round cuts. The latter can nevertheless be a good economical choice and every bit as satisfying as the most expensive cuts when carefully prepared (ground for beef tartare, for instance, or quickly sautéed and served with a fat-based sauce).

Beef can be eaten raw (tartare, carpaccio), but commercially ground beef can contain pathogens, most notably the dangerous *E. coli* bacteria, which exist on the exterior of the meat, not within the muscle. Children and anyone with compromised health should avoid raw commercially ground hamburger. When making raw beef preparations, it's advisable to buy whole cuts of meat, rinse and salt them, and do your own cutting and grinding.

Benriner: See Japanese mandoline.

Berries: Berries are a flavorful and versatile product in the hands of the cook. They can be served as they are if they're fresh, served with some cream or crème anglaise, used as garnish, or to make superlative dessert sauces and even vinaigrettes. Sauces made from berries are exceptional given how simple they are to make: cooked with sugar, pureed and strained, then adjusted for seasoning; because cooking alters the flavor, some chefs prefer sauces made from uncooked berries. Cooking berries is an especially good way to put to use extra berries or berries that will soon be on their way out; they're best combined with the sugar then left to macerate overnight before being cooked.

Beurre blanc and *beurre rouge*: These simple, versatile butter sauces flavored by wine and aromats are easy because butter is already an emulsion, and thus nearly a perfect sauce as it is—the wine simply flavors the butter. The basic method is to combine minced shallots and aromats with a delicious white or red wine and reduce till it's almost dry (*sec*), then whisk in butter a chunk at a time, season to taste, and you're good to go. Other acids such as vinegar or lemon juice can be added to the reduction, as can additional aromatics such as pepper or herbs; cream can be added to enrich it and smooth it out; the sauce can be strained for elegance, and fresh herbs can be added for flavor and color to finish it (volatile ingredients such as herbs or berries or aromatics should be added *à la minute*)—but it really is as simple as it sounds, butter mounted into reduced wine. Because the sauce is delicately flavored, both white and red butter sauces are customarily served with fish or other lean, mild, tender preparations.

Beurre composé: See compound butter.

Beurre fondue: See *beurre monté* and fondue.

Beurre maître d'hôtel: a compound butter (sometimes called "hotel butter") containing salt, pepper, lemon, and parsley, an excellent all-purpose sauce or accompaniment for countless fish, meat, starch, or vegetable preparations.

Beurre manié [*bur mahn-YAY*]: butter into which an equal volume of flour has been rubbed and kneaded becomes an easy, effective way to thicken small amounts of sauces while also enriching them. Slurries, pure starch and water, may be quicker and more widely used, but they don't enrich or add flavor—butter does. *Beurre manié* is especially suited to thickening pan gravies, meat stews, fish stews, and the poaching liquid in which fish has cooked (sometimes called *cuisson;* see also shallow poach), and should be used *à la minute,* just before serving.

Beurre monté [*bur mohn-TAY*]: *Beurre monté* is the term used in restaurants referring to butter that's emulsified into a little water, then held for use throughout service for enriching sauces, reheating vegetables, and basting meats, derived from the phrase *monté au beurre,* mounting (melting and whisking) butter into a sauce. Sometimes called *beurre fondue.*

Beurre noir [*bur nwoir*] and *beurre noisette* [*bur nwoi-ZET*]: These are related terms for brown butter and are sometimes used interchangeably. *Beurre noir* means black butter and often designates a sauce made with brown butter (*beurre noisette*), lemon juice, capers, and parsley (in effect a delicate vinaigrette, often served over lean, white, sautéed fish). *Beurre noir* should never be cooked until it actually turns black. *Beurre noisette* refers to butter cooked till the butter solids brown, and the butter develops a nutty aroma and flavor (thus its name, hazelnut). The trick with making a brown butter sauce is to recognize the right color and aroma, then to stop the cooking by adding the acid which cools the hot butterfat. Brown butter is a versatile preparation, whether as a *beurre noir* or *meunière* sauce, or as a kind of seasoning for vegetables, pasta, potatoes, or even sweet preparations such as custards and cakes.

Biscuit: a type of cake made with flour and liquid, approximately a 3 to 2 ratio, with solid fat first "rubbed" into the flour before the water is added as with a pie dough or *pâte brisée.* They can be free-form or rolled and cut. Some of its leavening comes from the fact that the fat remains in chunks and separates layers of dough (in the same way a pie crust becomes flaky).

Bisque: A thick, creamy, crustacean-based soup. Once bread-thickened, bisques are now more commonly thickened with roux. Restaurant menus and contemporary cookbooks occasionally use the word to describe a non-shellfish-based soup such as a vegetable puree. This usage is what H. W. Fowler, a respected commentator on English usage, would have called a slipshod extension; when bisque becomes simply a synonym for "thick and creamy," its meaning is diminished; thick, creamy vegetable purees should be called purees; thick, creamy shellfish soups should be called bisques.

Bistro: A word that has become a virtual synonym for "casual" when referring to restaurant styles, and therefore all but meaningless, bistro should be used to describe a style of restaurant that originated in Paris in the early nineteenth century. A bistro was then and remains today a restaurant serving economical French fare including sandwiches, egg dishes, soups, stews, roasts, and quickly prepared dishes using inexpensive ingredients (dishes that can meaningfully be grouped under the heading *bistro cuisine*).

Bivalves: Bivalves—clams, mussels, oysters—can be eaten raw or cooked. Clams and mussels are best simply steamed until they open, often with some white wine, garlic, and thyme. Oysters are prized as a raw food (it may be the only creature we commonly eat while it's still alive), but they can be broiled, roasted, fried, or used as a component in any number of dishes. All bivalves are filter-feeders and often trap toxins; it's not unwise to know where they came from and how they've been handled and, once you have them, keep them cold and eat them fresh. With all bivalves, freshness is paramount—the sooner you get them once they've left the water, the better.

Bladder (pig's): the sturdy sac is an extraordinary cooking vessel (to enclose, for example, a stuffed chicken in the dish *poulet en vessie*) and further proof of the pig's elegant efficiency.

Blanch: This word has several different meanings depending on who's using it, so it almost always needs some qualification or explanation. Technically, to blanch means to plunge a fruit into boiling water for a minute or less to make the skin easy to peel (as with a tomato or a peach) or to change, or "set," a green vegetable's color from flat to vivid green while keeping it, in effect, raw. Some kitchens use the word to mean parboil, to cook a vegetable halfway, then shock it so that it can be finished later. French fries are often blanched in low temperature oil so that they can be finished quickly (and crisply) in hot oil later. Many chefs use it to mean plunging a vegetable into heavily salted water that's at a rolling boil (1 cup of kosher salt per gallon is a good ratio), fully cooking that vegetable, then removing it to an ice water bath (see shock). To blanch can also mean to cover bones with cold water and bring them to a boil, then strain and rinse them in order to clean them for a white stock.

Blanquette: A blanquette is a white stew, often veal, in which the meat is first blanched to prevent impurities from compromising the cooking liquid, notable for its elegance and refinement. A fricasse, by contrast, is a white stew in which the meat has been sautéed without color to begin the preparation.

Bleach: Keeping a mild bleach solution for occasional use is a good way to keep boards, countertops, and sponges sterile. Clorox recommends 3 tablespoons per gallon of water for a kitchen cleaning solution. Bleach is volatile, so make such a solution regularly in small quantities.

Blender: A blender is one of the most important tools in the kitchen, used for making soups, sauces, and quick emulsified butter sauces, emulsifying vinaigrettes, and pureeing food for drinks. It can even be used in conjunction with a chinois in place of a vegetable juicer (vegetables can be pureed in a blender and the liquid passed through the sieve). (See also immersion blender.)

Blind bake: Blind bake means to bake a pastry shell or pie crust before it's filled. When a pie shell or *pâte brisée* is to be filled with a liquid mixture (a quiche, for example) or a mixture not to be cooked, the shell must be baked first. In order to prevent the bottom of the shell buckling up, some kind of weight is put into the shell to keep it flat as it cooks. Pie weights are made expressly for this purpose and are convenient, but a pound of dried beans on top of a piece of parchment paper or aluminum foil will work just as well.

Blood: Blood can be either a detriment or an asset. In stock and stews, it's an impurity we take out, usually after it has coagulated and floated to the top early in the cooking. But toward the end of cooking, blood can be added to a sauce to thicken and enrich it (often in the case of game birds and game stews such as civet). And in certain sausages blood is the defining ingredient; its delicate, custard-like texture, and rich, deep flavor make an extraordinary sausage called *boudin noir* (black pudding).

Bloom: 1) Bloom can mean to hydrate gelatin, which, whether powdered or in sheets, must absorb water before it can be melted and added to whatever it is you're thickening or gelling. 2) Sometimes chefs refer to putting spices or aromatics in oil so that they bloom, or release their flavor into the oil. 3) Bloom can refer to beneficial flora that can grow on some fruits and vegetables (grapes, cabbage). 4) Bloom can refer to the chalky white coating (separated cocoa butter) of improperly stored chocolate.

Body: What we mean when we say that a liquid has body is that it has a degree of weight and texture on the palate. Body does not reflect flavor. Think of water as the zero mark—water has zero body. If the liquid has almost the feel of water, it's doesn't have much body. If it feels more substantial, say a rich chicken stock, then we say it has body.

Boil, boiling, boiling point: About the only foods that should be boiled are green vegetables, vegetables needing peeling, bones for white stock (see blanch), and pasta—that is, items requiring the highest possible moist heat. In most other instances, and even sometimes in these instances, the high heat and vigorous agitation of boiling water cooks exteriors too fast, breaks things apart, and emulsifies impurities into the cooking liquid, effects that a cook should be aware of. This is why potatoes and dried beans should be cooked gently, why stocks are cooked at a mere tremble.

The boiling point—the temperature above which water cannot rise—is another idea to be conscious of and to put to use, most notably in the form of a water bath, a *bain-marie;* vessels (including food wrapped in plastic) can be cooked in water to ensure steady gentle cooking.

It should be noted, too, when even a small amount of water is in a pan, any food touching that water cannot be heated above the boiling point, 212°F; you can't sear or brown meat if there's water in your pan.

Bone marrow: An underappreciated ingredient in the kitchen, bone marrow makes an extraordinary garnish to a sauce, or it can be cooked and spread on a toast point as a canapé; it will flavor a savory custard or can be served roasted in the bone, seasoned with coarse salt, and served as an accompaniment to a beef dish. It should be soaked in salted water to remove residual blood, which will discolor and coagulate when it's cooked.

Bone out: To bone out is chef-speak for "remove the bones from" or to describe meat that has had the bones removed (e.g., a boned-out leg of lamb).

Bones: Bones are valuable because they are composed mainly of connective tissue that adds gelatin, and therefore body, to stocks, stews, soups, and braising liquids. Bones don't contribute good flavor, so they are almost always used in conjunction with flavorful ingredients such as meat and vegetables. Bones of animals bigger than chickens are often roasted or blanched before being used to make stock to coagulate the surface protein and reduce the amount of impurities released into the liquid, and, in the case of roasting, to add flavor.

Botulism: Botulism is a serious kind of food poisoning caused by the toxin released by the bacterium *Clostridium botulinum,* which only grows in an oxygen-free, warm, low-acid environment, such as in a can, food held in oil in jars, such as garlic, and dry-cured or smoked sausages. It is prevented in canning by rigorous sterilization and in food by sodium nitrite. The three important parts of the botulism equation are these: botulism spores, abundant in soil, are not toxic, nor are they easy to kill; given a room temperature oxygen-free environment—canned beans, a hanging sausage—the spores can produce the bacteria, which aren't dangerous in themselves. But give the bacteria the conditions and time to multiply, and they will produce the deadly toxin, which is immobilized only at high temperatures. (See also bacteria.)

Boudin, blanc **and** ***noir*** [*boo-DEHN blahnk, nwoir*]: *Boudin blanc* and *boudin noir* are special kinds of sausages with a delicate texture—pudding-like, thus the name *boudin. Boudin blanc* is typically made with pork and an abundance of egg and cream and seasoned with *quatre épices,* and is distinct from Cajun *boudin blanc,* which is seasoned differently and often contains rice. The primary ingredient for *boudin noir* is pig's blood, which solidifies and binds interior garnish such as onion, apple, and diced, blanched fatback.

Bouillon: Bouillon is the French term for broth.

Bouquet garni [*boo-KAY gar-NEE*]: A *bouquet garni* is a bundle of aromatics bound together with butcher's string so that it can be easily removed from the food, like a *sachet d'épices,* after it's flavored the food. It customarily includes parsley, thyme, bay leaf, leeks, celery, or other aromatics.

Brains: See offal.

Braise, braising: To braise means to sear meat in hot fat, then submerge it in liquid and cook it slowly and gently. The method is used for tough cuts of meat, shoulders and shanks, muscles with a lot of connective tissue that must slowly be dissolved into gelatin before the meat will be tender. It's sometimes called a combination cooking method, using dry heat (that is, very hot fat) followed by moist heat (lower than boiling temperatures). Compare with stew, which does not necessarily imply searing, and usually refers to the cooking of smaller pieces of meat.

The key factors of excellence in braising are these: Meat is seared for flavor, color, texture, and for clarity of the cooking liquid. Raw meat cooked in liquid will release blood and proteins as a kind of gray scum. Meat can either be blanched (as in a blanquette) or seared; both methods diminish the amount of impurities that wind up in the finished stew. Meat is first seasoned with salt and pepper, floured, then seared in a pan large enough to give the meat room and also retain enough heat to brown the meat. Using too small a pan will crowd the meat, thereby trapping moisture, and cool the pan so that the meat steams rather than browns. The second step is to combine the meat, stock, and aromats, bring the liquid to a gentle simmer on the stovetop, then cover, loosely, with a lid or with parchment paper (which allows some reduction of the stock, and keeps the liquid from boiling vigorously; a covered pot in the oven will be about 20 degrees hotter than an uncovered one; see McGee), and put it in an oven no higher than 300°F. The liquid should not boil—the ideal temperature in fact is about 180°F. The meat should be cooked until it is fork tender (braises are overcooked when the liquid has leached all the meat's flavor and the meat has become dry and stringy), then allowed to cool while still submerged in the liquid. Last, the fat should be removed from the braising liquid either by skimming it off immediately or by chilling the braise and allowing the fat to congeal, which makes it easier to remove. Braises should be gently reheated and always served very hot. (See also stew.)

Brandade: See salt cod.

Brandy: Brandy is a spirit distilled from wine; the best tend to be from the Cognac and Armagnac regions in France. Brandy is a powerful flavoring device, not only for adding to custards and flaming over sweet crepes, but also in savory preparations, such as for a country pâté. As with any alcohol used in cooking, quality matters. Use in your food only alcohol that is excellent to drink on its own.

Bread: The quality of bread is expressed through its aroma, color, density, crust, crumb, and flavor. Pay attention to these attributes when buying bread. Breads can be categorized in terms of lean doughs (doughs that don't use fats) and doughs that use a variety of additional ingredients that may include eggs and fat, which tend to make the dough softer, and sweet-eners and flavorings. Breads are also distinguished by the type of flour used—whether it's refined, or whole wheat, or rye, the latter two making a denser, more nutritious bread. We tend to think of bread on its own, eaten as is or as an independent part of a dish, for a sandwich, for croutons, or even saturated with a custard and baked to make bread pudding. But remember that bread, often in the form of crumbs, is a versatile ingredient, beyond coating items for frying, one that thickens or gives texture to sauces and soups, eggs, and salads. For this you should use fresh crumbs you make yourself. To make your own crumbs, avoid flavored breads and breads using fats or eggs. Use lean breads such as a country loaf with a high ratio of crumb to crust. The best bread for crumbs is day-old bread. Remove the crust and process in a food processor, spread the crumbs on a sheet pan, and toast them gently in the oven until golden brown (avoid the common problem of burning them by keeping your oven at 225°F or lower, below Maillard browning temperatures).

Bread flour: See flour.

Breading, standard procedure: The procedure for breading food that is to be fried is common: flour the item so that it is completely dry, dip it in egg, which clings to the flour, then dip it in bread crumbs, which stick to the egg. While the order and logic of standard breading procedure rarely varies, the details can vary greatly. The flour can be all-purpose, whole wheat, almond, or a pure starch such as cornstarch. The egg can be light-ened with water or seasoned. The bread crumbs too can be seasoned; they can be soft bread crumbs or hard bread crumbs (see panko), or they can be substituted with another cereal or a ground nut. Given standard procedure, breading is open to the imagination.

Break, broken: When ingredients that do not readily join have been com-bined into a homogenous mixture, we call this an emulsion, and when the various ingredients separate from each other, we call this emulsion *broken*. Butter is an emulsion, and if you get it hot in a pan, it will break, the clear fat separating from the water and milk solids that were once held homoge-nously. Preparations that commonly break are emulsified sauces, a hol-landaise, or a mayonnaise, fat emulsified into a small amount of water and egg yolk—when, in a once creamy luxurious sauce, the fat breaks out of the water and recombines with itself into a soup of fat. The reasons for such a sauce's breaking is typically that too much fat is added; too much heat will also break an emulsified butter sauce; an improperly mixed sauce will be unstable and may break. Broken sauces can be fixed by beginning the emulsion anew, starting with new yolks and adding the broken sauce as you would the fat; the emulsification should return. (See McGee for a thorough description of the structure of an emulsion.) Meat mixtures such as sausages and pâtés in which the fat is distributed uniformly throughout are considered to be emulsions, and this too can be broken when it is cooked—the fat separating from the rest of the mixture. The cause for this is commonly that the meat and fat got too hot before they were mixed together or during mixing. A broken forcemeat such as this, however, cannot be fixed after it's been cooked.

Break down: To break something down is butchering vernacular for reducing larger cuts or whole animals to individual cuts.

Brigade [*bri-GOD*]: The *brigade* system, described by the French chef Auguste Escoffier, organizes the professional kitchen in terms of duties; each chef is assigned to a particular task—one to the preparation and cooking of fish (*poissonier*), another to sauces (*saucier*), general preparations (*commis*), et cetera—to make the work more efficient.

Brine: A brine is salt in solution. Brining is a powerful technique that not only seasons meat and fish, but can also cure it or add complementary flavors. Fresh vegetables can be brined at room temperature for a natural pickle, one in which the acid is generated by bacteria. Brine strength, the ratio of salt to water, can vary but a good working ratio is a cup of kosher salt (between six and eight ounces) per gallon which, depending on the type of salt you use, will result in a 5 percent to 6 percent brine. For an exact brine, it's easiest to use metric measurements—50 grams of salt per liter of water results in a 5 percent brine. Always use kosher or sea salt, and it's best to weigh the salt rather than measure it by volume. A 5 percent brine is also an excellent liquid in which to cook green vegetables (see salted water) and the ideal strength for natural pickles. A small amount of sugar is often added to a brine to counteract the harshness of salt. Aromats can be added to the brine to complement the flavor of the meat or vegetables (tarragon and citrus for chicken for instance, garlic and sage for pork chops, garlic and chillis for pickled vegetables). Aromats should be simmered in the brine while the salt dissolves to infuse the water. Brines should be completely chilled before the meat or vegetable is added and should be discarded after they've been used (never reuse a brine). The brined item should rest after being removed from the brine to allow the salt concentration to equalize within the meat. A brined piece of meat, which has absorbed water, will result in a 10 to 15 percent greater yield and often juicier finished meat.

Broil, broiling: Like grilling, broiling is a dry-heat method of cooking that requires neither fat nor water as part of the cooking medium. It's used for meats that are tender and flavorful on their own and introduces additional flavor and texture by browning the exterior of the meat without adding the flavors of smoke that you get from grilling.

Broth: Broths (bouillons) are distinguished from stocks in that a broth is intended to be served as is whereas a stock is the foundation for other preparations. Thus, a broth should have a deep flavor of the meat and aromatics used and be well seasoned. Because stocks and broths get their flavor from meat (and develop body from bone and cartilage), broths should be made with plenty of meat and aromats.

Brown, browning: We brown foods to enhance their flavor (see also sear). A distinction should be made between browning and caramelizing, which refers to the transformation of sugars in high heat. Browning refers to the transformation of everything not sugar, otherwise known as the Maillard reaction. This reaction, which mainly concerns proteins and carbohydrates, is responsible for the char on a grilled steak, the golden brown skin of a roasted chicken, or the crust on bread, and results in all kinds of complex flavors. Even the sight of such browning is appetizing. Browning requires high heat, well above water's boiling point, so browning won't happen if you've got water or juice in your pan, or even if the sides of a pan are too high and collect a lot of vapor around the meat.

Brown butter: Butter becomes brown when it's cooked till the water evaporates and the milk solids, which separate from the clear butterfat, can turn brown; the butter takes on a complex nutty aroma (see *beurre noisette*). Brown butter is flavorful on its own as a sauce, and useful in both savory and sweet preparations; acid and aromats can be added to it to create a more dramatic sauce.

Brown sauce: See *espagnole* sauce.

Brown stock: Brown stock is made from bones that have been roasted; skin and bones and meat that have been browned in the oven or in a pan give stocks their brown color and a complex roasted aroma and flavor. Often the mirepoix is browned before being added to the stock for an even deeper flavor and color. In restaurant kitchens brown stock often signifies brown veal stock. Some kitchens that want to introduce roasted elements *after* the base stock is made color their stock with some form of tomato (usually paste), but usually brown stock means stock made using roasted bones.

Brûlé [*BREW-lay*]: French for burned, this term usually applies to a coating of sugar that has been finished beneath a broiler or with a blowtorch to transform it into a hard caramelized shell (créme brûlée is the most common example).

Brunoise [*BREWN-wahz*]: *Brunoise* is a decorative vegetable cut, a tiny dice, between 1/16 inch and 1/8 inch. Restaurant kitchens often prepare them today by julienning vegetables on a Japanese mandoline, and cutting the dice from these.

Buffet: Buffet is a style of service in which people serve themselves and thus determines a specific kind of cuisine: food that can be offered at room temperature—charcuterie, *à la grecque* vegetables, vegetable and bean salads, custards and tarts—or hot food that holds well, such as roasted meats and braises. A buffet is not appropriate for dishes that are best made or completed *à la minute*: lean fish, risotto, hot green vegetables.

Burnt, burned: Many kitchen mistakes can be fixed, amended, saved. Burnt is one that cannot. With only rare exceptions, burned bits of food ruin a dish with bitterness that is usually impossible to get rid of or hide. Some chefs add a *oignon brûlée* to a stock or a soup, a half onion blackened on a flattop or in a pan, for color; tomatoes for sauce can be charred for flavor; red peppers can be burned over a flame in order to remove their skin. Most chefs, though, like to keep anything burnt out of their food. Be careful when a thick soup or sauce sticks to the bottom of the pan; it can affect the flavor of the entire pot.

Butcher's string: Cotton butcher's string is a valuable kitchen tool, used mainly to truss birds and tie meat, which helps the meat to cook more uniformly, maintain the shape while it's cooking, and result in a better-looking finished product. Using butcher's string is something that's not difficult to learn and worth the effort. It has numerous uses, from tying *bouquet garnis* and *sachets d'épices* to supporting roulades to tying sausage links.

Butt: Butt typically refers to pork shoulder butt, often called Boston butt, the shoulder of the pig. This is an inexpensive but versatile cut that must be cooked low and slow to break down the connective tissue. It's the cut used for pulled pork and, because of its good marbling, ground for sausage.

Butter: Butter is one of the most special ingredients in the kitchen, certainly the most versatile and delicious kind of fat. Few kitchen staples have such a powerful impact on the flavor and feel of food. And the preparations are few that cannot be improved with a little butter. Butter is an effective shortener in doughs (see shorten) that's also enormously flavorful. Because it's a fat that's solid at room temperature it can also be used for its leavening effect on doughs in which layers of butter separate layers of dough (as with flaky pie crusts or laminated doughs, such as puff pastry). But it can also be softened at room temperature so that it is as pliable as mayonnaise (herbs can be incorporated into butter this soft for hotel butter or it can be folded into cooked salmon to make a rillette). Chunks of it can be added to the loosely cooked custard ingredients, eggs and sugar, so that when beaten the custard becomes smooth and velvety and extraordinary on cakes, cookies, and other pastries; its unique softening temperature and structure is what gives buttercream is voluptuousness. Cook those custard ingredients further, whip in butter, and the butter will help the custard set up into a tart filling as it cools. With its low water content, it will gently cook, or sweat, vegetables, a flavorful cooking medium. When it's heated, the fat and solids break out of the emulsion. These solids will brown and become complex and nutty (*beurre noisette*). If these solids are removed as the water cooks out, you will be left with pure, clear butterfat, called clarified butter. Clarified butter is an extraordinary cooking fat, not only adding flavor but also capable of becoming very hot without burning and so is excellent for sautéeing meats and frying crisp potatoes. This clarified butter can also be emulsified into some water and egg yolks for classic emulsified butter sauces, such as hollandaise and béarnaise (though whole butter can be used as well). It's possible also to melt the butter and maintain the emulsion of fat, water, and solids (*beurre monté*), which can be added to sauces or used to baste meats or even to poach meats and fish. And of course, it's good spread on bread and drizzled over popcorn or used plain like a stiff sauce with some roasted chicken or to enrich some radishes. Some butter is salted to enhance its flavor. Most chefs prefer unsalted butter because it gives them more control over the seasoning of their food. The quality of butter varies; good, flavorful butter is worth seeking out.

Buttercream: Buttercream is a preparation in which sugar (often a hot syrup), whipped egg whites, or whole eggs and butter are combined to make a rich luxurious confection often used as an icing or filling for cakes. Buttercream methods are determined by how the buttercream will be used and vary in how the sugar is handled and in the ratio of yolks to whites. One part softened butter added to two parts pastry cream (see crème pâtissière) will give you one form of this versatile and varied preparation.

Butterfat: Butterfat is the primary component of butter, usually about 80 percent. When it's separated from the water and milk solids in whole butter, it is called clarified butter, a translucent flavorful fat that enriches emulsified sauces and is also a superlative cooking fat.

Butterfly: To butterfly is a butchering technique of opening a whole muscle so that it spreads out, lays flat. It's often done to remove a bone, such as from a leg of lamb. Butterflied meat can be cooked splayed but, more interestingly, the cook can in effect season the interior of a butterflied piece of meat, or stuff it, and then tie it back up close to its original shape with butcher's string, a way of influencing the interior of a cut of meat before you cook it.

Buttermilk: Buttermilk is the liquid by-product of making butter. More commonly today buttermilk refers to the cultured milk sold in grocery stores that is thick and acidic. Like natural yogurt, buttermilk is useful as a flavoring device, and in batters its acid reacts with baking soda to release gas and leaven the batter.

Butterscotch: Butterscotch is a sauce and flavor distinguished from caramel by the use of brown sugar instead of white and the addition of vanilla. Perhaps because it has been so thoroughly embraced by boxed pudding mixes, it's become, regrettably, an uncommon preparation. It is more complex and richer than caramel and is enhanced if cider vinegar or lemon juice is used as a seasoning to balance the intense sweetness.

C

Cake: Cakes, one of the primary categories of preparations in the sweet kitchen (though things such as cornbread and biscuits are forms of cake, as well), fall into subcategories depending on the ratio of egg, sugar, flour, and fat, how those ingredients are combined, and the type of leavening used. Arguably, the method with which they're mixed is the primary determiner of the category and kind of cake those basic ingredients become: *Straight mixing* of the ingredients all together at once, usually leavened chemically (pancakes, muffins, quickbreads); the *creaming method,* in which the sugar and fat are mixed together to a creamy paste, that is, mechanically leavened (often followed by the addition of eggs one at a time), after which the remaining ingredients are added (brownies, pound cake, cheesecake); and the *foaming method* in which eggs are beaten (sometimes with the sugar) until they've increased substantially in volume (again, mechanical leavening), and the remaining ingredients are folded into the eggs, a strategy that takes advantage of the egg's extraordinary capacity to hold air and thus result in a light delicate crumb. There are subcategories of the foaming method as well. Angel food cake is made by whipping egg whites only, adding some of the sugar to them to make a meringue, then folding in the flour (no yolks, no fat)—the flour simply gives support to the structure of the meringue. With chiffon cakes, yolks and whites are separated, a batter is created out of all but the whites, and the whipped whites and batter are folded together. Sponge cakes combine whole eggs and sugar that are whipped over heat till they become frothy, after which the remaining dry ingredients are folded in.

Boxed cake mixes have rendered actual cake-making all but obsolete in the home kitchen, a regrettable circumstance given that boxed mixes tend to be bland and dry relative to the flavorfulness and richness you can bring to a cake made with the basic ingredients egg, sugar, flour, and fat.

Cake flour: See flour.

Cake pans: A variety of cake pans in differing materials are now commonly available. Because aluminum transmits heat most readily, this is the optimal material in which to bake. The heavier the gauge, the more evenly it will cook the food. Various nonstick surfaces and silicone molds are also widely available. It's a good idea to have a couple of good all-purpose cake pans; buy specialty pans—a ring mold, a springform pan, a jelly roll pan—according to what you like to make.

Calves' feet: The feet of calves, young cows, are especially rich in gelatin and can be added to meat stocks, especially veal stock, for additional body and for enhancing flavors without contributing new ones.

Campagne [*kahm-PAN-ya*]: French for country, this modifier suggests a rustic or simple preparation; it usually refers to a pâté that's coarsely ground and includes some liver or it can refer to bread that is large and hearty with a thick crust.

Canadian bacon: cured smoked pork loin. It's a good substitute for ham (not bacon), a lean cut that's easy to cure at home.

Canapé: Technically a canapé is a savory preparation served on a bite-sized piece of toast, but the meaning has broadened to include any form of individually portioned bites served before dinner. Compare hors d'oeuvres: dishes served before the meal that aren't individually portioned (olives and nuts or a charcuterie plate, for instance). Canapés should be approached with imagination—virtually anything can be manipulated into a canapé, from the common (canapés originated as mini open-faced sandwiches) to the more elaborate (soup, for instance, served in demitasse cups).

Candy: To candy is a technique typically brought to bear on savory items to give them a sweet counterpoint and, sometimes, additional crunch. Nuts are often candied by being cooked in a light glaze of butter, sugar, and seasonings, then roasted, or by being coated lightly with a starch, sugar, and seasonings, and deep-fried. Candy often suggests that sugar has been used to create a crunchy surface. Sugars are sometimes added to starches such as potatoes and yams, and these dishes can be called candied.

Canola oil: Canola oil is a neutral oil derived from a plant called rapeseed, originally made and marketed in Canada. It's an excellent all-purpose cooking oil. (See cooking oils.)

Caper: These flower buds from the Mediterranean, usually sold brined but which are also preserved in salt, are a salty acidic seasoning device used variously in sauces from the hot brown butter sauce (*beurre noir*) to the cold gribiche or as a garnish in, say, raw beef or cured salmon preparations.

Capon: Capon refers to a castrated chicken. These are rare in markets today but are prized for the fact that while they grow so big, up to eight pounds, they are still tender, delicate birds. Excellent for roasting.

Capsaicin: Capsaicin is a chemical concentrated in the white interior flesh of chillis responsible for the "heat." To reduce the heat when cooking with chillis, remove the white flesh and seeds before using. If you're working with a lot of peppers, it's a good idea to wear latex gloves; the chemical is hard to get off your fingers and easily finds its way to your eyes. If the sauce you're making is too hot, you can make an additional sauce without the capsaicin-carrying peppers and add it to the sauce, or the heat can be mitigated somewhat by the addition of a starch (such as potato) or a fat (butter).

Caramelization, caramelize: Technically, caramelization is the name we give to what happens to sugar molecules when they get hot, decompose, and begin to form new compounds. When we caramelize plain sugar, the sugar takes on many different hues and complex flavors. We often refer to the browning and sweetening of onions and other vegetables (and almost anything that browns as it cooks, for that matter) as "caramelization." But in most instances the browning is more likely the result of Maillard browning (the reaction of protein and carbohydrates to heat) and not actual caramelization. But the word *caramelization* remains a meaningful and less awkward term to describe the browning of fruits and vegetables during cooking than the more cumbersome term Maillard browning.

Carbohydrate: Carbohydrate is a broad category of food matter that includes sugars, starch, cellulose, pectins, and gums—pretty much everything we eat that's not a protein or a fat. Fruits and vegetables (all plants, really) are composed primarily of carbohydrates. Humans break down most of the carbohydrates we eat into sugars, which we convert to energy. We do not digest cellulose (fiber), the substance that provides structure to plants. (See McGee and Davidson for in-depth descriptions.) Several types of carbohydrates from potatoes to seaweed are used for thickening and gelling liquids.

Carpaccio: Carpaccio is often used to designate any thinly sliced raw meat, but its original form, sliced pounded beef, is its most valuable—a superb method for serving an inexpensive cut of beef (eye of round is best, rather than tenderloin, which can become mushy when pounded) in an elegant way. Use organic or grass-fed beef if it's available to you and beware potential clichés. "Carpaccio, a popular culinary idiom that promises a plate lined with thinly sliced meat, fish, or whatever the cook intends to glamorize, has suffered from overexposure, but this does not dim the luster of the brilliant original dish," writes Judy Rodgers in *The Zuni Cafe Cookbook*. "Easy to overwhelm, carpaccio shows best in restrained counterpoint, with careful contrasts of flavor, texture, and temperature."

Carrot: Carrots are a fundamental aromatic vegetable, used in countless preparations for their sweetness. They make up one-quarter of traditional mirepoix and can be used in most stocks, stews, and soup bases. It's hard to imagine a stock or stew that would not benefit from carrots. If they are to be used as a primary ingredient—they make a great pureed soup, and they are excellent glazed, grilled, and roasted—you should buy bunch carrots, carrots with their tops still on, which are usually fresher and a higher quality (but not always) than bagged carrots, often called "cello" carrots or "horse" carrots.

Carryover cooking: a fundamental idea and a matter of fact in the hot kitchen. Food doesn't stop cooking when you take it out of the oven or off the flame—it races. Big roasts get hotter inside. Brown butter can go from exquisite to bitter-black in a moment unless it's dumped from the pan or you add some cooling lemon juice. A crème brûlée in its water bath, if it has hit its perfect jiggle of doneness there in the oven, may overcook because carryover will take it past perfection. Nuts, toasting, with their high fat content, should be removed from the oven just before they appear to be done. Carryover cooking is as important a consideration as color, as aroma, as touch in evaluating when something is done. The rule of thumb is to plan on a 10 degree rise in temperature once the item is out of the heat. But many factors come to bear on the amount of carryover. How big is the item, how much fat, how much water, what is the ambient heat of its resting place, and how long will it rest? Carryover cooking can range from 5 degrees to 30 degrees depending on the circumstances; the larger the cut the farther it's likely to carry over. (See also resting.)

Cartilage: Cartilage is composed mainly of connective tissue, collagen, which, when cooked gently in a stock or stew, partly dissolves into gelatin, which gives great body to the liquid. When making stocks, a good proportion of joints to meat and bone will ensure that the stock has excellent body.

Cashew: In addition to being a great nut to eat roasted, cashews are a valuable cooking nut because of their sweet flavor and their capacity, when ground, to thicken and flavor sauces due to their high starch content, most notably in Indian dishes.

Casing: Casing usually refers to natural casing, typically from the digestive tract of sheep, pigs, and cows, though manufactured collagen casings are available. They vary in size according to the animal, from small sheep casing used for sausages like breakfast links and chipolatas, to the common hog casing for fresh sausages, to the very large beef bung caps for preparations such as bologna and mortadella. Most are edible, but some are too thick to be eaten. Casings can be ordered by mail or through the meat department of most grocery stores. They typically come packed in salt and will keep, refrigerated, for a year or more. Edible casings from hogs and sheep are especially valuable because they are both delicate and strong, they brown well, and provide a pleasing snap when they're eaten. Also, they're porous, and so allow specially prepared sausages to dry for dry-cured creations such as salami and soppressata. Caul fat, a membrane of connective tissue from pigs and sheep, veined with fat that surrounds the stomach and viscera, can be used as a kind of casing as well, as can pig and sheep bladder, the skin from duck and goose necks, and plastic wrap.

Casserole: While casserole can refer to a baking dish and lid as well as to the food that cooks in it and is served from it, the term denotes a baked dish (rather than a braise) and is reminiscent of the American kitchen in the 1950s, 60s, and 70s, when casseroles were in vogue; today the term is less common. The original *Joy of Cooking* lists an entire column of dishes under the heading casserole; in the revised and rewritten *Joy* (1997), the term is not listed, but makes a return in the 2006 edition, perhaps suggesting a comeback of sorts.

Cast iron: When properly maintained, cast iron pans are superlative cookware. They are inexpensive and durable, and because they're so dense they're slow to heat, but when they do, they get very hot and stay that way. When they are properly "seasoned," they are virtually as good as the fanciest nonstick sauté pan, better, in fact, because they can take a beating. They do react to acid and salt, however, so you wouldn't want to salt food down in cast iron, and the acid in tomatoes will actually draw iron into a tomato sauce (iron is good for you but tomato is bad for the pan).

To season cast iron, pour a half-inch layer of oil into it, put it over high heat until the oil is very hot or put into a 300°F oven for an hour or so, then let it cool completely. Pour off the oil and wipe dry with a paper towel. (In fact, if you make fried chicken or deep-fry potatoes in your cast iron, it will season itself.) Never use soap on it, only an abrasive (a copper scrub pad or some kosher salt), and it will stay seasoned and glossy indefinitely. If you neglect it, it can be re-seasoned. Even old and abused cast iron pans can be cleaned, seasoned, and reborn as first-rate cookware.

Enameled cast iron is cast iron that has an enamel coating—therefore it is nonreactive to salt and acid and should not be "seasoned"—and is also an excellent cooking material. It can be used on the stovetop or in the oven and is especially suited to braising because, while its surface is semi-non-stick, it still allows food to brown and the bottom develops a fond.

Caul fat: Caul fat is a membrane of connective tissue, veined with fat, that surrounds the stomach and other viscera in pigs and sheep (its medical name is omentum). It's a handy cooking device generally, enclosing a meat in a fatty membrane that virtually melts away during the cooking. It can be used to help shape meat and keep it moist during cooking (braised meats that have cooled can be wrapped and reheated in caul fat in a hot oven); it can wrap sausage (*crepinette*) or hold together different ingredients (a package of roasted vegetables and a chicken breast, for example); it can give a protective layer of fat to roasts, serving as a barding device. It must be special-ordered from the grocery store, or ordered via the Internet, or sometimes it can be found in specialty markets.

Cauliflower: Cauliflower is an underused vegetable that's an excellent carrier of garnishes and sauces. It's delicious roasted (it caramelizes well, especially when basted with butter while roasting), boiled and served with an emulsified sauce (though cheese sauce is traditional), and simmered and finished in the oven with garnish. It's crunchy and satisfying raw, and has mild, almost nutty, artichoke-like flavors when roasted. Its subtle cabbagelike flavors can be a good foil when garnishing rich seafood such as shrimp or lobster, and deep earthy flavors such as truffle. Cauliflower is also suited to pureed soups and sauces.

Cayenne powder: From the cayenne chilli, this hot powder is a good all-purpose heat source that's commonly available on the grocery store spice rack. But cooks should also consider other, less commonly available chilli powders as well, which can give more complex, sweeter, fruitier forms of heat, from dried chipotles ground to a powder to Espelette powder.

Celeriac: Often referred to as celery root, this is a wonderful aromatic root vegetable that's often pureed like—and with—potatoes. It's delicious roasted or boiled or poached and is excellent for use in soups. It's also an excellent aromatic to use in stocks and soups.

Celery: Celery is one of the traditional aromatic vegetables in mirepoix along with onion and carrot, used to enhance all manner of stocks, stews, and soups. Raw, its main attribute is its crunchiness, though it is also good braised. Its use as an aromatic should be evaluated by the cook—some chefs do not include it in mirepoix, feeling that it contributes too much bitterness to the flavor of the stock. It can be cooked in a variety of ways—its main obstacle is the long fibers running through it. Depending on how you're using the celery, you may want to peel away the fibers; otherwise they should be tenderized through long cooking.

Cellulose: Cellulose is a structural material in vegetables, fiber, a substance we don't digest but that is nevertheless good for our digestive tract. For very refined dishes, the cellulose is often removed—vegetable sauces and soups strained through a chinois, for instance.

Ceviche: A preparation in which raw slices of fish or shellfish are coated with an acid, often lime juice, along with other aromats for a short time before serving. The acid coagulates the proteins on the surface, firms the flesh, and seasons it without obscuring the raw-flesh flavor. Only very fresh fish should be used (taste a slice raw to evaluate its quality); the fish best suited to ceviche are fish from tropical waters around South America where this preparation originated, such as snapper, as well as fluke, tuna, salmon, and shrimp.

Champagne: Champagne is sparkling white wine made in the eponymous region of France. While the name alone carries its own cachet, there are many excellent sparkling white wines that do not originate from that region. Champagnes and good sparkling whites can be used to good effect in sauces.

Charcuterie: Charcuterie refers to cooked meats, primarily pork, including sausages, pâtés, dry-cured sausages, and hams as well as beef and lamb, con-

THE ELEMENTS OF COOKING A TO Z   85

fits, and rillettes. Charcuterie (derived from the French words for flesh and cooked) once referred only to cooked pork products but has since broadened to include all manner of cured and preserved foods, from smoked salmon to beef jerky to pickled vegetables. The word can also refer to a shop in which these products are sold.

Chaud-froid: Chaud-froid is a preparation in which cooked and cooled meat (the words are French for hot-cold) is coated in a thick sauce, typically a white sauce rich in gelatin that will set when cooled, then glazed with aspic. Sometimes the portions are decorated after the white sauce sets up and then are glazed with clear aspic. It's not only showy on a buffet but also a convenient way to serve a meat with two different sauces built into the dish. A classic chaud-froid dish is chicken with tarragon sauce. Chicken is poached and cooled, then coated with a chicken velouté that has been infused with tarragon and seasoned aggressively because it will be eaten cold. When the sauce has set up on the chicken, a chicken consommé to which gelatin has been added is poured over the pieces, giving them a lacquered shine.

Cheek (meat): Beef cheeks are a succulent, flavorful cut of meat; because they're well-used muscles (and therefore tough), they should be braised. Fish, such as cod and halibut, often have excellent cheek meat, boneless and compact, that is cooked as the fish is cooked. (See also jowl, an outstanding cut from the pig that is often cured and used like pancetta.)

Cheese: In the kitchen, cheese functions a couple of ways. For all dishes, it's an enricher. Cheese is composed of milk fat and you should think of cheese as you would any fat. Parmigiano-Reggiano is used to finish risotto for instance, adding flavor, richness, and body to the dish. Cheeses can be added to sauces and will incorporate well provided the sauce includes a starch and is not boiled (wine or lemon juice can help keep the sauce smooth as well). Cheeses also melt and brown well and so add color, flavor, and texture to dishes that are finished au gratin. Some cheeses, ricotta for instance, don't melt but rather dry out. These cheeses, like any hard cheese, can be grated over food. When you use cheese, you do so to add richness, flavor, texture, and sometimes color to a dish.

Cheesecloth: A valuable kitchen tool, cheesecloth is used for straining liquids, for making sachets, and generally for keeping aromatic herbs and spices out of the finished food they've enhanced. It's used as well for wrapping food that will be poached—a pâté, for instance, or foie gras *au torchon* (French for dish towel). It's a good idea to rinse cheesecloth first to get rid of stray fibers. Remember that other types of cloth will do the same work, often better and more economically. A few new handkerchiefs bought and marked for the kitchen are excellent straining devices (and can be reused, unlike cheesecloth); cloth napkins and cotton dish towels are also useful.

Cheese course: Cheese customarily concludes the savory bulk of the meal. Some fine-dining restaurants use a cart to serve cheese; an alternative to serving a variety of cheeses is to create cheese-specific courses.

Chef: Chef means leader. Chef de cuisine means head of the kitchen. A chef who no longer cooks in his or her restaurant should be referred to as chef-restaurateur. Executive chef typically refers to one who oversees an entire kitchen or food operation. (See also *brigade*.)

Chef's knife: Perhaps the cook's most valuable tool, a chef's knife, sometimes called a French knife, is between 8 and 12 inches long with a broad blade about 1¾ inches wide that tapers to a point. A good chef's knife can be used for most cutting jobs. A chef's knife and a paring knife are the only two knives that are fundamental to the cook. They should be composed of high-carbon stainless steel, and feel solid and comfortable in the hand. As important as the knife itself is the way you grip it: pinch the blade between index finger and thumb for control of the blade, wrapping your last three fingers around the handle itself. (See the essay Tools, page 35.)

Chicken: The most common protein cooked in this country, chicken is also one of the most variable in quality and often the most overcooked. From very inexpensive agribusiness chicken to the hand-raised chicken at a farmers' market at boutique prices, and from mealy and bland to chewy and gamey, you have a range of choices available to you today. This text advocates buying pasture-raised livestock, and chickens are no different. The USDA recommends that chickens be cooked to a finished internal temperature of 165°F, though if you buy from smaller producers, the breast should be cooked a little less, and should be juicy. Whole chickens are best roasted uncovered and at a very high temperature. Breasts are best cooked on the bone because they tend to be juicier when cooked this way; they're very easy to overcook off the bone (the boneless chicken breast of factory raised birds is an insipid cut, one of the most commonly overcooked cuts of meat, and should be avoided). The legs and wings are excellent braised as well as roasted, fried, or grilled. Bones, either raw or cooked, are excellent for making stock. Chicken skin can be roasted till crisp and used as a garnish.

Chiffon: a type of cake made by combining a batter (using vegetable oil instead of a solid fat) with meringue for a light spongy crumb. (See cake.)

Chiffonade: Chiffonade is an elegant cut, like a julienne, used primarily with herbs that will become part of the garnish of a dish. To chiffonade basil or sage or any other leaves, stack them, roll them into a tight bundle, and slice them crosswise into very fine ribbons.

Chilli: Chilli refers to a variety of pungent fruits often called chile peppers or hot peppers. A wide variety is commonly available at grocery stores, both fresh and dried (and sometimes canned, as with chipotles in adobo sauce). All have their own flavors and heat levels. They are extraordinarily versatile and add great flavors and verve to countless dishes. The heat in chillis (capsaicin) resides in the white flesh to which the seeds are attached and this, along with the seeds, is typically removed and discarded when preparing fresh chillis. Fresh chillis—poblanos, jalapeños, serranos, habeneros are common—are customarily stemmed and seeded. Dried chillis—ancho, chipotle, guajillo, cascabel, for example—are best if they're lightly toasted to enhance their flavor and completely dehydrate them. The stems and seeds are then removed and these peppers can be chopped or more commonly ground to powder in a spice mill or coffee grinder. Alternatively they can be rehydrated in warm water, then stemmed, seeded, and chopped and used in sauces. The late food historian Alan Davidson uses the native word for this important fruit in his *Oxford Companion to Food,* and his colleague Harold McGee joins him in using the term exclusively for what we've referred to as chili peppers, chile peppers, and hot peppers. "Given the many possibilities for confusion," writes McGee in *On Food and Cooking,* "I agree with Alan Davidson and others that we should refer to pungent capsicums with the original and unambiguous Nahuatl name *chilli.*"

China cap: kitchen slang for a conical metal strainer, used to strain out larger ingredients or ingredients that need pressing, such as lobster or shrimp shells, to extrude as much flavor as possible. Further straining can be done via a chinois.

Chinois tamis: French for Chinese sieve and usually referred to simply as a chinois (as distinct from a tamis, or drum sieve), this cone of fine mesh is an invaluable device for straining stocks, sauces, and soups. It's a tool of refinement; it will take a thick rough sauce or pureed soup and transform the texture into one of velvet. Raw vegetables pureed in a blender can be transferred to a chinois and pressed against the mesh to attain just their juice. For ultimate refinement when straining sauces, rap the chinois on its rim to pass the liquid through the mesh. Don't ram a ladle into the bottom; pressing the solids with a ladle this way will force the minute fibers that you're trying to remove from the sauce through the mesh and back into the sauce.

Chlorophyll: The green pigment in plants can be effectively freed from the plant and concentrated by grinding the plant leaves (spinach, parsley, watercress, for example), and soaking, simmering, and straining them. The resulting paste can be added to sauces and other preparations for an intensely green presentation.

Chocolate: Chocolate is a remarkable substance for the complexity of its flavor and luxury of its texture. Better-quality chocolate for cooking and baking has never been more widely available to cooks. Chocolate is also very easy to work with, more or less a finished product you add to your preparation for flavor and texture. The simplest of all chocolate preparations is ganache, otherwise known as chocolate sauce. Chop 8 ounces of chocolate, pour 8 ounces of hot cream over it, wait a few minutes, and stir. The quality of the result is dependent primarily on the quality of the chocolate. For cooking and baking, semisweet or bittersweet chocolate are most commonly used (the terms for all practical purposes are interchangeable). Quality is often implied by the percentage of actual chocolate (cocoa solids, the flavor, and cocoa butter, the fat) in the bar. Standard semisweet/bittersweet contains about 55 percent chocolate (the rest is mainly sugar). Chocolate with between 62 percent and 70 percent chocolate is now commonly available and may have a more complex and powerful flavor. As a rule, you get what you pay for. Taste and compare brands such as Scharffen Berger or Callebaut Bloc. If the confection you're planning is dependent on the flavor of your chocolate, choose a high-percentage chocolate you like.

Cholesterol: Cholesterol has negative connotations because high levels in our blood are associated with heart disease. But it's important to distinguish between blood cholesterol and the cholesterol in foods. While the dangers of high blood cholesterol are not disputed, remember that cholesterol in the food we eat (eggs, meat) doesn't necessarily raise our blood cholesterol; saturated fat is more often the culprit here. Technically, cholesterol is a lipid; lipids are fat-related substances that are among the primary structural components of cells.

Chop: an all-purpose term for breaking food down into chunks (as opposed to slices or finer cuts), used when the shape of the food is irrelevant. "Rough chop" is a common instruction for vegetables that will be used as aromatics in a stock or a sauce—anywhere from a half-inch to an inch. While the shape of the chop isn't important, the size can be: bigger chunks will take longer to yield their aromatic influence than smaller ones, the primary consideration when chopping. If what's being chopped will remain in the finished dish, smaller is usually better than bigger. (Compare dice and mince.)

Choux paste: See *pâte à choux*.

Chowder: A type of soup that can also be thought of as a method of preparation. Traditionally, chowders are based on seafood and potatoes, contain salt pork for flavoring, and are packed with ingredients, almost like a stew. They can be water- or stock-based and are sometimes thickened with a roux and creamed. But chowder today—whether with tomatoes (Manhattan-style), cream (New England–style), or vegetables (corn chowder)—denotes a thick, garnish-rich soup.

Chutney: Chutney is most commonly referred to as a condiment, a mixture of fruit, vegetables, or herbs, seasoned with acids and heavy spices, cooked to concentrate the liquids and flavors, a sweet-sour sometimes spicy-hot mixture often associated with Indian cuisine. But many chefs use the term to refer to any kind of thick chunky sauce, and it's useful to think of it this way when you're planning a menu and considering what to pair with meat or fish. In this way it's not much different from salsa, the Spanish word for sauce that, here, connotes a savory, chunky, vegetable-based sauce. Both chutney and salsa should be part of a cook's arsenal of sauces.

Citrus: In the kitchen, citrus refers to a group of salutary acids that add excellent flavor, freshness, and vibrancy to any number of preparations. It's a fundamental category of seasoning. Citrus juices can also form the base of vinaigrettes, and they can be reduced and used as the foundation for a sauce, sweet or savory.

Clam: See bivalves.

Clarification: A clarification is an egg white mixture used to remove particles from a stock, wine, or juice, any liquid that will be served perfectly clear. (See consommé.) The egg white mixture, which can also contain ground meat, mirepoix, tomato, and eggshell, is added raw to a liquid that is subsequently brought up to heat; as the egg white coagulates, it forms what is referred to as a raft, the final stage of the clarification, a disc or mat of coagulated meat and egg white, which in fact is a net of protein and collects the particles that make a stock opaque. After the stock has simmered for an hour or so (gently so as not to destroy the raft), the stock is ladled out of the pot (or for large quantities, siphoned), and passed through a coffee filter. It's possible to clarify stock using only egg white, but the protein net dilutes the stock's flavor somewhat, so it's important to include additional meat and aromats to the egg white mixture.

Clarified butter: Clarified butter is whole butter from which milk solids and water have been removed—pure, translucent butterfat. It's an excellent cooking fat. Whole butter is usually clarified by heating it gently; the butter will break, and the milk solids and water will foam to the top, where they can be skimmed off; a skin will also form on top, which is removed; the heavier, milky water that sinks, gradually bubbles to the surface, where it, too, is skimmed. When virtually all of the unwanteds are removed, the butterfat is strained through cloth to remove any remaining particles. It is among the most flavorful fats available and is excellent for sautéeing and frying because of this flavor and the fact that it can get very hot without burning. (The solids in whole butter will heat rapidly after the water has cooked off, first resulting in brown butter and then burnt butter.) Clarified butter is the traditional fat used for emulsified butter sauces and results in a very fine and elegant flavor. Butter can be cooked a little further so that the butter is both clarified and browned, in which case it's an excellent flavoring for both savory and sweet dishes. It's used in many cuisines, notably

Indian, in which it's called ghee (and is somewhat more complex than whole butter that's been clarified but not browned).

Clean: perhaps one of the most important adjectives for food and kitchens and also one of the most important verbs as well. Clean flavors are always to be pursued, flavors that most purely represent the food being cooked. Clean also denotes a harmony of flavor pairings. Stocks are said to be clean when they are relatively clear and fresh. Sauces are said to be clean when they have been properly cooked and strained and used, and not muddy, old, gluey, or off, as they can become if not cared for.

Cleaning is among the most important activities in the kitchen. A common refrain among chefs is "always be cleaning." Keep your food clean, your stovetop clean, your work surfaces clean. The unusual and fascinating dynamics of cooking are such that cluttered or dirty surfaces work their correlative clutter into the food.

Clean is also a state of mind and a description of a cook's abilities, as in the common phrase "working clean"—which means a cook not only looks clean and is keeping his or her work surfaces clean and organized, but is also working efficiently, is in control, with no wasted moves.

Clostridium botulinum: See botulism.

Cloth: Cotton cloths, cotton napkins, dish towels, handkerchiefs bought for culinary uses are valuable kitchen tools for straining stocks and sauces. See cheesecloth.

Coagulate, coagulation: Proteins coagulate, meaning they mesh together under a few specific circumstances. Proteins in meat and fish coagulate when they are cooked, resulting in stiffer flesh, dairy proteins coagulate to form curds, and egg proteins coagulate to form scrambled eggs and custards. Salt and acid cause some proteins to coagulate, but the main coagulating mechanism is heat. Various proteins coagulate at different temperatures, from 120° to 180°F (see McGee for specific proteins). The strength of coagulation increases as the temperature increases; a delicate mesh can clump into a tight knot. Scrambled eggs can become rubbery, a custard can curdle, meat and fish can become dry. Protein coagulation is omnipresent in cooking, an important concept with many nuances that are useful for the cook to understand.

Coconut: Unless you live where coconuts grow, you probably don't use them often, though because of their durability, they travel well and can be found throughout the country. The meat of the coconut has a sweet, nutty taste. Peeled from its woody shell and skin, it can be pureed with the coconut water to make coconut milk. The flesh is good to eat and to cook with and the milk, with its high fat content, makes it a great addition to both savory and sweet sauces, as well as a superb poaching liquid. Coconut fat, which has a melting point similar to that of butter and chocolate, is available in Asian markets and can be added to confections instead of, or in conjunction with, butter or cocoa butter.

Cod: Cod is arguably the most important fish in the history of human endeavors, in large measure because it is preserved so easily (see salt cod). It has become so popular in fact that we're in danger of overfishing it. Cod is a fish of great versatility; its flavor is mild and so pairs well with any number of sauces and garnishes; its flesh is firm, abundant, and nutritious. Cod is a fish to be appreciated and revered.

Coddle: Meaning to cook gently, coddle almost always refers to eggs in their shell, in a ramekin or in an enclosed container cooked in a water bath (*bain-marie*) until the white is just set.

Coffee: While coffee is a splendid beverage, it is also an effective seasoning device to be used in sauces and stews. Its complex flavor, notably its compelling bitterness, gives a perfect balance to the sweet acidity of concentrated tomatoes, in a tomato sauce or in a tomato-based sauce, such as a barbecue sauce, not to mention "red-eye gravy" (a sauce that traditionally uses coffee rather than wine or stock to deglaze a pan and form the base of the sauce). It can be used to flavor custards and cakes, as well. Concentrated coffee flavors, such as espresso extract, or instant espresso powder dissolved in an equal part boiling water, can also be used. If a sauce or custard to be infused with coffee flavor will be strained, freshly ground or chopped coffee beans can be used; if not, then freshly brewed coffee should be used. The flavor of coffee is especially volatile. It hits its peak and then deliquesces. Coffee is easily overcooked. It can be exquisite very hot or very cold but is unappealing in between. A powerful and unusual tool in the kitchen.

Cognac: Brandy made in the area of the eponymous town in western France, Cognac can be among the finer kinds of brandy, excellent for seasoning. (See brandy and alcohol.)

Colander: An essential kitchen tool, it's good to have at least one sturdy metal colander rather than a flimsy plastic one.

Cold smoke: to smoke food without cooking it. This means smoking meat, fish, or cheese at temperatures below 90°F. Salmon is typically cold smoked. Some items, such as cheese, are often smoked at refrigeration temperatures, below 40°F.

Collagen: a protein that gives structure and stability to muscles; connective tissue that makes up skin, tendon, cartilage. Collagen, when heated in the presence of water, dissolves, or comes apart, resulting in gelatin that gives body to stocks and sauces and in enough concentration creates meat gels, sometimes called aspic. The collagen in fish is much more delicate and easily broken down, dissolving at 120° to 130°F as opposed to that in meat, 140°F and higher (see McGee).

Combination cooking: Combination cooking uses two different forms of heat, often "dry" heat and "moist" heat, and is used in traditional braises in which a meat is seared in hot fat, then cooked till tender in liquid. An appliance referred to as a "combi" oven (combination oven) uses more than one form of heat, often steam and hot air for very fast, effective cooking.

Commis: The French word for clerk or assistant, *commis* is the incoming rank of a cook in professional kitchens; used most often in high-end and French kitchens, a more common term for *commis* is prep cook.

Common sense: A valuable maxim in the kitchen is that we cook with our senses: we evaluate the appearance of our food, we touch it, we listen to the amount of sizzle in a pan or the notes of dough turned by a hook in a mixer, our sense of smell helps us to determine doneness, and we must always be tasting as we cook. But common sense should be included in the list of important senses in the kitchen. It means: think about what your other senses are telling you. It means figuring it out on your own. Common sense is doled out unequally at birth, as surely as our other senses, but it is developed in a cook by trial and error, simple repetition, and by paying attention to the effects of heat and cold and time on your food, the behavior of your cooking tools, by keeping your eyes open and registering and remembering what you see.

Composed salad: The composed salad is a category of preparations—not to mention an excellent strategy for simple, satisfying, and balanced meals—whose backbone is lettuces and greens but whose components are diverse enough to comprise an entire meal, and can include cooked and chilled vegetables, meats, dairy, and starches, the sauce for which is customarily a vinaigrette. The ingredients in a composed salad are typically separate from the greens, consciously arranged, rather than tossed randomly together. Cobb salad and *salade niçoise* are common examples of the form, but really these salads can be composed of virtually any thoughtful combination of foods.

Compote: Compote is a loose term denoting fruit cooked with sugar. A compote can use fresh fruit or dried, the sweetness can be in the form of white sugar, brown sugar, honey, and seasonings and aromatics can include wine and herbs. Compotes can be served by themselves as a dessert, can accompany a dessert, serve as the sauce for a dessert, and they can also accompany savory dishes, such as grilled or roasted meats and game, or be used as part of cheese or charcuterie platters.

Compound butter: Compound butter, whole butter flavored with aromats, seasonings, and acid is one of the most easy and satisfying sauces available to the home cook. It's especially good with grilled meats and fish and a smart strategy given that grilling doesn't create, as a by-product of the cooking, a sauce base the way braising or pan roasting do. A compound butter can be made to pair with virtually anything. And because butter is usually on hand in the fridge, it's a great sauce or garnish to use in a pinch. The most common form is called *beurre maître d' hôtel,* or hotel butter (parsley, lemon juice and zest, salt, and pepper). Butter mixed with shallot and *fines herbes* would be excellent with roast chicken, butter mixed with citrus zest would be excellent atop poached salmon, or combined with minced chipotle peppers, lime juice, and cilantro on grilled steak, et cetera. When composing compound butter, you should think of it as you would a sauce—seasoning it with salt and pepper, adding an acidic component for balance and contrast (citrus or wine, for instance), together with appropriate aromatics—fresh herbs and shallot are most common. To make a compound butter, use a rubber spatula to press and fold the seasonings and aromats into room temperature butter. It can be served out of a ramekin but restaurant kitchens typically form the creamy butter into a log using plastic wrap, and chill it in an ice bath to maintain its cylindrical shape as it hardens; it can then be sliced into appealing discs when ready to use.

Concassé: *Concassé* is French for pounded, but in kitchen parlance the term refers to tomato that is peeled, seeded, and chopped. Tomato *concassé* is used to finish any number of sauces or dishes, adding color and flavor.

Condensed milk: The main forms of milk from which water has been removed are evaporated milk, sweetened condensed milk, and powdered milk. Their main benefit is shelf life—they keep for ages at room temperature. "Condensed" milk is sweetened with sugar and cooked until it is as thick as sauce. It can be used to sweeten coffees and teas, and has myriad culinary uses—as a custard base, drizzled on cookies and baked, and, gently heated, it will turn into a rich caramel at low temperatures.

Condiment: A condiment is a sauce served not on a dish but with it, sauce on the side, whether it's mustard served with a charcuterie platter, chutney with Indian dishes, chillis in fish sauce with Thai dishes, or ketchup with a burger. Derived from the Latin word meaning to pickle, condiments are associated with a powerful balance of sweet, sour, acidic, and spicy flavors.

Cone: See cornet.

Confectioners' sugar: See sugar.

Confit: Confit, the French term for preserving, refers to a cooking technique in which meat is first salted for a day or more, then rinsed and cooked gently in fat until tender, then cooled and chilled in the cooking fat. The meat is removed from the fat and reheated to serve. The technique originated for reasons of preservation: meat properly salted, cooked, and cooled this way could be kept in a cool cellar for months without spoiling; indeed, it tended to improve over time. While we no longer need to cook food this way to preserve it, the technique continues to be valuable because the results taste so good. Duck and goose is often confited in its own fat, but pork is excellent cooked this way; any meat that benefits from long slow cooking can be confited. The confit results in meat that is very rich and succulent and tender, and skin, if it is reheated properly, that is very crisp and tasty. Generally speaking, anything referred to as a confit— lemon confit is simply lemon packed in salt—has been preserved.

Confiture: French for preserved fruits and jams, confiture, which comes from the word meaning to preserve, can reasonably be used to refer to any fruit that is cooked with sugar and cooled, a process that will, to varying degrees, preserve the fruit. Making a confiture is an excellent strategy if you find yourself with an abundance of fruit on the tail end of ripe.

Connective tissue: Connective tissue either connects or supports other tissue in all animals. Types of connective tissue include bone, tendon, and cartilage. Connective tissue is a mixed blessing to the cook. It's valuable because it's a rich source of a protein called collagen, which, when cooked, breaks down into gelatin that gives body to liquids, from delicate to firm. But connective tissue is the stuff that makes certain cuts of meat tough. Because connective tissues usually only break down and become tender at temperatures that are considered well beyond well-done for meats, tough cuts of meat—such as the shoulders and shanks of animals—are often cooked in liquid (meaning, at temperatures below 212°F) for hours and are served with that liquid to which they've contributed abundant gelatin and flavor.

Consistency: The thickness, or lack thereof, of a sauce or a soup is a quality we tend to think about after we've got the seasoning and flavor right, because we can adjust it, thickening via a slurry, thinning with stock or water, but it helps to think about consistency of your liquids at all stages of cooking. Indeed, some chefs consider such adjustments an indication of an error in the cooking of a sauce. The proper consistency in a sauce is every bit as important as the flavor and seasoning. And often consistency tells us when something is done, especially with egg-based sauces.

Consommé: Technically, consommé is a clear soup or broth, and a "consommé double" is one that has been clarified with egg whites and fortified with additional meat and aromats. Generally, though, consommé refers only to a stock that has been clarified. The word has an appealing double meaning: it can mean finished or completed (a finished stock), but it can also mean consummate or perfect, and so we can think of consommé as stock brought to the ultimate state of clarity and flavor, stock perfected. It should be crystal clear, clear as a distilled liquid. Any clear stock (stock that hasn't been made cloudy from too vigorous cooking) can be clarified using the consommé method: a clarification, ideally including mirepoix, aromats, and lean ground meat in addition to egg whites, are combined with stock in a pot and brought up to heat as the pot is stirred continuously (to prevent egg white from sticking to the bottom of the pan) until the raft forms. The soup is simmered gently for about an hour, then carefully ladled through a coffee filter into a clean pot or container. The soup can usually be cooled and reheated without losing its clarity. Garnishes range from diced custard to julienned vegetables to grains and pastas and even Parmigiano-Reggiano (see Escoffier, which lists nearly 150 consommé variations), though care must be taken to prevent the garnish from clouding the crystal clear broth. Consommé can also be served cold (often as gelled consommé).

Convection oven: A convection oven is an oven with a fan in it; in some ovens the fan circulates heat emitted by the elements, in others the heat emanates from the same vent the fan blows through. The circulation ensures a uniform temperature within the oven, which otherwise has hot and cool spots. Convection heat has many benefits, among them a decreased cooking time, uniform heat, and increased dehydration of what's being cooked (such as the skin of a chicken). But it can also accelerate the cooking and dry out delicate surfaces, such as on custards and cakes.

Cook: one who cooks, nothing more, but this includes chefs who cook, as well (see chef). Any chef worth his salt is a cook first and foremost. Men and women who work in kitchens are cooks; the leaders of sections of the *brigade* are chefs, that is, leaders, of their area.

Cookie: The defining components of a cookie are, with some exceptions, flour, sugar, and fat, and how we vary and add to these components define specific cookies. Flour gives a cookie structure; sugar gives a cookie both structure and sweetness and sometimes crispness; and fat shortens the dough and gives a cookie unctuousness, suppleness, flavor. Seasoning, leavening, mixing method, shaping method all affect a cookie, and the three base components can be varied or even replaced—almonds might replace some of the flour in a sugar cookie, egg whites create the structure in a macaroon. These are flourishes—chocolate chips, eggs, oatmeal and raisins, citrus and poppy seeds, sweet spices, fun shapes, colorful decoration—benevolent and necessary flourishes, certainly, the paint not the canvas.

Cooking oil: The main criteria for oil used for cooking, neutral oil, is how hot it can get before it smokes and burns, and after that, the flavor and feel it adds to the food it's cooking. The chief benefit of a cooking oil is that it can get very hot; that combined with its density makes it an effective vehicle for heat transfer. Refined cooking oils such as vegetable oil, corn oil, canola oil, peanut oil, and grapeseed oil can reach up to 450°F before they begin to smoke (see McGee), at which point they begin to break down rapidly and develop bad flavors (and even catch fire). Animal fats begin to smoke at about 375°F. The most neutral-flavored oils tend to have higher smoke points; these also tend to be lower in saturated fat, less expensive, and more easily available than animal fat. But animal fat can impart a delicious flavor to the food. Olive oil can be used for cooking, but depending on how it's made, it can have a low smoking point (expensive cold-pressed extra virgin olive oils should not be used for high-heat cooking). Also it's a very flavorful oil, a flavor you may or may not want to add to your food. Olive oil is more expensive than neutral oils and so less efficient from a cost standpoint. Many chefs prefer grapeseed oil because it has a high smoke point and a clean flavor, but it's expensive. Peanut oil is an excellent oil, as well, but also slightly more expensive than all-purpose canola or vegetable oils, which considering issues of cost, usage, flavor, and health, are the best all-purpose cooking oils. Hydrogenated fats (vegetable shortening) can be used; they have high smoke points and a long shelf life, but can contribute an oily feel in the mouth and given health concerns regarding trans fats, are not the preferred choice.

Cook off: To cook something off is kitchen vernacular for cooking and cooling food so that it's ready for service (as in, "I'm going to cook off the green beans before I break down the chickens").

Copper (pots, pans, and bowls): Copper pots and pans are prized for how well and evenly they conduct heat. They're beautiful, too. But they're expensive and they're a nuisance to keep bright. Copper bowls do help in stabilizing whipped egg whites (see McGee).

Corkscrew: While there all kinds of ingenious devices for removing a cork from a bottle, a wine key, the pocket-sized opener restaurant servers tend to use, is the best choice of corkscrews. They're inexpensive, space-efficient, and have few moving parts and so tend not to break; also they last a long time. They do require a small amount of practice, but their advantages make learning to use them worthwhile.

Corn: One of the world's most-produced grains, one that gives us products as diverse as oil, starch, sugar, and even plastic, is also one of the most versatile ingredients in the kitchen. Beyond use as a sweet vegetable boiled or gently sautéed, corn is an excellent garnish, adding visual and textural contrast to soups, sauces, salads, and stews. It also pairs well with most meats and lean fish. Frozen corn can be used in a pinch, but corn is best cut straight from the cob. Corn today is so sweet, it requires little cooking—it more or less just needs to be heated through. Corn can also be pulverized in a blender or food processor and strained for its juice, another excellent use of corn that has many applications (as a sauce, as an enrichment to risotto, for example). Other forms of corn are also available, from corn nuts to dried white corn, which can be used like a legume (soaked, then simmered, for dishes such as pozole), to popcorn.

Corned beef: See cured meats.

Cornet: French for horn, the cone is a convenient shape, or device, for serving food. Most Americans are used to filling theirs with ice cream, but tuile batter can be shaped around a cornet mold for a kind of canapé base. Classical French preparations include shaved ham and thinly sliced cured salmon shaped using such a mold, and sweet preparations include puff pastry wrapped around the mold, baked, and filled with some form of cream.

Cornichon: French cornichons, small elegant cucumbers, cured (pickled), and seasoned with tarragon, are tart and crunchy and excellent as a condiment for pâtés and cured meats and are also excellent chopped and added to cold sauces such as a gribiche or rémoulade. These are usually preferable to the American version, called gherkins, which tend to be more sweet-and-sour rather than elegant and tart.

Cornmeal: See grains.

Cornstarch: Cornstarch is mainly used to thicken liquids, everything from sauces to pie fillings. For sauces, it tends to break down with long cooking, so its usually used *à la minute* (see slurry). It can be used to create a very thin crisp coating on deep-fried food. Cornstarch can also be added to flour to reduce a dough's proportion of gluten for a more tender (lower-gluten) pastry dough.

Corn sugar: See dextrose.

Corn syrup: Corn syrup, a viscous sweetener, is valuable for the consistency it provides, adding chewiness and preventing the crystallization of other sugars in pastries and candies. It disperses more easily in liquids. It's considered less sweet, its effects less cloying than granulated sugar, and so is often used to sweeten tart preparations such as sorbets.

Coulis: Coulis is a sauce with a thick smooth consistency, most commonly used to refer to fruit sauces. Older definitions describe it as the juice from vegetables and shellfish and others include meat juices. Escoffier includes a recipe for an onion coulis. The term came into vogue at the height of nouvelle cuisine, when raspberry coulis was everywhere on menus. While chefs looking to diversify menu terms may apply it to any manner of puree used as a sauce, today it most usefully describes a sauce of raw or cooked fruit that is pureed and then strained (though some chefs dispute whether a sauce can be described as a coulis if it is cooked).

Country (style): The term country denotes rough cuts, coarse textures, robust flavors, and inexpensive ingredients. A country pâté, for instance, or country loaf (*pâté* or *pain de campagne*). It's useful in terms of setting expectations for a dish but the term country should not suggest a lack of quality or care.

Court bouillon: Literally, short or quick stock, court bouillon is made by heating aromatic herbs and vegetables in water acidulated with vinegar, wine, or citrus, to create a flavorful cooking medium, most commonly used for fish. Water, acid, mirepoix, and a *sachet d'epices* will make a standard court bouillon, but the technique can be varied depending on what's being cooked and how you you want to use it. Chilli peppers and citrus zest might be added to the water for poaching shrimp, for instance, or, for a different effect, garlic, scallions, and ginger.

Covering (pots and pans): Covering pots and pans, it should be obvious, keeps more heat in. Sauces boil harder and water comes to a boil faster in a covered pot. Stew in the oven will be hotter in a covered pot than in an uncovered one. Always boil green vegetables uncovered (though it's okay to cover the pot momentarily to help the water return to a boil if you're using too small a pot). Covering a sauce partially or completely will inhibit reduction of your sauce—so if your sauce is reduced enough but not cooked enough, continue to cook it covered. To retain some heat but allow some reduction (in a braised dish, for instance), the cover can be set ajar; a parchment paper lid can be cut to fit a pot to allow some reduction, prevent a skin from forming, and retain heat.

Couscous: See pasta.

Cracklings: Animal skin that's been slowly cooked until it's dehydrated and most of its fat has been rendered and it has become golden brown and crispy is called cracklings. The most common form of cracklings are made from pigskin, which has abundant fat and collagen. The skin must be slowly cooked until it's tender, scraped of residual fat, then can be cut into strips and fried. It can be slowly roasted as well until it's crisp. Duck and chicken skin also make extraordinary cracklings and can be used as a crisp rich garnish, in salads or bean dishes, for instance, as will fatty fish skin. Cracklings from poultry skin are best made by laying the skin between two Silpats and roasting until golden brown and crisp.

Cream (noun): Cream—that is, heavy cream or whipping cream ("light cream" has half as much fat and will not whip as well)—is an all-purpose enricher; it adds fat without adding substantial flavor or oiliness to countless preparations. Its thick consistency creates exquisite texture. From savory to sweet dishes, from sauces and soups to risottos, pastas, and potatoes, to all manner of vegetables, stews, dessert sauces, and custards, it would seem that more dishes than not can be improved with a little bit of cream. If, when evaluating a sauce or dish, it does not satisfy in quite the way you had hoped, one of the questions you should ask yourself is whether or not there's enough fat; if not, is cream an appropriate way to get more fat into the dish? Cream can be gently simmered and reduced by about half to make what's called double cream (*crème double*), concentrated cream used to finish sauces *à la minute*. If you have an abundance of cream that you won't use, you can whip it in a food processor until the fat and water separate; you'll be left with what amounts to butter and water, and the butter will keep much longer than the cream or can be frozen.

Cream can be whipped to increase its volume and lighten its texture. The colder it is, the easier it is to whip. Whipped cream is often sweetened and used as a dessert garnish, but it can also be used in savory dishes, seasoned with aromats, spices, acid, and/or herbs. If the dish it's enriching is hot, the whipped cream will quickly return to its liquid state.

Cream, sweetened, is practically a ready-made dessert and so there are countless desserts that are just that, cream and sugar combined with some sort of thickening procedure (cooked yolks, whipped egg whites, gelatin, cornstarch). Think of cream as a kind of dessert mother sauce.

Cream (verb): In baking, to cream means to combine sugar and fat into a uniform mixture. Creaming results in a fine texture (or crumb) in cakes (from cookies to muffins to pound cake); creaming is so fundamental that such preparations can be defined by the method, the creaming mixing method (see also cake). Creamed butter and sugar should appear bright and airy. Often eggs are mixed in one at a time following the creaming stage. Occasionally, creaming may refer to combining sugar and egg yolks and mixing till the sugar is uniformly dispersed.

Cream of tartar: Cream of tartar, a by-product of wine making, is, in effect, powdered acid. It's sometimes added to egg whites to help stabilize meringue (lemon juice will do the same job), and to preparations that use baking soda for leavening.

Cream out: kitchen slang for finishing a soup or sauces with cream *à la minute*.

Cream puff: See *pâte à choux*.

Cream sauce: béchamel sauce finished with cream; it sounds boring but is in fact elegant, delicious with delicately flavored lean white meats, or as a base for cream pasta sauces or cream soups.

Crécy: in classical French cuisine, a term that denotes carrots are a main component in the dish or is the main garnish (see similar terms *Du Barry* and Florentine).

Crème anglaise [*krem ahn-GLEZ*]: Crème anglaise—vanilla sauce, custard sauce, or simply anglaise—is the dessert workhorse sauce but there is nothing pedestrian about it when it's prepared correctly. Delicious by itself, served hot or cold, it can also be treated like a mother sauce and seasoned with anything from brown butter to sweet spices to distilled spirits; it can be the base for or accompany countless desserts. Serve it hot with a soufflé or as the sauce for an apple tart, or cold over berries. Freeze it and it's vanilla ice cream. Cook it in a water bath and it's crème brûlée. Add butter and sugar and it becomes a delicious buttercream filling. Thicken it with starch and it's a sturdy pastry cream. It couldn't be more basic: milk or cream, egg yolks, sugar, and vanilla (preferably a fresh bean but extract will work). The basic ratio, while variable to taste, is one cup of liquid to three yolks to a quarter cup of sugar. The method is standard: cream half the sugar with the eggs while the liquid and remaining sugar heat in a sauce pan (with vanilla bean if using); add a little hot liquid to the yolk-sugar mixture to temper the yolks, then add the yolks to the hot milk or cream, and stir the mixture continuously while it heats and thickens. When it hits *nappé* consistency, strain and chill it. Vanilla extract or other seasoning can be added during cooking or after, depending on the seasoning (spices or aromats that need time to infuse should be added to the milk or cream as its being heated). Crème anglaise is one of the fundamental preparations in the sweet kitchen, and left unsweetened, can be used for savory preparations as well.

Crème brûlée, crème caramel [*krem brew-LAY, CARE-ah-mel*]: Dessert custards garnished with caramelized sugar, crème brûlée and crème caramel are anglaise sauce cooked in a water bath. The texture, their great pleasure, should be luxurious and smooth. In the first, the cooked custard is coated with sugar and torched till the sugar forms a golden brown crust; in the second, the caramel is cooked first, added to the cooking vessel, and allowed to cool before the custard mixture is added, cooked, cooled, and unmolded.

Crème fraîche [*krem fresh*]: Crème fraîche is a cultured cream—that is, a cream in which acid-generating bacteria have been introduced to create a stiff, sour cream. Crème fraîche is stiffer than sour cream and has a more delicate, sour quality along with a hint of sweetness as well. Its texture and flavor make it an excellent all-purpose enricher, especially to hot preparations, soups, and sauces, because it can be heated without breaking. Crème fraîche is now widely available, but it can be made at home by combining two parts heavy cream with one part cultured buttermilk and leaving it to stand in a cool kitchen until the right consistency is reached, one to three days.

Crème pâtissière [*krem pah-TEE-see-air*]: Also known as pastry cream, crème pâtissière is essentially sauce anglaise, vanilla sauce, thickened with starch (flour was once used but cornstarch is more common now) so that it has considerable body for use as an all-purpose dessert filling (cakes, éclairs, fruit tarts). The method is much the same as that for crème anglaise, adding about 2 tablespoons of cornstarch per cup of liquid to the sugar-egg mixture and cooking till very thick, too thick to strain. In some cases whole eggs are used instead of yolks, or milk only and no cream, and it's usually flavored by vanilla extract rather than by a bean. Additional flavors can be added immediately after cooking it.

Crepinette: sausage wrapped in caul fat and roasted, usually as a patty, though Escoffier recommends shaping them into rectangles. Think of the crepinette as a technique, a way of serving loose sausage in an elegant way. Often herbs or other garnish are placed on top of the sausage beneath the caul fat, which becomes transparent after cooking.

Cross contamination: Avoiding cross contamination, transferring harmful bacteria from one food to another, or one surface to another (a shipping box to a cutting board), is mainly a matter of common sense in the home kitchen—wash cutting boards thoroughly, don't store raw meats above the salad in the fridge—but certainly not something to be ignored, and it's a watchword in busy professional kitchens.

Crosshatch: Crosshatching usually refers to decorative grill marks on meat, though it can also refer to the overlapping cuts in skin, such as on a duck breast, which facilitates the fat's rendering and the skin's crisping and, secondarily, an appealing visual effect. Cross marks should not be at right angles to create squares but rather obliquely, to create diamonds. To make an appealing crosshatch, start with your blade at five o'clock, then for the crosshatch, shift it to seven o'clock. The same for grill marks—start your meat at five o'clock and shift it to seven o'clock (the grill or grill pan must be very, very hot to make good grill marks).

Crouton: Literally, bit of crust, we tend to think of croutons as crunchy cubes of bread in a salad, but a crouton can be a slice of bread that is heated until it's crisp all the way through, as with the crouton in traditional onion soup. Store-bought croutons are almost invariably pale and/or badly seasoned versions of actual croutons, with very little flavor and stale herbs. If the crouton matters to the dish, it's best to make your own. Cut flavorful bread, season it if you wish with a flavorful fat, such as olive oil, and salt, or leave dry, and put it in a very low oven to toast. You can avoid burning your croutons by keeping the oven temperature at around 275°F or below.

Fresh bread can also be sautéed in a pan in oil or butter until golden brown and crisp.

Cru [*krew*]: raw or uncooked. Jambon cru is ham that's been dried but not cooked. Cru is a useful term in that it's more elegant than raw or uncooked.

Crudité [*krew-di-TAY*]: Raw vegetables, usually served as hors d'oeuvres, are popular because they score high in all the categories pre-meal food requires: one- or two-bite items with good visual appeal and variety of tastes and textures; they're healthful and won't fill you up, and they're easy to prepare. Freshness is key, as is a good sauce or sauces, usually fat-based for lean vegetables; vinaigrettes work well, or the sauce could be as simple as a good butter served with radishes and coarse salt. Tougher green vegetables are best blanched and shocked to tenderize them slightly and bring out an enticing color.

Crumb: Crumb is the word bakers use for the interior of a bread or a cake. When a baguette has an airy interior with uniform circular air pocks and a fresh fragrant aroma, it's got a good crumb, or a cake may be said to have a fine crumb, a coarse crumb, or a dry crumb.

Cuisinart: See food processor.

Cuisson [*kwee-SOHN*]: *Cuisson* literally signifies cooking process—*cuisson à la ficelle* means cooked on a string, *cuisson à la vapeur* means steamed. And it can also mean the cooking liquid—the sauce a braise cooks in, for instance. But it carries a useful extension of that secondary meaning in some kitchens: cooking liquid that, after it's done its job, is then reduced to become a part of the finished sauce for the item that cooked in it. It's most commonly used as part of the shallow poach technique; when the fish has poached, it's removed from the pan and the cook reduces this *cuisson,* adding herbs and butter, with a little starch to thicken it, to make an *à la minute* sauce.

Culture: A culture can refer to live bacteria that might be added to, or developed in, milk, sausage, dough, or brine to initiate fermentation. A product that is cultured, such as crème fraîche or yogurt, has had beneficial bacteria added to it; the bacteria feed on sugars in the food, and generate acid as a result, which not only gives a pleasant tang to the food but also helps to preserve it.

Curd: When acid is added to or develops in milk, specific proteins called caseins clump together; the clumps are called curds. Curds are what give us cheese, and this curdling action is what makes yogurt and crème fraîche thick. (See McGee for a complete description of the curd and curdling.)

Curdle: the act of proteins clumping together, coagulating, or more generally, any homogenous mixture that separates into clumps and liquid. Sometimes curdling is desired (cheese), and sometimes not, such as a custard that overbakes or a hollandaise that breaks.

Cure: 1) To cure means to preserve. Almost always, it's salt that cures food, often followed by a secondary treatment, cooking or drying. (See salt cod, bacon, prosciutto.) 2) The salt mixture used to cure meats, which can contain sodium nitrite, sugar, and other seasonings. Cures can be dry (salt and seasonings) or wet (also called a brine). A "dry" cure should not be confused with dry curing, which indicates that a food has been cured with salt and then hung to dry in order to preserve it.

Curing salt: Curing salt is a salt containing a small amount of nitrite or nitrate, also called sodium nitrite or, generically, pink salt, which is often sold under various brand names. Sodium nitrate is pink salt that includes nitrate, an important component of dry-cured sausages, required to prevent the growth of the bacteria that causes botulism. Potassium nitrate, saltpeter, was used for dry-cured sausages but has been replaced by sodium nitrite and sodium nitrate (depending on the item being cured) because of their consistency and reliability.

Curry: Curry is a generic term, derived from the word for sauce, referring to a range of dishes common in India and Southeast Asia, usually specified as an Indian curry or a Thai curry and denoting a fragrant sauce with an abundance of spices, often very hot.

Curry powder: Curry powder is a blend of ground spices used to flavor sauces, usually associated with cuisines of India. High-quality blends from the grocery store are acceptable if they're very fresh; they become insipid over time. It's better to find a recipe you like and make your own fresh, to your own taste. Spices common in curry powders include cumin, chillis, coriander, cardamom, cinnamon, nutmeg, ground ginger, and turmeric, which gives a sauce the neon-yellow color associated with Indian curries.

Custard: The most basic definition of custard is simply liquid thickened by eggs, a fundamental preparation, and idea, in both the savory and sweet kitchen. Custards give us some of our best dishes—quiches, crème brûlée, and crème anglaise (sometimes called custard sauce). Because they're so prevalent in desserts, we tend to think of custards as sweet, though standard custard technique—liquid, eggs, seasoning, mixed and baked in a water bath—can be applied to virtually any flavor to which you want to bring the custard texture. An herb custard to garnish a savory soup, olive oil custard with *à la grecque* vegetables, tarragon or bone marrow with beef. Escoffier added a diced custard (called a *royale*) to consommé. The liquid might be partly vegetable or fruit juice, though fat is a large part of the custard's exquisite texture and shouldn't be avoided altogether.

Custard sauce: See crème anglaise.

Cutlery: See knives.

Cutting boards: The best surface to cut on is wood, a sturdy wood such as maple (what some of the best boards are made of), rather than a very hard wood. Avoid completely any cutting board that is harder than your knife. Polypropylene and rubber boards are acceptable (but they get ugly). Avoid boards that don't get scratches or nicks; they're harder than your knife and will ruin it; if you can hear your knife blade come down on your board that's a bad sign. Avoid so-called antibacterial boards. The belief that wooden boards are less sanitary than plastic ones is misleading. Avoid bacterial contamination by cleaning your boards with very hot soapy water and letting them dry thoroughly upright. Use a light bleach solution for ultimate sterilization. To reiterate: use wood cutting boards. They're better to work on—better on your knives, better on your food, better on your hands, better on your eyes.

D

Dacquoise [*dah-KWAHZ*]: Dacquoise is a meringue flavored with nuts, usually almonds, and baked till crisp, or a dessert featuring them. (See also meringue.)

Dance: Used by professional cooks, "the dance" is an affectionate description of line cooking when it's done right and well, when a team of cooks is in elegant synchronicity. It's often recalled with a kind of strange euphoria unique to the profession.

Danger zone: Danger zone is a food safety term that refers to temperatures at which bacteria don't simply exist, they thrive, multiplying at an exponential rate. Most bacteria are dramatically slowed at refrigeration temperatures, 40°F and below. Above 40°F the speed with which they multiply increases. At temperatures around 100°F they are thriving. After 120°F they begin to become less effective. Most don't survive for very long at temperatures above 140°F. Thus, the range of temperatures between 40° and 140°F is called the danger zone with respect to bacterial contamination and food safety. This is the reason food prone to harmful bacteria, chicken and eggs, ground meat, should not be held for long periods at temperatures in the danger zone.

Daube [*dohb*]: Beef braised with red wine and vegetables is a preparation called *daube de beouf*. Originally made in a vessel specific to the dish, called a *daubière* (not unlike New England chowder cooked in a chaudière), the meal was distinguished by the regional vegetables of Provence and the way that they were layered in the vessel. *Daubes* can be served hot or cold; when cold, the liquid is gelatinized and the beef dish is called *daube en gelée*.

Dauphinoise: Potatoes sliced and baked with cream, seasonings, and cheese—scalloped potatoes, potatoes au gratin—are not only an enduring and cherished way to prepare potatoes, *dauphinoise* is an excellent strategy for cooking potatoes in advance of serving them; that is, cooked, chilled, and reheated, they're as good as if not better than when they were initially cooked. They're also extremely versatile; other ingredients such as sautéed mushrooms or peppers or leeks can be added for flavor and a seasonal touch to this all-purpose preparation. (Not to be confused with potatoes *dauphine,* which are like croquettes, mashed potatoes mixed with egg or with *pâte à choux* and fried.)

Debeard: Mussels grow tough fibrous strands, the beard, in order to attach themselves to stationary objects in tidal areas. To debeard means to remove these dark fibers, which originate from within the mussel, gently tugging them off by hand.

THE ELEMENTS OF COOKING A TO Z   109

Decant: Decant means to gently pour wine from the bottle into another container, a decanter. Any liquid can be decanted to separate it from its sediment (such as oil from the herb used to infuse it). Wine is decanted for this reason but also because it can improve, via oxidation, a wine's flavor and aroma. While it's associated with old expensive red wines, decanting can have a good effect on big young reds as well (Zinfandel, for example); conversely, decanting can detract from wines whose assets are particularly volatile (Pinot Noir, for example).

Deep-fry: To deep-fry means to submerge food completely in hot oil, usually around 350°F, the more oil the better (without losing sight of the fact that oil is expensive and needs to be used economically). Deep-frying is an especially fast way to cook because the density of the oil makes the heat transfer especially efficient; it's also very tasty, adding its own flavor and texture and making a food's exterior golden brown and crisp. But it requires a lot of oil, so cost is a factor, and it billows into the air clouds of minute particles that stick to everything as grease and so can smell up and dirty a kitchen or an entire dwelling if you don't have good ventilation. But the results are so good many consider it worth all its disadvantages. Technically, the deep-fry method is classified as a dry-heat method, which signifies cooking without additional water in direct contact with the food. Food that has been deep-fried should be clean, crisp, and flavorful. It's not necessarily any more unhealthy than pan-frying or sautéing; the fat should not saturate what you're cooking. The high temperature heats the food's water, which rushes out in bubbles of steam. Bad results are usually due to poor oil quality or improper temperature control. Thermometers are best for determining if the oil is hot enough, though a chopstick will do (the wood should bubble almost immediately when the oil is hot enough). Using enough oil is important because when a lot of cold food is added, the temperature will drop precipitously and the food might not cook quickly enough. Smoking oil is too hot—dangerous, in fact, because the fumes can ignite (don't panic, do cover the burning oil with a lid and allow to cool). Oil can be strained and, if it has not developed off odors or been used too much, reused.

In professional kitchens proper maintenance of the fry oil (is it filtered daily? is it only kept hot during service? is attention being paid to its diminishing quality?) is important from the food-cost standpoint and the standpoint of the finished dish.

Deep-poach: To deep-poach means to submerge food completely in a flavorful liquid and to cook it gently, below boiling temperatures, as low as 160°F. The technique, in the moist-heat category (implying low temperature), is usually used for chicken or fish, a meaty fatty fish (salmon is often deep-poached), though any protein that doesn't require the color and flavor of browning (achieved with dry heat, high heat) can be deep-poached. When poaching fish, it's customary to do so in a stock or a court bouillon, a quick stock made with water, herbs, aromatic vegetables, spices, and wine or vinegar. Court bouillon is not customarily used as part of the finishing sauce (as the liquid from shallow poaching is), but meat stocks used to shallow poach chicken or beef usually are.

Deglaze: To deglaze means to add liquid to a hot pan encrusted with browned juices and vegetable and tasty bits of meat and skin. The liquid used to deglaze a pan, which can be anything from water to wine to stock, boils off the tasty fond, bits and pieces and particles of what had been cooked in the pan, extracting their flavor. Pans are deglazed to create sauces to accompany the item that gave it the fond in the first place.

Degrease: Degreasing—removing the fat from a stock, soup, or sauce—is important to the clarity, texture, and flavor of the finished liquid and can be done in various ways. Stocks are degreased using a ladle; the bottom is used to push the clear fat to the edges of the pot, then the ladle is dipped just low enough to collect the fat and as little stock as possible. Degrease stocks early in their cooking: the bit of stock removed with the fat is less concentrated and therefore less valuable, and removing fat early gives it less chance to become emulsified into the stock. Consommés with just a few discs of fat floating on top can be degreased by dragging a paper towel across its surface. Braised dishes almost always need to be degreased; because braises tend to improve after being chilled, it's most efficient to remove the fat after it's congealed.

Demi-glace: Brown stock—usually veal, but it can be any roasted meat and bones or even caramelized vegetables—that's substantially reduced is used as the base for or to fortify myriad *à la minute* sauces. In classical French cooking, demi-glace, sometimes simply called demi, is a reduction of brown veal stock and *espagnole* sauce, which serves the same purpose. (See also mother sauces and derivative sauces.)

THE ELEMENTS OF COOKING A TO Z   111

Denature: The word denature is usually used in the kitchen with regard to protein molecules. Proteins are tightly coiled; but by breaking the bonds that maintain their shape—mechanically, with heat, or with acid—they uncoil into long strands. These long strands can then recombine or coagulate in ways that can be useful or harmful to the food, whether in a clarification, a meringue, a custard, a piece of meat or fish, depending on the skill of the cook. McGee provides extraordinarily clear and detailed descriptions of protein denaturation and its results.

Derivative sauces: Derivative sauces, sometimes called compound sauces, are those that use a mother sauce as a base to which aromats, seasonings, acid, and fat are added, usually *à la minute,* to finish the sauce. Brown sauce derivatives are the most abundant and diverse, though béchamel and veloutés—the base for cheese, cream, and white wine sauces, for instance—are likewise excellent beginnings for derivative sauces.

Devein: Devein refers to the removal of the intestinal tract of shrimp, which runs along the back, though it can logically refer to removing the veins from any item. The most common and easy way to devein shrimp is by slicing the back lengthwise with a sharp paring knife. Shrimp are available deveined; they cost a little more, but this can be a good time-saver.

Devil: generally, to make piquant (via mustard) and spicy, used mainly today to refer to a hard-cooked egg preparation and to a ground ham preparation, though leftover bones with plenty of meat scraps remaining (as from a beef rib roast, for instance) can be coated with spices and mustard—deviled—broiled to reheat and eaten as is.

Dextrose: This corn-derived sugar is sold powdered and most notably is used in fermented meats (dry-cured sausages) because it's believed to be more readily broken down and available to the bacteria that cause fermentation. The impact of dextrose is less intense than that of table sugar, though table sugar can usually be substituted.

Dice: To dice means to cut into uniform cubes or refers to the cubes themselves. The size of the die varies. According to the Culinary Institute of America, large dice are ¾ inch square, medium dice ½ inch square and small dice ¼ inch square. Large dice—chunky and inelegant—are typically used for vegetables for stocks or preparations that will be cooked for a long time and will eventually be discarded; large dice can be suitable in a stew or for preparing root vegetables to roast. The smallest dice are *brunoise,* ⅛ inch square, and fine *brunoise,* ¹⁄₁₆ inch square; the latter are typically made by julienning the vegetable on a mandoline and dicing the julienne, and are typically used as an elegant, flavorful garnish.

Die: A die is the plate through which meat is ground. While professional grinders come with dies of varying sizes, most grinders for the home come with two, large and small, ⅜ inch and ⅛ inch. The large die grinds coarse; the small die is the one used most often. For meat that must be finely ground, for a refined pâté or emulsified sausage, for instance, it can be helpful to grind it twice, first through the large die, then through the small die. Wash and dry dies and blades by hand, and store them securely so that they don't become dull. Blades and dies should be professionally sharpened periodically.

Direct heat: Direct heat refers to cooking over coals, directly over the coals as opposed to off to the side, which would be using indirect heat. Direct heat is the grill's equivalent of sauté—high heat, dry heat, used to develop a flavorful surface on a naturally tender item. For food that needs more time or a gentler temperature, indirect heat should be used. Except for items that require very little cooking, a combination of direct heat (for flavor) and indirect (for uniform cooking) is best.

Distilled water: water that has been distilled to remove minerals and other impurities. Distilled water can be important to use when working with live cultures, when the impurities in tap water might harm the bacteria, as for adding dried cultures to sausage to initiate fermentation. On the other hand, distilled water can be harmful to yeast and should not be used with yeast-leavened products.

Done, doneness: Determining "doneness"—or when something is done, when it must come out of the heat, which can rarely be forecasted by a recipe—is one of the most important skills a cook must learn. Because it's a skill, it can never be perfected absolutely; rather a cook refines his or her skill by paying attention to everything cooked and always adding this accumulated observation into an understanding of when something is done. With some meats, doneness can be objective, cooking a sausage to, say 150°F, for instance. But a thermometer is only as good as the person using it. Pulling a standing rib roast from the oven at 120°F will yield different results depending how hot the oven was and how cold the meat was when it went in. If you determine a custard is done and thus pull it from the oven, that custard may well overcook once it's out of the oven; it's "done" shortly before its final temperature is reached because of carryover cooking. Braised dishes offer a broader window for doneness than lean roasted items, but it's still a window and overcooking and undercooking are possible without some care from the cook. A cook should use all his or her senses when determining doneness. Learning to evaluate the doneness of meats by touch is an important skill and can only be achieved by practice. Because an important part of cooking meat is allowing it to rest, one doesn't necessarily remove it from the heat when it's done, rather, it's done after it's rested. A handy tool for testing doneness is a long thin needle or cake tester that can be inserted into the center of a piece of fish or meat, then held to your skin (wrist or below your lower lip) to know whether an interior is cold, warm, or hot.

Double-boiler: A bowl within a pot that allows you to cook over steam is used for gentle cooking. Some form of double-boiler is a kitchen tool that's very handy for preparations that benefit from gentle heat such as melting chocolate and cooking yolks for emulsified butter sauces. You can buy a pot with a double-boiler insert but a steel or glass bowl that rests partially inside a saucepan works just as well.

Double cream: Heavy cream that we reduce by about half is called double cream or *crème double*. We do it to save time; double cream can be added to sauces at the last minute to enrich them and the sauces don't require as much further reduction. Double cream is essentially repasteurized; because of this cooking and its reduced water content, double cream may keep longer than fresh cream.

Dough: Dough implies flour and liquid, with some gluten formation, whether lengthened for elastic bread dough, or shortened for crumbly cookie or pie dough, and it's usually not so loose that it can be poured like a batter but instead is shapeable.

Dredge: Dredge means to cover an entire item uniformly in a dry coating, usually by dragging it through a bowl of the coating and pressing the coating into the item to ensure an even layer. Dredging implies a forcefully applied, concentrated coating.

Dress, dressed, dressing: three similar words with different meanings. Dress is a verb that means to coat with a sauce. It can also mean to clean and prepare game for cooking. Dressed can mean that a salad has its vinaigrette, but it also refers to fish that have been gutted and cleaned and are ready to be cooked; a cleaned and trussed chicken is sometimes referred to as "dressed." Dressing has long referred to the sauce that accompanies salad and is also used as an alternative to stuffing. In the interest of clarity, stuffing should be used to describe the mixture that goes inside the turkey; if you don't put that mixture in the turkey, but cook it separate from the bird, call it dressing.

Dried herbs and spices: While fresh herbs are almost always preferable to dried, dried herbs are a valuable staple to have in your pantry, especially to use in seasoning soups and stews and other preparations that are cooked for periods long enough to rehydrate them and extract their flavor (which is considerably different from the flavor extracted from fresh herbs). This presumes they have flavor to begin with. It's common that the dried herbs in home kitchens are pale and flavorless, having sat for years in the same spice rack. It's wise to buy dried herbs and spices, those that you don't use frequently, in the smallest available container so that they're less likely to get old. When using a dried herb or spice, if you can't remember the last time you used it, it's a good idea to observe, smell, and taste it to evaluate its freshness; dried herbs and spices should have a sharp, rather than dull or faded, color; dried herbs should have a clear aroma—if you can't smell them you won't be able to taste them. Taste spices—if they have no flavor, it's time to get fresh ones.

Drum sieve: See tamis.

Dry cure (noun): a mixture of salt, sugar, and seasonings used on meat and fish to preserve it, and to enhance its flavor and texture. (See also brine.)

Dry cure (verb): To dry cure meat means to allow it to dry in such a way that it is preserved. Meats and sausages that have been dry cured are not typically cooked but are sliced thinly just before serving and are dense and powerfully flavored (salami and prosciutto, for example). Before ubiquitous and easy refrigeration, techniques of dry curing could ensure an efficient use of a community's food supply. We continue to dry cure meat and sausage today because items handled this way can taste so good. The ability to dry cure food is now considered an artisan craft of a high order. Meat and sausage that is to be dry cured is almost always salted first to begin the process of dehydration and to create an inhospitable environment for the bacteria that cause meat to decay. Often some form of sodium nitrite or sodium nitrate is also included in the cure to prevent botulism poisoning.

Dry heat (cooking): Dry heat refers to cooking without water—sauté, grill, broil, roast, and deep-fry—and implies high temperatures, usually 350°F and above, temperatures at which excess water will have evaporated. (See moist heat (cooking), its counterpart.)

Dry rub: a mixture of spices, seasonings and/or aromats that's rubbed onto the surface of meat or fish before the meat or fish is cooked as a way of boosting an item's flavor. Meat or fish to which dry rub is applied is often oiled first so that the oil coats the particles of dry rub; oil encourages more dry rub to adhere to the meat, distribute the flavor evenly, and helps to cook the dry rub spices (if they remain dry, they can burn).

Du Barry: in classical French cuisine, a term that denotes cauliflower is a main component in the dish or is the main garnish (see similar terms *Crécy* and Florentine).

Duck: Domestic duck is a very flavorful bird that's underused in the home kitchen. Except for boneless breasts, duck is best cooked slowly at low temperatures. It can be slow roasted; this helps tenderize the tough legs and render the copious fat. Legs are excellent braised. Braised duck legs can be removed from the bone and added to salads, soups, and stews. They are extraordinary confited. Breasts can be sautéed or pan-roasted, or skinned and grilled. It's necessary to begin breasts skin side down over very low heat in order to render the fat and ensure a crisp skin; chefs tend to serve duck breast medium rare. Crisp skin is one of the great pleasures of eating duck. Skin can be scored to facilitate rendering. Rendered duck fat is an exquisite cooking medium. Duck bones will make excellent stock. Wild ducks behave differently; their skin doesn't get crisp, the legs must be braised to make them tender, and their breast meat is very dark, rich, and gamey and should not be cooked much beyond medium rare or, like squab, it can take on a liverish taste.

Dumpling: Dumpling typically refers to dough or batter cooked in liquid. They can be savory or sweet. Dumplings are, in method and effect, like quick pastas (the French term for dumpling is *pâte cuite,* cooked pastry) and can be thought of that way. Spaetzle, a loose dough or batter, is a kind of dumpling, and feels more like a pasta (it's often sautéed after it's boiled to develop more flavor); gnocchi is more dumpling than pasta. Chinese dumplings are more like raviolis than what we think of as dumplings; potstickers are in effect poached and then fried. (Davidson, in *The Oxford Companion to Food,* calls the English translation of "dumpling" for the Chinese technique a "heinous excursion.") American dumplings are usually simple flour-and-liquid doughs that include some leavener and are cooked in stews; these are more like boiled biscuits than the European and Asian pasta-like forms. Sometimes the dough includes cooked potato or egg. Dumpling dough can also be used to enclose a filling. In whatever form, from little knots to large knobs to delicate enclosures of elaborate fillings, the dumpling, whether cooked first and added to a dish or a plate or cooked with it or eaten on its own, offers a versatile strategy for carrying additional flavors and ingredients in an intriguing and satisfying way.

Dutch oven: A Dutch oven is a deep pot with a lid, often made of enameled cast iron that's used for stewing and braising. Its important attributes are a heavy material that facilitates even cooking and a lid. It's the vessel of choice for braising, allowing the cook to sear the meat and cook it in the same pot. It's a valuable cooking tool, but not, strictly speaking, essential; any heavy-gauge pot with a lid will do the same job.

Duxelles [*DUX-el*]: Chopped sautéed mushrooms, *duxelles* is a valuable and versatile *appareil* that adds flavor and texture to countless dishes. It makes a superb *farce* for ravioli, meat, fish, or vegetables or, even more simply, an elegant, flavorful bed or garnish for virtually any meat or mild fish. White wine and veal stock can be added to it to create a fine mushroom sauce; *duxelles* simmered in some cream and blended will make a simple and delicious mushroom soup. The key to flavorful *duxelles* is to get a very good sear on the chopped mushrooms before the mushrooms can begin dumping their water; use a heavy bottomed pan, make sure it's screaming hot, don't skimp on cooking oil, and don't crowd the pan with mushrooms (they'll steam instead of brown). Minced shallot is an excellent aromatic to include (added after the mushrooms have begun to cook to avoid burning it), as is chopped parsley, along with aggressive use of salt and pepper. Once the mushrooms have been seared, the pan can be deglazed with white wine to add more flavor (most of the liquid should be cooked off; *duxelles* is typically very moist but not liquidy). The *duxelles* can be used immediately or spread on a tray or plate to cool before being reused. If reheating it, do so gently with a little butter; a few drops of lemon juice will enhance its mushroominess. Any mushrooms can be used but because the mushrooms are finely chopped, the inexpensive button mushroom is the common choice.

E

Earthenware: Cooking vessels made of clay—slow to heat up, slow to cool off, and nonreactive—are especially suited to the long gentle cooking of stews and braises. They can crack so are not typically used for high direct heat but can be used, with care, on the stovetop (the tagine, a shallow earthenware dish with a conical lid, is customarily used on the stovetop). Because they hold heat so well and thus keep the food hot, they're excellent serving vessels as well. Many Asian braises are labeled "cooked in a clay pot." Also noteworthy, whether the vessel is in use or not, is the visual and textural appeal of the earthenware itself, especially if it's handmade; there's an appealing symmetry to preparing food in a handmade pot.

Eau de vie [*OH de VEE*]: A distillation of fermented fresh fruit, *eau de vie* is a clear, powerfully flavored spirit. *Eaux de vie* are not aged (like brandies, distilled wines) and are meant to convey the flavor of the fruit. Because of their cost and high alcohol content, they are not used often in cooking but can, like brandy, be used as a seasoning device, especially in finishing dessert sauces, ice creams, and sorbets. Examples of *eaux de vie* include kirsh (cherry), Poire William (pear), and *framboise* (raspberry).

Egg: The chicken's egg, ubiquitous, inexpensive, nutritious, versatile, and delicious, is the kitchen's greatest ingredient and food tool (see the essay Egg, page 22). It's used in countless ways—to thicken, to enrich, to leaven, to flavor, to color—and can be brought to many fine ends in and of itself. It can be main course or garnish, pedestal or focus. Its shape is aesthetically appealing and symbolizes life. Bird eggs differ primarily in size from quail to duck to ostrich, but behave similarly in cooking. Except for lobster roe, which is often used as a seasoning device in sauces or a vivid garnish, the eggs of fish are usually eaten raw rather than used in cooking, or salt cured and used as a seasoning (bottarga, for example).

Egg beater: An egg beater is a convenient kitchen tool but not recommended given its limited uses; meaning you can do a lot more with a whisk and should learn to use that valuable tool well. Egg Beaters is also a commercial product, a low-fat egg substitute; also not recommended—use the real thing.

Egg wash: Egg, beaten, usually thinned with milk or water, is called egg wash. Egg wash is typically brushed on dough before cooking the dough to give the crust a golden brown sheen. Egg wash can also refer to the second component of standard breading procedure, in which case it can be seasoned according to the dish it will coat in addition to being thinned. Whole eggs are usually used for egg wash, but yolks or whites alone may be used.

Egg white: See albumen.

Eighty-six: restaurant kitchen slang of obscure origins that indicates a dish is no longer available. In better restaurants, it's a matter of staff pride not to have any item offered on the menu eighty-sixed. It can also refer to an item that has been discarded, a fired employee, or an idea that's been abandoned.

Emulsified sauce: a category of sauces in which fat is emulsified into a small amount of water-based liquid and aromats. Emulsified butter sauces—which can use whole butter or, for a more refined sauce, clarified butter—are among the most flavorful, satisfying, and versatile in the sauce oeuvre. Traditional emulsified butter sauces (see the essay Sauce, page 12), such as the hollandaise or its relatives, are as thick as mayonnaise but can be lightened or thinned according to the cook's taste. Vinaigrettes are often emulsified into a stable, homogenous sauce so that the oil and vinegar don't separate. *Beurre blancs* and *beurre rouges* are *à la minute* emulsified sauces, which take advantage of the emulsifying properties of butter, which itself is a water-in-fat emulsion.

Emulsifier: Given enough mechanical power, any two substances can be emulsified, but the cook with his whisk or his blender or mixer makes use of emulsifiers, substances that prevent two opposing liquids from separating. Lecithin, in egg yolks, is a common one. Mustard will help to maintain the emulsification of a vinaigrette. Additional starches and proteins can also help to stabilize an emulsion. (See McGee for a complete description of how emulsifiers work.)

Emulsify, emulsion: An emulsion is a homogenous mixture of two substances that don't naturally combine, or, more precisely, a suspension of one substance within another. To emulsify means to combine two substances into a uniform mixture. In cooking, the most common emulsions are fat within water emulsions, mayonnaise, for example. Milk is an unstable emulsion and unless homogenized will separate, the cream, the fat, rising to the top. Often vinaigrettes are emulsified. Fat combined with protein and water is another form of emulsification, used to make baloney or hot dogs. Understanding the chemistry of an emulsion is useful in making them, maintaining them, and repairing them when they break. A fat-in-water emulsion is composed of countless microscopic bits of fat separated from one another by sheets of water via an emulsifier, such as those in egg yolk. The water keeps the countless particles of fat from grouping together, which is what happens when an emulsification breaks (ironically, breaking is actually a coming together). (See McGee for a detailed discussion and illustrations of emulsions.)

En croûte [*ohn KROOT*]: Literally, in crust, *en croûte* signifies that something has been cooked in a crust, almost always a pastry crust, typically pâtés, though whole pieces of meat are sometimes cooked *en croûte,* such as salmon in a dish called coulibiac and beef tenderloin in a dish called Wellington. When cooking something *en croûte,* it's important either to leave the ends open or to create one or two steam holes so that the crust exterior is crisp and not soggy.

En papillote: See *papillote.*

Enzyme: Specific proteins in plants and animals called enzymes act as catalysts for various chemical reactions and are responsible for many good and bad changes in food. They're what make an apple bruise, an artichoke blacken, a green bean turn from bright to dull, and make fat rancid. But enzymes are also why aging meat can make it more tender, are active in the fermentation process, and are often responsible for food aromas. More often than not, the cook wants to limit the effects of enzymes, which slow down in cold temperatures and are inactivated at high temperatures. But as McGee points out, before they are inactivated by heat, enzymes become vigorous as the temperature rises—thus the importance of cooking those items that are hurt by enzymes (green vegetables, for example) as quickly as possible. Enzymes require oxygen to work, and some are slowed or inactivated by high concentrations of salt and acid—creating low-oxygen or salty or acidic conditions can slow the effects of enzymes.

Escallop: the French term for meat that's sliced thin and is sautéed or sometimes breaded and pan-fried.

Escoffier, Auguste: The most celebrated chef of his time (1846–1935) is noted today not for his cooking in the great hotels of Europe but rather for his magnum opus, *Le Guide Culinaire* (1903), published in English as *Escoffier: The Complete Guide to the Art of Modern Cookery*. It's an extraordinary work, comprising 5,012 recipes, that in many respects has set a standard of classical French cooking that remains valuable today.

***Espagnole* sauce:** *Espagnole* sauce, also called brown sauce, is arguably the most important of the mother sauces and best describes the power of the derivative-sauce method (see derivative sauces). Made of brown veal stock, browned mirepoix, and tomato, thickened with a brown roux, *espagnole* sauce can be transformed into countless *à la minute* sauces. (Escoffier, who calls them "compound' sauces, gives recipes for more than fifty.) *Espagnole* sauce is also the base for classical demi-glace, which is a reduction of equal parts *espagnole* sauce and brown veal stock. (See the essay Sauce, page 12.)

***Étouffée* [*AY-too-fay*]:** *Étouffée* is the French term for stew and stewing in a covered pot; the term is especially common in Cajun cooking.

Evaporated milk: Milk that's been concentrated by half is often used in recipes to enrich custards or sauces (not to be confused with sweetened condensed milk). It's convenient because it has a long shelf life—not to mention a slightly caramelized flavor—and so it's a dairy product you can always have on hand. But fresh whole milk or cream or a combination can be used in its stead.

Expedite, expediter: restaurant-kitchen parlance for the act of receiving orders from the dining room and organizing the sequence and timing of when those orders are cooked by his or her *brigade* and sent to the dining room. The chef who does this is called the expediter.

F

Fabricate: To fabricate a food is kitchen vernacular for cutting a large item into smaller items or otherwise preparing an item so that it's ready to cook (often abbreviated as "fab" or "fabbed"). It's usually used with respect to meat and fish.

Factory raised: This relatively recent descriptor refers to livestock such as pigs and chickens that are raised and processed by agribusiness conglomerates. It denotes high volume production and often signifies a lower quality animal raised in unnatural conditions. (Compare farm raised.)

Farm raised: A descriptor that denotes livestock that has been raised using traditional farming methods. Sometimes called "hand-raised" or "free-range," farm-raised animals have been raised in an environment and on a diet appropriate for their system, and have not endured an unusual amount of stress during their lives or before slaughter. The results of farm raising, according to the people who do the work, tend to be happier animals and superior meat. (Compare factory raised. See also organic.) Farm raised is also a term applied to fish but with less benevolent connotations. Fish "farms" are increasingly common, but their advantages and disadvantages are still being evaluated. Wild fish is still generally preferable to farmed fish. (See aquaculture.)

Fast food: There's nothing wrong with fast food per se, as long as it's good food. For years, though, just about all fast food was unhealthy—high in fat, sodium, and chemical additives, low in nutrition, and generic in taste. While this kind of food remains the dominant form worldwide, an increasing number of fast food businesses are paying attention to their customers' hunger for better ingredients and handmade food. Fast food one day may not signify bad, unhealthy food but rather a style of food and the nature of the place where it's eaten.

Fat: Fat is one of the four building-block categories of all food (water, carbohydrates, and proteins are the others), is arguably responsible for the most pleasure and the most pain in our diets, and is a fundamental cooking tool. In the kitchen, we cook with fat, whether vegetable derived (canola or corn oil) or animal derived (butter, lard); its capacity to get very hot without breaking down allows us to cook food till it's crisp. Different fats have different flavors and qualities that must be considered when choosing a cooking fat—canola oil is neutral and less expensive than the flavorful butterfat. Fat "shortens" dough, which makes pastry tender rather than breadlike. Fat enriches, whether it's the oil in a vinaigrette on vegetables, cream added to a soup, butter mounted into a sauce, olive oil drizzled on bread. It's the rare dish that cannot be made more tasty and satisfying by adding a little more fat. In this way, fat can be thought of, in addition to a medium and an ingredient, as a kind of seasoning. When evaluating food, the cook should ask himself or herself, does the dish have the appropriate amount of fat in it? Whether cooking with it or seasoning foods with it, fat should first be thought of in general terms rather than specific ones; that is, only after you've acknowledged that a fat is called for, should you then narrow your choice of the type of fat ("I'd like this tomato sauce to be richer and so need more fat—now, should that fat be butter or olive oil?").

Fats are broken into categories, saturated and unsaturated. Saturated, mainly from animals, is associated with health risks; the level of saturation is evident in how hard the fat is at room temperature—duck fat is very soft, while the more saturated beef fat is hard. Unsaturated fats, those from plants (tropical nut fats excepted), are pourable at room temperature and have less health risks associated with them. Hydrogenated fats are liquid fats processed to be solid and stable at room temperature (margarine, vegetable shortening), but these too can contain trans fats, which have the same risks associated with saturated fats. All natural fats are recommended (from rendered beef fat to canola oil) and hydrogenated fats are not recommended.

Remember with regard to animal fat that there are different qualities to the fat depending on where it comes from on the animal. The pig, for instance, offers us jowl fat, leaf fat from around the kidneys, and back fat (in addition to intramuscular fat)—all of which have different properties.

Among chefs, this is the dogma: fat means flavor. Remember also that fat doesn't make us fat, too many calories make us fat. In the kitchen, fat is your best friend.

Fatback: A layer of fat, which can be as thick as two or three inches, runs the length of a pig's back and is called fatback. Pig fat is a versatile fat in the kitchen (whether rendered into lard for cooking and shortening or ground for sausage), and fatback is the purest expression of that fat. The clean creamy fatback is used to enrich sausages and pâtés, either ground or diced, as well as lean whole cuts of meat (see lard and bard). Fatback from naturally raised hogs can also be cured and eaten by itself, thinly sliced, a preparation called lardo.

Feet: Animal feet—calf, pig, chicken—are a rich source of gelatin when simmered slowly in a stock or a stew. A foot appropriate to the stock being made, chicken for chicken, calf for veal or beef, will give the liquid additional body. Because of their neutral flavor, calves' feet can be added to any kind of stock for additional body and flavor.

Ferment, fermentation: Fermentation is the transformation of molecules by microorganisms, such as yeasts and bacteria, and helps to create some of the most wonderful foods and drink known to humankind. Yeasts feed on sugars and turn them to alcohol, acetic acid bacteria feed on alcohol and turn it into vinegar, lactic bacteria feed on the sugars in dairy and create yogurt and crème fraîche. Yeasts feed on the sugars in dough and release carbon dioxide and alcohol, raising the dough for bread and adding aromatic compounds from the alcohol and other by-products. And bacteria feed on the sugars in a sausage mixture to generate acid that will help to preserve it as it dries and add an acidic tang to its flavor. All are examples of fermentation, which gives us wine, cheese, leavened bread, and salami, to name a few examples.

To ferment food—to use microorganisms in a semi-controlled way to enhance its flavor and preserve it, whether pickling your own vegetables with salt and water, or raising your own yeast to make bread—is one of the pleasures of cooking available to all cooks. Uncontrolled fermentation by undesirable bacteria, molds, and yeasts will spoil food.

Fiber: Fiber is the general term for the component of vegetables and seeds that our bodies can't break down and absorb, such as cellulose. Fiber is good for our digestive tracts, so a diet that includes plenty of natural fiber is important to maintain. Fiber is also something that a cook removes from food when making refined dishes. Among the impurities caught in a chinois when straining a pureed sauce, for example, is fiber, the stuff that gave the vegetable structure and helped to contain all the valuable color and flavor of the vegetable but has little flavor and a rough texture.

Ficelle, à la [*fee-SEL*]: This is the French term for cooking food by allowing it to dangle from a string (*la ficelle*) in front of a fire. A technique often associated with leg of lamb, cooking *à la ficelle* is more work than cooking the meat in an oven—it should be basted regularly and carefully tended to ensure all sides are evenly cooked but not overcooked and dried out. The technique is valuable because the meat picks up extra flavor from the fire and it's also a pleasure to behold a leg of lamb or a pheasant cooking slowly in front of a fire.

Farce, farcir [*farse, far-SEAR*]: *Farce* is French for stuffing, and *farcir* is the verb for to stuff. In professional kitchens, the term *farce* is used instead of stuffing—a cook would make the *farce* for the ravioli, for instance. The anglicized form of the word is forcemeat, which kitchens use as well, though some prefer to use the French term because it has a more refined and elegant sound.

Filet, **fillet** [*fi-LAY*]: *Filet* means to remove the bones, and a *filet* indicates a single portion of boneless meat or fish. Used by itself, it usually refers to a cut of beef tenderloin, also known as filet mignon.

Fines herbes [*feens erbs*]: A combination in equal parts of Italian parsley, tarragon, chervil, and chives, the *fines herbes* combination is an elegant flavor to enhance delicate dishes, from eggs to meat to fish to sauces. Tarragon and chervil, both anise-flavored herbs, combine with the bitter back notes of parsley and the sweet onion from the chives. The herbs are easy to grow and are an excellent mainstay in the kitchen.

Finesse (see the essay Finesse, page 45): 1) Refinement, elegance, and delicacy of execution, performance, or artisanship is an important concept in the best kitchens. It can refer to the chef's actions, the act of cooking; it can refer to a specific cooking technique that elevates the quality of a dish. In French kitchens, the word used is *soigné*. In general terms, finesse refers to the small extra efforts or movements that result in excellence and refinement. 2) Finesse can be used as a verb indicating a step in a preparation requiring special attention (e.g., "The *beurre rouge* is a tricky sauce that must be finessed to be successful"—that is, careful attention and movements are required to ensure a good emulsion and an elegant appearance).

Finish: To finish means to perform the final step in a dish's preparation, to make the *à la minute* adjustments to a dish that bring it to its peak immediately before serving (sauces are often finished, for example, by being mounted with butter).

Fire: In restaurant-kitchen parlance, to fire means to cook. The chef or sous chef "fires" orders as he or she is ready to send the orders to the dining room. The term firing time, as in "the soufflé has a twenty-minute firing time," indicates how long a dish takes to cook from the time it's fired.

Fish: Fish is such a big topic it nearly defies inclusion in a cooking glossary, but there are a few basics all cooks should understand about the categorization of the earth's underwater, finned creatures. First, perhaps, is an appreciation of the fact that fish is the last group of wild animals still available to most of us, though with the advances in aquaculture, this is increasingly less true with the most popular fish such as salmon and most freshwater fish.

Categories of fish are broken down into round and flat. Flat fish, bottom dwellers such as sole, halibut, turbot, and flounder are lean, mild, white fish (because they don't do a lot of swimming). Round fish, bass, cod, snapper, et cetera, are in continual motion and so have a firmer, meatier, and more flavorful flesh. The more powerful swimmers, salmon and tuna, for instance, develop red muscle and often include more fat than the white-muscled fish. Fish may also be categorized in terms of fat content, from lean to fatty to oily (mackerel, for instance, another powerful swimmer). Flat fish and round fish are gutted and filleted differently and if you have access to fresh whole fish, it's helpful to feel comfortable filleting each.

Fish should smell clean and fresh when you buy it—don't be shy in asking to smell the fish you're about to purchase. Optimally, fish should be stored as close to 32°F as possible. This means refrigerating it on ice, in a container that allows water to drain out so that the fish doesn't soak in water; whole fish should be stored in the ice, belly down, while fillets should be wrapped in plastic to prevent contact with water. Fish should be bought as near to the time you intend to cook it as possible.

Fish is extremely delicate, so handle it gently. Most fish, because it's naturally tender, needs to be cooked gently. Some fish can stand up well to higher heat longer, such as monkfish and grouper, but as a rule you're more likely to overcook fish than to undercook it. Unlike red meat, most fish does not benefit from resting and should be served shortly after its cooked.

Some fish is best not cooked at all or lightly "cooked" with acid, as with sashimi and ceviche (tuna, salmon, fluke, snapper, for instance).

Fish sauce: This condiment made from fermented fish, ubiquitous throughout Southeast Asia and smelling cleanly of low tide, is a vital part of Asian culinary tradition. But fish sauce can be important to any pantry for its extraordinary seasoning effect, a flavor-enhancing impact often associated with umami. While it's excellent simply mixed with hot chillis and used to finish beef or chicken or simply rice, a few drops add dimension to tomato sauce, macaroni and cheese, chicken soup, and countless other dishes. Quality varies considerably; it's best to shop for it in Asian markets rather than in American grocery stores. It goes by other names in other countries: *nam pla* in Thailand, *nouc mam* in Vietnam, *tuk trey* in Cambodia, *ngan pya-ye* in Burma, *patis* in the Philippines.

Fish skin: Fish skin can be a flavorful and dramatic component of fish if handled properly—which usually means cooking it till it's crisp. Soggy fish skin is not generally appealing, but if you gently squeegee with a knife the cleaned skin on, say, a fillet of bass or rouget, back and forth until the mucus and water are removed, the moisture will cook out of it more quickly and allow you to crisp up the fish skin before you've overcooked the fish. From a flavor, textural, and visual standpoint, crispy fish skin can be an exciting part of the fish to serve.

Fish stock: A valuable base preparation for fish dishes, from soups to sauces, a stock for which there is no substitute or common, store-bought counterpart. Fish stock should be made with the bones of white fish and should be cooked gently and briefly. (See the essay Stock, specifically page 6 for notes on basic preparation.)

Flambé: This word designates that a dish will be finished with alcohol, then set aflame. The technique is used only for show; it doesn't have a substantial impact on the flavor of a dish nor does it cook off the alcohol in a substantial way.

Flan: the Spanish term for crème caramel (see custard and crème brûlée, crème caramel), though it can also refer to various pastry tarts, both savory and sweet in the United Kingdom, so it can be confusing. When referring to crème caramel, use the unambiguous term crème caramel, when refer-ring to a custard, use the unambiguous term custard.

Flatbread: Flatbreads—a broad and intriguing category of bread making which at the most basic level implies simply flour and water and salt, the staff of life—can be leavened or unleavened, soft and chewy or crackerlike, and may be the easiest of breads in the home cook's repertoire. Styles of flat-breads include Italian focaccia and Middle Eastern pita, which are leavened with yeast, or Indian roti and Mexican tortillas, which are unleavened. Any bread dough can be rolled flat and baked into flatbread.

Flattop: While some stovetops use burners, others use flattops, heavy steel or cast iron panels heated from below that get very hot and stay very hot. They work just as well as gas burners if the bottom of your pans are flat (pans that are regularly put smoking hot under running water can eventu-ally buckle and will be less effective on a flattop). Many chefs today prefer what's called a graduated flattop, a flattop that's heated in the center so that the cook can adjust the temperature on his or her pan by moving the pan closer or farther from the center of the flattop.

Flavor: arguably the most important element of a dish. All other elements of the craft of cooking, doneness, seasoning, texture, presentation, all are in support ultimately of flavor. Flavor is paramount.

Florentine: In classical French cuisine, Florentine denotes that spinach is a main component in the dish or is the main garnish (see similar terms *Crécy* and *Du Barry*).

Flour: Refined wheat flours are distinguished mainly by the percentage of protein in them. All-purpose flour has more protein than cake flour and less than bread flour. Can you make bread and cake from all-purpose flour? Yes, but the result will not be quite the same. The significant proteins in flour are glutenin and gliadin, which come together when water is added to form gluten. Bread flour's high gluten results in an elastic dough, dough that can stretch when bubbles of gas are released by yeast within it, and thus makes the best bread. Cake flour, or pastry flour, has a lower gluten content, thus the more tender result, desirable in a cake. McGee notes that you can add cornstarch or some other pure starch to all-purpose flour to reduce its protein percentage or add dried gluten to raise it. Whole wheat flour, which includes the bran and the germ from the wheat grain, results in a denser and more nutritious result. Other grains and cereals—corn, rice, rye—can be turned into flour for varying preparations from noodles to breads.

Flute, fluting: Fluting means to carve decorative grooves, often used on mushrooms or, in pastry, a fluted pastry wheel makes a grooved, decorative edge in the dough.

Fluted pastry wheel: A pastry cutter with a fluted, or grooved, wheel is not a fundamental kitchen tool but it can add a meaningful touch to the edges of pastries and pastas.

Foam: Foamed food, a hallmark of avant garde chefs, popularized by Spanish chef Ferran Adrià, became a trend in the early years of this century. While foam does have its uses (foamed milk in coffee is a good example), it can feel affected or gimmicky when used for the sake of itself rather than as an integral part of the dish. Foams can be simple—blending a viscous liquid or sauce with a hand blender. Or they can be more complicated—very thin liquids can be foamed by being whipped with gelatin, for instance. Restaurants often use a nitrous oxide or CO_2 whipped-cream canister to foam liquids (such devices and techniques are inexpensive and easy to use at home).

Foaming method: a technique used for batters in which eggs are beaten to incorporate air, which serves as the leavening in cakes; afterward flour, sugar, and seasonings are folded into the fluffy egg mixture, and the batter is baked for a light and tender crumb. (See cake.) The key point in the technique is good *mise en place*—have all the components ready (hot oven, greased pans, dry ingredients sifted) so that after the eggs are aerated, the dry ingredients can be immediately incorporated and the cake put in the oven immediately to avoid losing as many air bubbles as possible.

Foie gras [*fwah-GRAH*]: French for fat liver, foie gras is the liver of geese or ducks that have been fed a high calorie diet specifically to produce this culinary delicacy. Prized for its rich flavor and elegant texture, it's one of those rare foods for which there's really no comparison in flavor, richness, and texture. It's unique also in that only a few producers in the United States

raise ducks for foie gras, which means that chefs order from the same purveyors as home cooks do—meaning home cooks can get the same quality
product as the chef. Foie gras, composed almost entirely of fat, is versatile:
it can be served hot—roasted, poached, or sautéed—and it can be served
cold, usually in the form of a terrine or *torchon*; it can be main course, hors
d'oeurve, or garnish. Though it's very expensive, foie gras is among the most
easy items to work with at home because you need to do so little to it to
make it great.

Animal rights activists have argued that the force-feeding, a process
called gavage, is inhumane and have called for outlawing it. Some like-
minded chefs have stopped serving foie gras. Other chefs believe that the
process does not hurt the duck or goose and is no more inhumane than any
other form of conscientious animal husbandry and serve it gladly. The sub-
ject remains controversial.

Fold: To fold means to incorporate one mixture or ingredient into another
gently. Gently is the operative word. It's used when one or the other ingredient or mixture is delicate and could be flattened or compromised by vigorous mixing. Dry ingredients are folded into whipped egg whites for an
angel food cake, for example, and other batters are folded gently to prevent
gluten from forming and making the finished product tough.

Fond: 1) Fond means foundation. Stock is said to be *le fond de cuisine*.
Fond can also refer to the bits of meat, skin, and reduced juices stuck to the
bottom of the pan in which meat has been sautéed or roasted; this fond,
deglazed, can become the foundation of an *à la minute* sauce. Fond is an
important word and concept in the kitchen. 2) Fond can also mean the literal base of an item, such as *fond de artichaut*.

Fondant: a pliable sugar mixture like a paste that is melted (and often flavored) for use as an icing or as a filling for chocolates or as a decorative covering. Chocolate fondant is a chocolate mixture used for chocolate icing or
for glazing fruits, candies, or pastries.

Fondue: Fondue is the French term for melted. When vegetables are
described as fondue—tomato fondue or leeks fondue—the word indicates they've been cooked gently and slowly until they are virtually melted.
Butter that has been melted or melted in a way that sustains its emulsion is
sometime called *beurre fondue* (see also *beurre monté*). Cheese and choco-

late fondue are, of course, dishes in which food is dipped into melted cheese or chocolate.

Food mill: The food mill is a valuable kitchen tool for pureeing fruits and vegetables. A hand-turned paddle presses the food through a die, mashing it and separating it from skin, seeds, or cellulose, resulting in a uniform puree. While other tools can perform similar work, its advantages are unique in that it's both a grinder and a strainer. A food mill's basin accommodates larger amounts of food (potatoes, for instance, are often passed through a food mill, which mashes them without making them gluey). Food mills have different-sized dies, which allows the cook to choose the coarseness of the puree.

Food processor: A multipurpose appliance for cutting, chopping, mixing, and countless other uses is an invaluable piece of equipment, but it can also compromise certain preparations. While it will pulverize onion in seconds for minced onion, it will turn some of the onion to juice and result in varying size chunks; mincing onion by hand results in a far better mince. It doesn't puree, like a food mill, but rather cuts. Before you use your food processor, think about what you are doing and why, and evaluate whether or not it is the appropriate tool for the work at hand. When a recipe directs you to "process" something, this means pulse it in a food processor; if a recipe directs you to "blend" ingredients, this does not mean blend them in a food processor but rather in a blender or even by hand. Different equipment has different effects on the food.

Forcemeat: Forcemeat refers to any ground or pureed meat, fish, fat, and/or vegetables used to stuff something else, whether ground pork in a terrine mold or mushrooms in a ravioli. The term is an anglicization of the French *farcir* and *farce,* to stuff and stuffing. The term is most commonly used to describe a mixture of ground meat, fat, and seasonings for a pâté or a sausage. Some chefs find the sound of the word rough and inelegant and prefer to use *farce.*

Forestière [*FOR-est-ee-air*]: In classical French cuisine, this term denotes that mushrooms are a main component in the dish or is the main garnish.

Fork tender: Fork tender is a term used to describe the doneness of tough meats in braises and stews. Fork tender means that when a fork is pushed into the meat, the meat gives no resistance to the fork, that a piece of meat will fall from a fork from its own weight.

Fortify: to intensify flavor or to make more powerful, usually by adding an additional substance, such as a sauce fortified with reduced veal stock or reduced wine, or by reduction.

Free-form: forming by hand, without the use of a mold. Tarts are often made free-form by pressing the dough into a disc and pinching the edges.

Free range: This term designates that the chickens have been allowed to roam and feed, are not factory-raised chickens, which are kept in tight quarters. Free range can indicate a high quality of raising and they are usually preferable to factory-raised birds (they're smelly and dirty even when they aren't packed into cages). Free range does not necessarily mean organic, nor does it guarantee a chicken has had abundant room to range, but it usually indicates a certain degree of care with regard to their raising and is usually meat with a better texture and flavor. In the best circumstances, it means not only better muscle texture from the activity, but better flavor in the meat if the birds have been allowed to forage for food, eating a diverse diet that can result in a more complexly flavored meat.

Freeze, freezer, freezing: The freezer is an invaluable preserving tool that we take for granted these days. But it is a tool that can be used well or used thoughtlessly. All items that are frozen should be well wrapped. Oxygen is the enemy in the freezer and the main culprit, along with time, of freezer burn. The best kind of wrapping is vacuum sealing, as you get with a Food Saver or similar product. Food will keep frozen well a long time this way. Most items will begin to pick up off odors if abandoned in the freezer. As a rule, items high in fat freeze well (butter, bacon, ice cream), again, if they're well wrapped; fresh bread, wrapped in foil, is also well preserved by freezing. Keep a Sharpie on hand in the kitchen and label and date your food (don't think you're going to remember what this well-wrapped lump is a month from now).

Freezer burn: Food that has not been well wrapped or becomes exposed to the air from being jostled around in the freezer will dry out. Frozen things that become dry will get freezer burn, will be discolored and have a bad flavor. You can see it; if it looks bad, it probably is. Wrap foods well and securely.

French, Frenched: a technique of preparing rib bones on lamb, pork or, generally, any protruding bone. Meat and connective tissue on the bones and between them is cut and peeled away, the bone scraped till it's white and dry, down to the eye of the meat or even beyond to the main chop (some butchers use a technique of wrapping butcher's string around each bone and yanking the meat and connective tissue off with it). The effect is aesthetic and does not affect cooking or taste. The bones of Frenched racks are often covered with foil before being cooked so that they don't burn and become discolored.

Fricasse: See blanquette.

Fritter: a batter or a dough packed with garnish—anything from fruit to fish to vegetables—deep-fried till crispy. These make great hors d'oeurvres, excellent garnishes for a main course, and when sweet, a satisfying dessert. If they have no interior garnish, then they are doughnuts. If they are not deep-fried they are dumplings. As with most deep-fried food, fritters are best eaten while hot from the oil, so plan on serving as they are cooked. A *pâte à choux* is a terrific dough to use for sweet fritters. A low-gluten flour or flour combined with a pure starch such as cornstarch can result in a lighter, more tender fritter.

Frizzled: Frizzled is a restaurant menu euphemism for fried that is almost always used to describe leeks that have been julienned, deep-fried, and used as a garnish. It does sound better than "fried" and can be applied to any julienned vegetable that's deep-fried.

Frosting: See icing.

Fruit: Technically, fruit is the mature and edible ovary of a flowering plant, which includes not only apples and oranges and bananas but also tomatoes and green peppers and cucumbers. But we still tend to think of fruits as sweet and vegetables as savory, a meaningful distinction.

Fry: To fry means to cook in fat, technically considered a dry-heat cooking method because it's done at temperatures exceeding the boiling point of water. But it's a vague term; the cook should distinguish the type of frying being done. If frying in a small amount of oil, enough to come halfway up the sides of the item being cooked, it is called pan-frying. If the item is

THE ELEMENTS OF COOKING A TO Z   133

completely submerged in fat, it should be called deep-fring. If you are using just enough oil to coat the bottom of the frying pan, the preferred word is sauté.

Frying pan: As cooking has advanced in the American kitchen, and cooking equipment has become chic, the term frying pan, once used to refer to any low-sided pan, is used less and less. We can and should use precise terms for low-sided pans to distinguish between them, such as sauté pan or *sauteuse* (sloping sides) and *sautoire* (straight sides), or cast iron (sometimes called a Griswold, the name of an early manufacturer).

Fumet [*foo-MAY*]: *Fumet* is fish stock that usually includes white wine. *Fumets* should be clean and light. They should be made with the bones of white fish—preferably flat fish (turbot, sole, flounder), or the fish the *fumet* will support in the finished dish, but bass and halibut are good as well—not fatty red-fleshed fish such as salmon or tuna. Gills, veins, eyes, and fins should be removed. The bones should be soaked overnight in ice water to draw out any remaining blood. Sweet aromatics in addition to onions often include fennel. Vegetables should be lightly sweated, then white wine is added and cooked until the alcohol fumes can't be detected. The bones are added, gently sweated, then water is added to cover and brought up to heat and cooked gently, a half hour or so, never brought to a boil or it will become cloudy. *Fumet* is used like any stock, as the base for a soup or sauce, or as a cooking medium in a stew or *cuisson*.

Fungus: Fungi are simple plants, a group that includes mushrooms, of course, but also beneficial yeasts and molds.

Funnel: Funnels are handy to have around, one small for transferring ingredients such as spices into small containers and a larger one for transferring liquids.

G

Galantine: A galantine is an old and special preparation in which a poultry forcemeat, or pâté, is rolled inside the skin of that poultry, tied, poached, chilled, and sliced to serve.

Game: Wild animals and birds, hunted and cooked, are usually different from their domesticated brethren. They tend to be leaner as a result of their own hunting work in the wild and their meat tends to have stronger, gamey tastes (richer flavors associated with blood and offal) from their exertion and a diet taken from their surroundings. Categories of game include venison (elk, deer, caribou, antelope, moose), bear, exotics (feral hog, sheep, goats), furred and feathered small game, and reptiles. There are cautions with some wild animals that don't apply to domestically raised livestock. Wild hogs and bear, which eat what they come across, including objects such as dead birds, can carry trichinosis (which you're unlikely to find in a domestically raised hog). And experts recommend staying away from spinal and brain tissues of venison. However, most of the food safety issues concern how carefully the animal was eviscerated; if the animal was cleaned and dressed by an expert, most cuts of game can be eaten undercooked or rare. This is important because game tends to be so lean. Larding and barding are good techniques for increasing the succulence of game, or, for those concerned about fat, gently poaching game in stock is another option.

Ganache: Ganache is a fancy word for chocolate sauce. It's usually made by adding hot cream to chopped chocolate and, after the chocolate has begun to melt, gently stirring it into a smooth emulsion. It can be made with other fats (such as butter) and with additional flavorings or forms of sugar (often corn syrup is used). A common ratio of equal parts by weight of chocolate and cream results in a thick chocolate sauce that is pliable when chilled. The less liquid used the harder the ganache will be when it sets up. Ganache is used for fillings, chocolate truffles, and icings. It's also perhaps the easiest dessert sauce to make and, if you use delicious chocolate, one of the best.

Garam masala: an Indian spice mixture that commonly includes cumin, coriander, and pepper as well as some "sweet" spices such as cardamom, cinnamon, cloves, and mace. This can be bought but making your own according to your tastes is easy and the result is superior to most store-bought mixtures.

Garde manger: Garde manger refers to cold-food preparation, from canapés and hors d'oeuvres to pâtés to salads. In restaurant kitchens, the garde manger station or the chef garde manger, prepares salads, canapés, starter courses, and other cold foods.

Garlic: Garlic is one of the great ingredients of the pantry, a bulb with numerous uses and varying flavors depending on how it's treated. Fresh garlic and garlic that's been properly dried is markedly better than the garlic that's been hanging around for a while with its germ green and protuberant. Choose garlic that is very hard, that looks like it's about to burst out of its skin. The best garlic is often found at farmers' markets, and is often of the hard core variety, the bulbs arranged around a stiff central shaft; grocery store garlic is usually soft core (no central shaft). Fresh hard-core garlic is worth the extra expense because its flavor is so much more fresh and vivid than the commercially grown garlic.

If you pay attention to the behavior of garlic you'll notice that how you cut it matters; minced garlic tastes different from sliced garlic. Garlic can be pressed; while most chefs wouldn't dream of this, it's acceptable if you first remove the germ—the green, growing part of the garlic—which quickly gives the smashed garlic an old or off smell and flavor. It's always a good idea to remove the germ from garlic that will be minced or sliced. If the garlic will be cooked for a long time (in a stock or a stew), removing the germ is not necessary. Garlic can be roasted in foil with some oil till it's tender and slightly caramelized; or it can be steam roasted—placed in a ramekin with a little water, covered with foil, and baked in a moderate oven; steam roasted garlic results in a milder, cleaner cooked garlic flavor without the flavors of caramelization, which can be abundant in this sugar-rich plant. Garlic burns relatively quickly and will become bitter. Burnt garlic should be discarded.

Garlic press: Provided you remove the germ first or add the garlic to a hot pan immediately, garlic presses are fine for home cooking. They are also controversial. In the chef world they're looked on as an amateurish tool, pressing garlic a regrettable compromise for the sake of convenience. This is because whole garlic cloves smashed through a press will rapidly develop an off flavor if not cooked immediately, apparently because the enzymes in the germ when mashed with the garlic go to work transforming the aroma and flavor of the garlic. If you remove the germ first, garlic can be pressed without compromise. Immediate high heat will also deactivate the enzymes, which is why you can even press garlic with the germ if it's going immediately into a hot pan. You should also know that the effect of garlic varies depending how it's cut; there are subtle differences in flavor between crushed garlic, minced garlic, and garlic paste made by mincing and smearing it with the broad side of a knife; use all these methods yourself and pay attention to the differences.

Garnish: Garnish is often thought of as a last minute visual flourish for a dish, but in restaurant cooking, garnish can refer to secondary but fundamental component of a composed dish rather than decoration. Garnishes should not be used solely for visual effect, but should add a harmonious flavor or textural element to a dish. For example, garnishes are the pearl onions, sautéed mushrooms, and lardons in a beef *bourguignonne;* pistachios and tart cherries in a classic pâté (called internal garnish); or the gremolata that might garnish osso bucco or a similar braise. While there are exceptions, it's a good idea to use only garnishes that you can eat.

Gas (burners): Gas burners are desirable because their heat is immediate, unlike electric burners or flattops, and they also provide the cook an immediate visual indication of their heat level. They aren't necessarily hotter than electric, only faster.

Gastrique: a reduction of sugar and vinegar (or any sweet liquid and any acid) that's used to season sauces for meat dishes, customarily ones that are paired with fruit, such as duck or venison.

Gastronomy: the craft, science, art, sociology, and anthropology of food, cooking, serving, and eating.

Gaufrette: wafflelike chips of root vegetables, cut on a mandoline.

Gavage: the force-feeding of ducks and geese being raised for foie gras.

Gel: to add a thickening agent such as gelatin or agar to a liquid or semi-liquid so that it sets up or holds its shape. Strengths of gels vary depending on whether the liquid simply needs a more substantial consistency or if it needs to be sliced (as with a vegetable terrine bound with a gelled liquid, for instance; see aspic).

Gelatin: 1) A protein derived from animals that's sold granulated and in clear sheets, used to solidify liquids or loose creams to varying degrees or to stabilize foams (see also aspic). Gelatin must be bloomed in water—rehydrated—so that it melts completely. Sheets of dry gelatin are soaked in water; powdered gelatin is sprinkled over three times its volume in liquid and allowed to bloom. 2) When the collagen that composes connective tissue is heated it will, given enough moisture, melt, resulting in gelatin. This gelatin is what gives stocks and sauces body. Some stocks will have enough gelatin in them to set up and become firm; if you want your stock to be this gelatin rich without adding powdered gelatin, add a calf's foot or pigskin, which have abundant collagen. If these aren't available, most tough cuts, joints, and feet (chicken feet, beef shank) can provide additional gelatin.

Gelée [*juh-LAY*]: French for aspic. *Oeufs en gelée* are eggs in a gelled meat stock. The quality of the liquid used, whether it's tomato water or stock, is critical to the success of the dish; if it's a stock it should be clarified (see clarification) and, because it will be eaten cold or at room temperature, it should be aggressively seasoned.

Génoise [*jzen-WAHZ*]: a cake made using the foaming method, here with whole eggs that are gently heated over hot water so that the sugar dissolves and the eggs reach their full volume when whipped. Dry ingredients are folded into the foamed egg-sugar mixture. Butter is added to enrich and flavor the cake and also shorten the gluten created in the initial mixing. (See also sponge cake.)

Germ (in garlic): the green growing part of the garlic clove. It's best to remove this immediately when working with garlic, as it can compromise garlic's flavor. It should always be removed if the garlic is going to be minced and held for any time. If it's to be heated immediately or if the garlic is going into a stock or a stew that will be cooked for a long time, removing the germ is less important.

Germ (in wheat): The germ, or the embryo of the wheat grain, is rich in protein and fiber and can be added to yeast doughs to fortify bread. Because the germ is high in fat, it's susceptible to becoming rancid and so it, as well as whole wheat flour, should be kept airtight in the refrigerator or freezer to prevent spoilage.

Ghee: the Indian name for clarified butter, a principle cooking fat in that country (among many other uses), traditionally made from milk that has been soured like yogurt, then churned to make butter, which is then gently cooked to preserve it (see McGee). Other methods include not skimming the solids that rise but rather allowing them to sink to the bottom and brown. Traditional ghee therefore is more complex than butter that's been clarified. For recipes requiring ghee, use clarified butter.

Giblets: the heart, gizzard, and liver of poultry. The heart and gizzard (the second stomach of the bird used for grinding partially digested food) are both strong rich muscles that require long slow cooking to become tender. The liver is best sautéed quickly. The heart and gizzard are often chopped and used to flavor gravies, but they're also good to add to stock made from the bird. Braised or confited giblets can be part of a composed salad or sliced and fried crisp and used as a salad garnish the way you might use bacon.

Glaçage [*glah-SAJZ*]: Technically, *glaçage* is a sweet frosting or glazing, but some chefs use the word to describe a savory technique wherein a dish is finished with a cream- or yolk-based sauce and quickly broiled or heated under a salamander, to give the dish a glazed appearance.

Glace de viande [*glahss de VEE-ohnd*]: The French word for ice cream, *glace,* is also the term used in kitchens for meat stock that has been substantially reduced—*glace de viande* or more commonly *glace*. Two quarts of good veal stock reduced to a cup will result in *glace*. It's used to fortify sauces *à la minute* and also can be added to forcemeats to enrich and bind them, or as a baste for roasted meats to enhance their depth of flavor.

Glands: Glands are parts of the body that absorb bodily matter, alter it, then secrete or excrete it. It's special tissue that is often distinctly flavored and textured. The liver and kidney are glands that can be very special to cook and to eat; the thymus gland, called sweetbreads on menus, is another excellent gland. When preparing pork shoulder butt for slicing or grinding, glandlike nodes, small fatlike discs about the size of a quarter, are often found embedded within; they can make the meat bitter and should be removed from the meat and discarded.

Glaze (noun): 1) A liquid concentrated to syrup consistency, usually used referring to a stock (meat glaze) or vinegar (balsamic vinegar glaze is a common preparation). 2) Any thin, dense, sugar-based coating for cakes and pastries, often one that gives food a luster or shine, can be called a glaze.

Glaze (verb): To glaze is a method of cooking root vegetables. It's important to understand that glazed vegetables does not mean candied vegetables. Glaze refers to the lacquered sheen the finished vegetable carries when properly cooked. It's an excellent technique that seems to have lost its fashion, probably due to bad technique (and therefore bad tasting vegetables). Proper glazing technique involves cutting the vegetables—onion or scallion, carrot, beet, turnip, parsnip, vegetables that are high in sugar—to a uniform shape, simmering them in a little bit of water with a pinch of salt, sugar, and butter, cooking off the water just before they're cooked through so that the sugar, butter, salt, and what is now a vegetable stock concentrate on the bottom of the pan, and coating the vegetables by rolling and tossing them in the pan. Glazed vegetables can be prepared several hours before serving and kept warm (not refrigerated) until reheating to serve.

Gluten: a mixture of wheat proteins, glutenin and gliadin (see McGee) which, when hydrated, combine into long strands that make a dough elastic, the quality that allows a dough to hold bubbles of gas released by yeast, giving us leavened bread. Gluten will also relax if you leave it alone. Gluten can make preparations such as pasta and pastries tough. We use a fat to shorten the gluten strands when making a tender pie crust. An alkaline, such as baking soda, will also weaken gluten.

Gnocchi: Little "lumps" of pasta, gnocchi are often made from riced potatoes held together with flour; gnocchi can also be made with flour and ricotta cheese or, in a version called Parisian gnocchi, with eggs and semolina flour, resulting in a pasta that's completely different from the Italian potato or ricotta gnocchi. Gnocchi should be firm but not tough and not pasty; when making potato gnocchi, add just as much flour as is needed to hold the potato together, being careful not to overknead.

Goose: Goose behaves much like duck, though they are most often roasted whole. Because geese are bigger, they require more cooking. Like duck they need long slow cooking to render the copious fat. Their rendered fat is an excellent cooking medium. The legs are especially good confited.

Gooseneck: Gooseneck is the restaurant-kitchen slang for a long spouted sauce dish.

Gougères: See *pâte à choux*.

Grains: The nutritious fruit of grasses—rice, wheat, corn, and a few others—comprise the bulk of the world's diet and are a prominent part of the cook's pantry. They can be taken in virtually any flavor direction you wish, have

myriad uses and variations, and so are extremely versatile. They are composed of a husk (the bran), the germ, and the endosperm, and often
only the endosperm is used, but they can be bought and used whole,
cracked, crushed, or powdered (flour). The husk is valuable for its fiber,
the germ for its high nutrition, and the endosperm for its carbohydrates
and protein. While there's considerable variation in terms of cooking
method, most grains are dry and so need to be hydrated, usually with
twice their volume in water (though dried corn, such as hominy and
polenta, needs more and some rices, such as basmati, need less), a 1:2 ratio
is the rule. The most important thing to know about cooking grains is that
they will be permeated and flavored by the liquid they cook in. So if that
liquid is water, that is how they will be flavored. It's almost always advisable to add salt and some fat (butter, a flavorful oil) to the cooking liquid,
if not aromatics or stock. A pinch of salt in two or three cups of water
won't usually cover the seasoning needs. Taste your water after you've seasoned it; that is the level of seasoning your rice or quinoa or grits or bar-
ley will hit when they are cooked. If the water doesn't taste pleasantly
seasoned, adjust it. Grains can be kept warm provided they don't dry out
and they refrigerate and reheat well.

Gram: A gram is equal to approximately ⅛ of an ounce; 28 grams equals
one ounce. Recipes generally translate the equivalent to either 25 or 30
grams per ounce for the sake of uniformity. Metric measurements are
more efficient because of their consistency and equivalency (50 grams of
salt in a 1,000 grams of water, that is, a liter—will give you a 5 percent salt
solution, for example). If you have the choice between using grams and
using American equivalents, use metric.

Granita: Italian for grained, granita, or *granité* in French, is a dessert or
intermezzo composed of sugar and flavored water, usually fruit or liquor;
it should be granular (its crystalline texture is one way it's distinguished
from the smooth sorbet), intensely sweet-and-sour, and refreshing, though
savory granitas are not uncommon. The crystals are formed by stirring the
liquid occasionally as it freezes.

Granulated sugar: This all-purpose sweetener, at the ready, is fine for baking and sweetening drinks and offsetting the harsher effects of salt. Convenience is its main strength. But because it's so convenient, it's easy to use it
without thinking; consider using brown sugar or honey instead. Table

sugar is a very simple sweet; when you cook it and it begins to color, you can taste the mounting complexities as the sugar molecules transform. (See also sugar.)

Grapeseed oil: Grapeseed oil is often chefs' cooking oil of choice because it's so clean and its smoke point is relatively high, but it's more expensive than other neutral oils, such as canola, and so not always the most economical choice (see cooking oil).

Grate, grater: Grating is a kind of utility cut, reducing a big object down to a specific size, like chopping for items that don't chop well, such as cheese or nutmeg. And a good grater, with different-sized grates, is a recommended kitchen tool. It's a lot more versatile than it's often given credit for, and the creative cook will use a grater for more than just cheese. It will take the meat from the skin of a tomato petal; garlic can be grated straight into a sauce; vegetables can be grated as quickly as they can be chopped and will infuse a stock or court bouillon much more quickly than diced mirepoix (see also Microplane).

Gratin, gratiné: *Gratin* and *gratiné* refer to a dish or the making of a dish that is broiled or heavily browned on top so that a crust has formed, usually of cheese, a way to introduce complex flavors and texture to otherwise soft rich dishes.

Gravlax: Literally translating as buried fish—a preserved and often fermented fish in old Scandanavia—gravlax now refers to cured salmon that's not smoked (compare with lox, which are typically brined and often smoked). Gravlax are easy to make at home and highly recommended if you have access to excellent salmon, preferably wild. Pack a side of salmon in a 2:1 mixture of salt and sugar (and any aromatics you wish, citrus zest, fresh herbs, spices) and let it cure for about a day depending on its thickness, rinse and dry it, and (the hardest part) slice it thinly.

Gravy: the American word for *jus,* more or less, the notion of using the available fat and juices from what's been roasted to make a sauce. There's never enough juices from a roast to create enough sauce for all the people a roast will feed, so it's helpful to have some stock or wine on hand to augment what's left behind by the meat. Use the fond in the pan to fortify the juices and stock, along with any additional aromatics you might want to add. Once you have the right amount of liquid flavored as you want it, a gravy, unlike a *jus,* is usually thickened with a roux or a slurry. In the case of gravy, it's best to use fat rendered from the cut of meat you're roasting to make the roux. (See the essay Sauce, page 12.)

Grease: Among the most nefarious by-products of cooking, grease refers to the airborne particles of fat that rise from hot cooking pans and collect on whatever they can find. Grease should not be used synonymously with fat. Fat is good; grease is evil.

Grecque, à la [*ah lah GREK*]: The term *à la grecque* refers to cooked vegetables that are served cold. An *à la grecque* salad is composed of cooked and chilled vegetables sauced with a vinaigrette. The technique is simple: cook vegetables in a court bouillon till they are almost, but not quite cooked through, and shock and store them in the chilled cooking liquid until ready to serve. It's an excellent technique, generally, and a good one to use if you need to prepare the food before serving it; it's especially appropriate during hot weather for buffet service.

Green vegetables: Green vegetables should be cooked as quickly as possible and served immediately or, to preserve their brilliant color and their flavor, shocked in ice water, drained, and gently reheated when ready to serve. Of course green vegetables can be roasted, grilled, pan-steamed, or broiled but generally, the fundamental technique for cooking a green vegetable is to plunge it into a vast quantity of heavily salted water, so much water that it doesn't lose its boil, and (if not serving right away) to stop its cooking as rapidly as possible by shocking it in ice water.

Gremolata: Gremolata is a simple, ingenious combination of aromatic seasonings—garlic, lemon zest, and parsley all finely minced—that is used to brighten braised dishes (that is, add fresh, distinct herbal and citrus flavors that contrast with the complex, caramel and roasted flavors of stews and braises). Because the garlic is raw it should be used on piping hot food; the freshness gives braised meats an incomparable boost. The traditional version of this is called *gremolada* and is briefly cooked with osso bucco (braised veal shank), also a superb use of this vivid combination. Variations on the *idea* of gremolata—fresh herb, citrus, garlic—are valuable, too, replacing the lemon zest with other citrus such as orange or lime, the parsley with basil or cilantro.

Griddle: a flat cast iron cooking surface, which gets very hot and holds the heat. Griddle can also be used as a verb, signifying the method of cooking, food being cooked directly on the large flat surface. Properly maintained, griddles develop an excellent nonstick surface.

Grill, grilling: an excellent dry-heat cooking method that differs from most other cooking methods in that it adds substantial new flavors to the food itself, the complex flavors of smoke. There are three fundamental choices to make when determining how to grill: high heat or low heat, direct heat or indirect heat, covered grill or uncovered grill. All of these are determined primarily by how long the food needs to be cooked and how gently it needs to be cooked. Use high direct heat if the food is tender and doesn't require a long cooking time (a steak, for example), which will result in a good flavorful exterior quickly. If the food requires a long cooking time (chicken legs, pork shoulder) or will be hurt by high temperatures (sausage) lower heat is used; often the best way to achieve low heat is through indirect heat (banking coals on the sides) or a combination of direct and indirect; if you're using indirect heat, it's usually best to cover the grill. Food grilled covered will also pick up a lot of additional smoke flavor. Covering a grill can also help you to control flames for meat that's rendering fat over coals. If the meat will render a lot of fat and juices (such as a whole chicken), it's a good idea to put a drip pan beneath the meat. Outright flames should be avoided because they result in bitter flavors and possibly the development of cancer-causing nitrosamines. Your choice of fuel—gas versus coal or wood—is a matter of personal taste.

Grill marks: Grill marks are an appealing visual element for food and do add some flavor from the charred surface. Traditionally, a good diamond-shaped crosshatch is favored; in order for home cooks to achieve good grill marks, either a very hot cast iron pan must be used or the grill surface, oiled, must be very, very hot.

Grind (noun): The grind of meat is important for pâtés, sausages, hamburgers. Most grinders come with at least two dies—the plate through which the meat is extruded—one large and one small, and more elaborate grinders have a variety of die sizes. The smaller the die, the finer the grind and smoother the texture will be.

Grind (verb): the term we use for meat and also for pulverizing spices (and coffee beans, of course). The act of grinding meat creates a lot of friction and therefore heat, which can cause the meat and fat being ground to separate when cooked. Always grind meat that is very cold. A grinder is a versatile tool for more than just cooked meat. Vegetables can be ground for quick extraction in making a stock; ground bacon becomes a flavorful elegant garnish when sautéed. If you want to get the most out of your spices, toasting them gently, then grinding them just before using them, is the way to do it. Spice or coffee grinders are the quickest and easiest way to grind spices though they can be ground in a stone mortar (or in a pinch finely chopped with a knife). Being able to grind your own spices quickly and easily makes a big difference in cooking and is highly recommended. Grinders are inexpensive enough that you can own one for coffee and one for spices.

Grinder: Grinders are available as stand alone appliances, manual cranks, and as attachments to standing mixers. Depending on the kinds of cooking you do, they can be very valuable, creating a texture in the meat that's not possible by finely chopping or by pureeing in a processor. The latter is sometimes an acceptable alternative to grinding, but the results of grinding and of pureeing are different. The blades and dies of grinders can easily become dull if they're not taken care of and compromise the quality of the meat you grind; it's best to wash and dry them by hand, and if you use them frequently, have them professionally sharpened.

H

Half-and-half: Half-and-half, a mixture of milk and cream, has about 12 percent milk fat, about a third what cream has. Half-and-half is acceptable to use for custards that call for mixtures of cream and whole milk, but not as a replacement for cream.

Ham: Ham is cured pork, cured usually with some form of nitrite. Sodium nitrite—also called curing salt or pink salt—is what gives ham its rosy color and hammy flavor. Without the curing salt, it's pork. (It should be noted that poultry will take on a hammy flavor if cured with nitrite, giving those who must avoid pork an option with similar flavor and texture.) We call a variety of cuts from the hog by the name ham—cured shoulder is sometimes called a cottage ham, the foreleg is the picnic ham—but ham usually refers to the big back legs. These can be dry cured—cured in salt, then hung to dry (often called prosciutto or jambon cru)—or cured in brine and cooked (a fresh ham) or smoked. Ham is good to eat as it is, hot or cold, but its most powerful and influential use may be as a seasoning, adding heft and complexity to countless dishes, from soups to beans to stews.

Ham hock: Ham hocks are cured, smoked hocks, the part of the leg just above the trotter, and are used to flavor and add body, via gelatin, to soups and stews. They don't have a lot of meat on them, but cooked till tender what little meat there is is excellent. The skin on the hock also adds substantial gelatin to the liquid in addition to the other connective tissue.

Hand blender: See immersion blender.

Hard ball stage: a term referring to a specific temperature of sugar, about 250° to 260°F, which, when chilled, results in a solid texture and is used for nougat, marshmallows, and rock candy.

Hard crack stage: a term referring to a specific temperature of sugar, around 295° to 310°F, which, when chilled, results in a very brittle texture and is used for butterscotch, brittles, hard candies, and toffee.

Haute cuisine [*oat kwee-ZEEN*]: *Haute cuisine* refers to classical French cuisine and/or denotes a level of technique brought to bear on food and its preparation resulting in complex, refined, elegant dishes. The term to some is synonymous with stuffy, old-fashioned, expensive French food. In fact, *haute cuisine* should be used to describe food and service in fine dining restaurants on which the highest level of care and effort has been brought to bear.

Head: The heads of animals often carry a lot of meat and collagen that will impart flavor and gelatin to a stock. Sometimes the head can be added to more bones as part of the stock but often it's a means to an end in itself (headcheese and *tête de veau,* for instance). Larger heads carry whole cuts of meat (hog jowl and beef cheeks) that are excellent braised. Heads are a valuable part of the animal and not to be dismissed.

Headcheese: Headcheese is a preparation in which slow-cooked meat and vegetables are packed into a mold and bound with gelatinized stock. Like a pâté, it can be sliced and served as part of a charcuterie platter or salad, with mustard or a vinaigrette. It's customarily made from the head of a pig because it is a convenient and tasty way to utilize the head from this animal: the bone and meat and connective tissue create a flavorful stock loaded with gelatin; the cooked meat is easily removed from the bone, the cartilaginous ears become tender and can be julienned together with spices and salt and aromatic vegetables.

Hearing: To hear your food is an important ability, more important than we often recognize. Listen in your mind to the sound of vegetables simmering in a little butter and water. The simmer will move from gentle to crackly as the water leaves the pan, letting you know that your vegetables will begin to caramelize now. Dough as it is mixing will make a different sound against the side of the bowl as it comes together, helping you to know how much longer you should mix it. Pay attention to the sound of your food cooking.

Heart: The heart may be the least "offal-ish" of the organ meats; it's a muscle and so resembles other muscles that give us such cuts as steaks and chops, as opposed to such organs as kidney or liver. Heart tends to be very lean and richly flavored. Because it worked so hard it can be tough; it's excellent to use to flavor stocks (and a great choice to add to the clarification of a consommé), but it can also be sliced thinly (a form of tenderizing), and briefly cooked as with any other lean muscle.

Heat: Heat levels are critical to excellent cooking and have an infinite range. The heat levels for sautéing vary in intensities according to what's being cooked. Home cooks are sometimes unsure about what low heat or medium heat actually means. When unsure a cook should consider what's being cooked and what the intended result is: a caramelized surface or a slow rendering of fat and some tenderizing? Is the item to be cooked tough (requiring low heat) or naturally tender (high heat)? Low heat on a stovetop is such that the food can spend a lot of time in the pan, which you want for, say, bacon or a sausage. High heat usually means bringing the cooking oil to smoking or just before. High heat will not only brown food, it has the secondary effect of preventing food from sticking to the cooking surface. When determining the heat level, or sussing out the meaning of a recipe, think about the food and use your common sense.

Heat diffuser: Some preparations require long, low heat. Heat diffusers mollify even the lowest levels. They can come in handy but if you don't have one, making a ring of aluminum foil to raise the pot above the heat is an adequate alternative.

Heavy cream: See cream.

Herbs (fresh): Fresh herbs are among the most important ingredients in the kitchen. It's difficult to overemphasize the significance of their effects; these featherweights pack a powerful punch and can single-handedly elevate a dish from good to great. Their uses are countless—from *fines herbes* that flavor a sauce or an omelet, added to butter (see compound butter), added whole to salads, included among the aromats in stocks and stews. Herbs are sometimes categorized by their stem—soft or hard. Chives, tarragon, parsley are soft-stemmed herbs; thyme and rosemary are hard-stemmed herbs. While you can substitute dried herbs for fresh, practically speaking there is no adequate substitute for fresh herbs. If there is any common error cooks make in how they use herbs, it's usually in their failure to use as much as they might. Fresh herbs are volatile and so should be cut as close to their being used as possible. To hold them in the refrigerator for a day or two, wrap them in a damp towel so that they are able to breathe but don't dry out.

Herbs (dried): While dried herbs should not be used as a substitute for fresh, dried herbs do have a variety of uses. The best dried herbs are often those you dry yourself; crushed over a chicken to be roasted or added to soups and stews, they're delicious. Two factors affect the impact of dried herbs. First, dried herbs do keep for weeks, but over time they become insipid. The fresher they are, the better. Home cooks should buy them in small quantities and always evaluate their freshness by smell and color. Second, dried herbs need time in the cooking to rehydrate and then offer their aromatic influence; they need to be added to the dish well before the dish is finished.

Hog: The hog is an animal so versatile from a culinary standpoint that a saying has evolved about it: everything can be used except the oink. Its meat has an extraordinary range of flavors and textures given myriad preparations, its fat is unparalleled, not only as an enricher of everything from pastries to pâtés, but also as a cooking medium; its skin is loaded with collagen (which gives us gelatin). Its offal is abundant and itself has many uses, from casings to organs. The variety of uses for the many parts of the pig is unparalleled in our livestock. This text recommends seeking out naturally farmed hogs—and eschewing the debased, factory-raised pork—when time, availability, and cost make this choice practical (available over the Internet and, more and more, in grocery stores).

Hold: To "hold" food means to keep food, but usually refers to the act of cooking or partially cooking food and holding it to complete its cooking later. To hold food well means to store it in a way that will keep it as close to the way it is at the moment as possible. Some food is held as a simple matter of storage. Other food is cooked long before serving and then held, one of the most critical skills a restaurant cook can have and a skill that has great advantages for the home cook. Knowing what food can be cooked and held without compromise allows the home cook to serve that food efficiently during busy weekday meals or weekend dinner parties.

Hollandaise: a warm emulsified sauce, sometimes called a mother sauce (though technically it's not). Whole butter or clarified butter is emulsified into yolks seasoned with a reduction of water, acid, salt, and pepper to create a thick, rich, vivid all-purpose sauce for vegetables, eggs, and fish. Variations include béarnaise (flavored with tarragon), *choron* (tarragon and tomato), and *paloise* (mint).

Homogenize: to mechanically combine two opposing liquids so they are uniformly dispersed; milk is homogenized to prevent the fat from combining with itself and rising to the top.

Honey: Honey is an excellent all-purpose sweetener, adding more complex flavors than table sugar. When you're sweetening something—whether it's whipped cream or tea or a marinade—it's a good idea to consider what kind of sweetness you want; honey's great floral notes might be just what you're after. Quality of honey varies; the most distinctive honeys often originate from wildflowers and the blossoms of fruit trees.

Hors d'oeuvres: Hors d'oeuvres are preparations served before a meal, usually those that are not individually portioned, such as nuts, cheeses, a *pâté en terrine*. Compare canapé, dishes that are served in individual portions.

Horseradish: It's important to distinguish the horseradish in a jar, a kind of horseradish-and-vinegar puree, from freshly grated horseradish. They're very different products. Freshly grated horseradish is heady and pungent and clean and with the addition of fat, commonly cream, it's the basis for a delicious sauce for meat and fish. It can also be grated or even finely julienned and used as a visual and flavorful garnish for rich meats, pâté, salad, or smoked fish. Prepared horseradish in a jar can be substituted for fresh, but the results will not be comparable.

Hospitality: Hospitality, which derives from the Latin word for house, is the core of the restaurant industry. Cooking, cleaning, and serving are all in the service of this single idea, that of pleasing the guest, making the guest comfortable. Whether you're a restaurant cook or a home cook, and regardless of the personal pleasures the act of cooking brings, it's useful to remember that cooking is usually in the service of others.

Hotel butter: See *beurre maître d'hôtel.*

Hotel pan: Hotel pans are rectangular steel pans of varying sizes and depths (a "200 pan" is two inches deep, a "400 pan" four inches deep, and so on), the kind that fill the inserts in a buffet steam table or that contain the *mise en place* of a line cook's station. Hotel pans are useful all-purpose containers for cooking, holding, and storing some food.

Hot smoke: Hot smoke means to cook the food and smoke it at the same time but at a low temperature, between 150° and 200°F or so, so that the item is both gently and evenly cooked while taking on a deep smoke flavor. Hot dogs and bacon are items that are typically hot smoked. (Compare cold smoke, smoke roast, and pan smoke.)

Hound's-tooth check: Hound's-tooth check is the traditional pattern on the professional cook's trousers, presumably used because it disguised stains; hound's-tooth check pants are sometimes casually referred to as checks.

Hydrate: See rehydrate.

Hydrogenation: the commercial process of forcing hydrogen into liquid fats so that the fat will be solid at room temperature. Hydrogenated oils can contain trans fats, which are believed to raise blood-cholesterol levels.

Hydroponic: Hydroponic refers to a method of growing plants in nutrient rich water and a controlled climate rather than in soil. The advantages are that produce can be grown indoors all year long; the produce tends to be pristine looking (it doesn't have to endure weather). Hydroponic farming is a very efficient method in terms of space and consistency, but hydroponically grown foods can have a generic flavor, lacking the complexities individual soils give to leaves and fruits and vegetables.

I

Ice: Because it has such an impact on lowering the temperature of food, ice is a great kitchen and cooking tool. It will rapidly halt the cooking of green vegetables and keep the temperature of ground meat down when making a sausage; measured and added as the water in a yeast dough, it will keep the dough cool if it's being mixed in a hot summertime kitchen; a pot of stock will drop from simmering to chilled in minutes when the pot is submerged in ice and the stock stirred. Ice can be used for temperature control, to stop green vegetables from cooking, or to cool the outside of a stockpot, and is usually used in the form of an ice bath.

Ice bath: Ice baths, plenty of ice in water, are used to cool food quickly. A good ice bath has about 50 percent ice and 50 percent water; an ice bath doesn't mean ice floating on the surface. Vegetables are typically shocked in an ice bath to halt their cooking, often so that they can be held and reheated later. Hot liquids can be stirred while their pot is in an ice bath to bring the temperature down fast. When cooling anything in an ice bath, it's a good idea to agitate the item in the ice bath to ensure that it's always surrounded by ice-cold water.

Ice cream machine: Ice cream machines will freeze most any liquid, custard, or puree, sweet or savory, and while their convenience is undeniable, given plenty of ice and salt, two containers, one that can fit inside another, and a wooden spoon or stiff spatula you can create the same effect if you need to.

Icing: Icings, typically composed of sugar and butter and sometimes egg, are often an important garnish for cakes and cookies. The simplest icings are made from confectioners' sugar and butter (4:1 ratio by weight, the consistency adjusted with liquid, such as cream). Buttercreams, though, are a more complex, richer icing. Buttercreams use some form of egg (whole, yolk, or white), which are cooked, and the sugar is typically cooked as well. Whole butter is whipped into the cooked egg-sugar mixture to complete the buttercream. Frosting and icing are interchangeable but icing tends to be the term professionals use while frosting seems to have more homey connotations.

Immersion blender: The immersion blender, a hand-held appliance with a whipping blade on the end that can be immersed in hot liquid, is an invaluable tool for pureeing soups in the pot, for blending sauces, or for mounting butter into them. Some come with attachments and chopper cups, which can be convenient.

Impurity: Just about anything we want to remove from liquids—coagulated protein, vegetable fibers, fat, foam—that is, any substance that adversely affects flavor and texture can be considered an impurity. Removing impurities by skimming and straining your stock, soup, or sauce is an act that should be done continually throughout the cooking.

Induction burners: An electromagnetic coil in induction burners causes the electrons in steel or iron to move rapidly, uniformly heating the cooking vessel—only the metal gets hot. This is an efficient way of cooking, because the only thing getting heated is the pot, and that happens very quickly. Another substantial benefit is that it doesn't heat the air the way gas and electric burners do, so induction burners are especially appreciated in hot climates, and they're easy to clean because food spilled on them won't cook. It will not heat glass or ceramics, so if you cook in a tagine or only have Pyrex pots, an induction burner may put you at a disadvantage, but most chefs who use them, praise them.

Infuse, infusion: To infuse means to add a flavor to something without adding the actual material that produces the flavor—infusing oil with the flavor of basil but not its leaves, for instance. Oils are commonly infused with herbs or spices; when you are using a *sachet d'epices* in a stock, you are infusing the stock with the contents of the cheesecloth, and milk and cream is often infused with sweet aromatics for dessert preparations.

Inlay: An inlay is a type of interior garnish that adds visual appeal and flavor to a dish, usually a terrine (though occasionally a dough or a cake). The item is usually used whole—a tenderloin in a meat pâté, a lobster tail or scallops in a seafood terrine, a sausage in brioche.

Intestine: Hog and sheep intestines, which give us a variety of casings for sausages and other preparations, are extraordinary for their qualities of being very strong but also very delicate. They contribute to a sausage's texture, flavor, and color. They determine its size (most purveyors designate varying diameters that are available). And while they are a superlative container for ground meats, they are sometimes used as a filling for a sausage, the andouillette. Beef intestines are also used but they tend to be larger and more fibrous, often too tough to eat.

Instant read thermometer: No kitchen should be without one. For those items that must be cooked to a precise internal temperature, or when you need water to hit a specific temperature for poaching, an instant read thermometer is essential in knowing when you're at the right point. Thermometers aren't foolproof. There's a saying: a thermometer is only as good as the person using it. To use a thermometer properly is important, especially when evaluating a large cut of meat. You must know what part of the meat your thermometer is giving you information about. Remember that the heat of the metal probe can slightly affect the temperature of the meat being measured. It's a good idea to make sure your thermometer is giving you accurate readings; check them by taking the temperature of an ice bath (32° or 33°F) and/or boiling water (211° or 212°F); analogue thermometers can be adjusted to show the correct temperature.

Interior garnish: Garnishes add visual, textural, and flavorful components to the main focus of a dish. But some items benefit from interior garnish, such as elements that are added to a pâté before it's cooked, garnish that is only seen after the food is sliced. Interior garnish can be divided into two categories: random garnish, mushroom, dried fruit, or diced, cured meat folded into the forcemeat; and an inlay, a single garnish carefully placed within the forcemeat.

Intermezzo: In culinary terms, intermezzo refers to a small dish that arrives between larger ones, often serving as a palate cleanser, an acidic *granita,* for instance. It should be refreshing.

Iodized salt: salt to which potassium iodide has been added, a procedure begun in 1924 to prevent the iodine deficiency prevalent in inland states. Iodized salt has a harsh chemical flavor; it's thus not recommended for use in cooking or seasoning food. American diets today are typically varied enough to obviate our need for iodized salt.

Iron pans: See cast iron.

Italian meringue: See meringue.

J

Jams and jellies: Fruit, preserved by cooking it with lots of sugar and a gelling agent such as pectin, becomes a jam or, if it's clear, a jelly. Jams are especially useful as a sweet addition to tarts and cakes and other confections not only because of their intense sweetness and acidity, but also because of their appealing texture. As we look to honey for a more complex sweetener than table sugar, we can also consider jams, depending on what is being sweetened. Clear glazes used to make fruit tarts shiny, for instance, often use a jam to enhance their flavor. Many jams contain seeds; when using them as a flavoring component, they can be passed through a sieve. Jams need not necessarily be fruit based; any vegetable or even a dairy product, cooked till it's the consistency of jam, can technically be referred to as a jam. Jellies is also a term that refers to candies delicately gelled with pectin.

Japanese mandoline: For thin uniform slicing and julienning, this tool is a kitchen essential. Many companies sell slicers with all kinds of extras, but the one professional cooks tend to use, the Benriner slicer or mandoline, is also the most simple and least expensive. Thickness is adjusted by a screw on the underside of the slicer; some slicers are wide enough to require a screw on either side; these are not recommended because it's difficult to get the two screws into an identical position, which results in uneven slices. The blades on these slicers are very sharp; either use a hand guard, though they can be cumbersome, or start slowly and gradually increase your speed so that you can slice and julienne without adding extra protein to your meal.

Jerk, jerked, jerk seasoning: a spicy, tantalizing seasoning paste, originating from Jamaica, that can season anything from chicken to pork to fish. It's composed of chillis, salt and pepper, sweet spices, notably the native allspice, and vinegar. When something is seasoned with it, it's said to be jerked.

Joints: The joints of animals are loaded with collagen, which breaks down into gelatin, given plenty of gentle moist heat. Joints are therefore excellent to include in stocks for the body they give it.

Jowl (hog): The hog jowl is prized for its flavor and ratio of fat. It can be cured like bacon into what's called *guanciale,* is often dried, and can be used like bacon or pancetta. The fat is rich and flavorful, and very good for sausage making.

Jus: French for juice, *jus* usually refers to the juices released by the meat during cooking or after cutting it, which can accompany the meat (meat served *au jus,* with its juices). But it can also refer to a quick sauce made in the pan the meat cooked in, with the fat and fond of the cooking. To make such a *jus,* excess fat is poured off, the pan is deglazed with wine or stock, herbs and any meat trim can be added along with enough stock (you'll always need additional liquid; whatever you're cooking won't release enough actual juices to create enough sauce); it is quickly cooked, strained, and served immediately. It should taste very fresh. *Jus* tends to get its body and richness from the fat left in the pan rather than from a starch or a reduction. If your *jus* is thinner than you'd like, you can lié it with a starch slurry.

Jus lié: stock that has been thickened with a slurry (starch and water mixed to the consistency of heavy cream).

K

Kimchi: a spicy Korean pickle mixture usually composed mainly of cabbage but many vegetables, such as turnip and radish, may be used. The pickle, often seasoned with garlic, scallions, and chillis, is easily fermented at home and may be the surest way to get a good quality kimchi.

Kitchenware: See the essay Tools, page 35.

Knead: We knead doughs to help develop the protein gluten, which gives them the elasticity they need to hold the bubbles of gas that leaven them. Dough can be kneaded mechanically (usually called mixing rather than kneading) or by hand. It's easy to overmix a bread dough mechanically; eventually a mixer will break down the gluten structure and the dough will be flabby—it will lose it's elasticity, won't spring back when pressed or pulled—and won't rise or cook properly. It's difficult to overknead by hand.

Knife sharpener: The best tool for sharpening knives is a sharpening stone. Either learn to sharpen your knives on a stone or have them professionally sharpened. Stones come in a varying degrees of coarseness and varying qualities, and require some form of lubrication, either water or oil. Regardless how you restore a sharp edge to your knives, use a steel frequently and you won't need to sharpen them as frequently (steels don't sharpen, they help to maintain a sharp edge).

Knives: Knives are the savory cook's main tool. While all kinds of knives are available, strictly speaking you only need two good ones, a big one and a little one. You can buy a whole set, and specialty knives can come in handy, but it would be better first to put the same money into two excellent knives, a chef's knife and a paring knife, and a steel, the metal bar or rod used to maintain a sharp edge. A good cook should be able use a chef's knife and a paring knife for virtually every task requiring a knife.

Kosher salt: Kosher salt has no iodine in it and so has a cleaner effect on food; other noniodized salts are available but the combination of kosher salt's being both inexpensive and widely available makes it the preferred salt for cooking and seasoning. It comes in larger grains or flakes and takes a little longer to dissolve on the surface of meat, but its size makes controlling the amount between your fingertips easy. Use the same brand, which will help you to use it consistently by touch. Remember that different salts have different volumes by weight, so it's recommended that you weigh kosher salt rather than measure by volume when using it in quantities larger than a tablespoon.

L

Lactic acid: the acid produced by bacteria in fermented dairy, dough, and meat products, which gives these items (yogurt, sourdough, salami, kimchi, and other fermented pickles) their distinctive flavors and in many cases helps to preserve the food.

Lactose: the sugar in milk, which, McGee writes, "is found almost nowhere else in nature." Some people don't have enough of the necessary enzyme to break down this sugar and are thus "lactose intolerant."

Ladle: Ladles are important kitchen implements. Many are made in volume measurements and these are especially handy for serving consistent portions of a sauce or a soup. It's helpful to have a 2-ounce, 4-ounce, and 8-ounce ladle in your kitchen.

Lamb: Like the meat of other land animals, lamb is divided into two broad categories, tough and tender. The meat is very flavorful, especially from those animals that are naturally raised and pasture fed (they're ruminants). Tender cuts of lamb can be eaten very rare, but most chefs believe that even tender cuts are most flavorful slightly above rare. Leg of lamb can be tough but the muscles themselves are tender and can be separated from the connective tissue that binds them and cooked like other tender cuts. The younger the lamb the more tender. Baby lamb that has yet to begin feeding on grass is especially so.

Laminated dough: A laminated dough is a dough into which a block of butter has been enclosed and, by means of folding the dough over on itself and rolling it out numerous times, has developed hundreds of layers of dough separated by fat; laminated dough puffs when it's cooked, thus its name, puff pastry, or in French *mille feuille,* a thousand leaves; laminated doughs are used for croissants and Danish and other pastries, both savory and sweet. Interesting variations result when you flavor the butter with herbs, spices, or even other fats such as cheese or chocolate.

Lard (noun): Lard is rendered pig fat and an exquisite cooking medium and ingredient that was once common but is now all but obsolete in kitchens. Properly rendered, it is excellent to use for sautéeing, pan-frying, deep-frying, and confiting. It is solid but soft at room temperature, making it an excellent shortening for pastry doughs (unlike butter, which is commonly used in pastries, it has no water, which encourages gluten formation, and so is a powerful shortener). Lard has a more neutral flavor than other animal fats and so is an excellent all-purpose fat.

Lard (verb): Larding means to insert fat using a larding needle through large lean cuts, such as big beef roasts, to give meat a richness and flavor it lacks.

Lardo: Lardo is cured fatback; the thick slab of creamy fat that runs along the back of the hog is salted and seasoned and allowed to cure. It is then sliced and eaten as is with some seasonings (olive oil, salt and pepper, maybe some fresh herbs) and bread but it can also be gently cooked and used as a garnish on a white pizza or served with eggs. Served raw it should be smooth and creamy and should have a mild, cured pork flavor.

Lardons: Cured pork belly, bacon, cut into batons, can be used as featured ingredients in a salad or a quiche, or they can be used as a seasoning device in stews. It's best to cut your own according to the impact you intend them to have—if they're garnish for a delicate salad or a pasta, smaller, for a stew, larger. If you're featuring them in a classic frisée salad, cut them substantially, a half-inch square. They should be cooked low and slow to render their fat, crisp the exterior, and tenderize the interior.

Leader: See chef.

Leavener: Anything that leavens a dough or batter—that is, helps to make it rise—is a leavener. A food (egg white), a chemical (baking powder), an organism (yeast), a mechanical process (whipping) are all leaveners. Folding and rolling a butter-and-flour biscuit dough will act as a kind of puff-pastry-style leavener. Your choice of leavening affects the texture and flavor of the finished product.

Lecithin: Lecithin is a type of molecule abundant in egg yolk that allows fat and water to form a creamy, homogenous, emulsified sauce. It works as an emulsifier, McGee explains, because it has a fat soluble section and a water soluble section; its fat soluble section embeds itself into the fat droplets and the protruding water soluble tail prevents them from touching one another and combining (which is what happens when you break an emulsified sauce).

Leek: Leeks are one of the treasures of the kitchen and used primarily for their aromatic qualities and gentle sweetness. They're great to add to stocks for flavor (McGee notes that they contain a special carbohydrate that gels and thus increases a stock's body). They're delicious gently sautéed and used at the beginning of a sauce or a soup (they have a great affinity for butter and cream). They can be julienned and deep-fried. The entire leek can be used in stocks, but if they are to be eaten, only the white part should be used. Leeks can have a lot of dirt trapped between their layers, so they should be halved lengthwise, leaving the root end on, and thoroughly cleaned with cold water.

Leg: The legs of animals usually contain plenty of connective tissue and are heavily used (and therefore fairly lean) muscle. Thus they usually require low heat cooking—as with traditionally braised lamb shank, osso bucco (veal shank), and rump roasts. Leg of lamb has several different muscles bound together by connective tissue; these can be separated from the connective tissue and cooked and sliced almost like a loin. Beef cuts from the leg can be relatively tender, depending where on the leg it is (top round for example). But generally, from rabbit to chicken to duck to the larger animals, legs benefit from longer gentle cooking.

Legume: Legumes are the plants with pods that give us beans and peas, distinguished by their variety and high protein content. They are eaten both fresh and dried. Combined with grains, they can offer all the amino acids the body requires, obviating the need to eat meat. (For more information on cooking, see beans.)

Lemon: Lemon, notable for its clean fresh flavor and tartness, is a wonderful all-purpose acid that can be used to season or flavor countless dishes from savory to sweet—raw greens to hot vegetables, to butter, to meats and fish, soups and stews, custards and creams. More dishes than not are improved with a judicious seasoning of fresh lemon juice. Or as chef Eric Ripert puts it, "Lemon saves zee ass of so many dishes." For its juice and its zest, lemon is an invaluable tool.

Lemon confit: Lemon confit is lemon that's been preserved in salt and is sometimes called preserved lemon. It's a beguiling seasoning device for everything from salads to roasted chicken to stews and is sometimes featured in Middle Eastern and North African cooking. Because preserving lemons is so easy to do, because it's such an interesting seasoning tool, and because it keeps indefinitely, it's worth making lemon confit a part of your pantry. Halve lemons and pack them in salt in a nonreactive container and cover. They'll be cured in a month; discard the flesh and the pith, which must be scraped from the skin, then julienne or mince the skin. If using raw, it should be blanched briefly to leach out some of the salt.

Lemon curd: Lemon curd (or custard)—lemon juice, sugar, eggs, and usually butter, cooked till the mixture becomes thick—is an excellent all-purpose dessert *appareil*—filling, topping, garnish, or featured item (as in a lemon tart). Lemon curd is traditionally made by whipping egg yolks, sugar, and lemon over simmering water to cook the eggs, then whipping in the butter piece by piece, though there are variations (it can be made in a microwave, for instance).

Lemon zest: Lemon zest is an extraordinary seasoning, imparting bright, lemony flavor without the acidity of lemon juice (see gremolata, for example). It's difficult to think of a dish that isn't improved by some gratings of lemon zest. When using lemon or any fruit zest—whether cutting by hand or using some form of zester or grater—it's important to remove the white pith (with the exception of candying, in which the pith gives the zest structure and prevents it from becoming too leathery or brittle). For very refined cooking, zest should be blanched and shocked before using, which removes the bitterness.

Lentil: Lentils are one of the legumes that can be cooked fairly quickly and need no soaking. Lentils come in many distinct and interesting varieties, but generally there are larger rounder lentils, green French lentils, or small flat disclike lentils that are common here.

Liaison [*lee-ay-ZOHN*]: Loosely speaking, a liaison is anything that binds, such as a slurry or *buerre manié*. A classical liaison is a mixture of egg yolk and cream, incorporated into sauces, soups, and stews to thicken and enrich the liquid. A traditional *blanquette de veau,* for example, is finished with a *liaison.* It should be added at the end of cooking after the sauce is no longer at simmering temperatures (you don't want to overcook the egg), and it should be tempered with some of the sauce before being added to the sauce. A common ratio is three parts cream to one part yolk, and three parts sauce to one part *liaison*.

Lié: To lié—French for tied, bound, connected—means to thicken a sauce, usually with a slurry. Sometimes it's used as a descriptor, as in *jus de veau lié*, which is a fortified veal stock that's been thickened with a slurry for use as a sauce.

Lime: Lime is a powerful, excellent, and perhaps underused seasoning device. It's among the most acidic of the citrus juices we commonly have on hand, as you've realized if you've ever made a lime vinaigrette; you need to balance its powerful acidity with more sugar or more fat than you would need for lemon or vinegar.

Lime zest: Lime zest is lime flavor without acidity, an excellent seasoning device. The same rules apply to it as to other zests—use just the zest, removing the pith, and blanch and shock to remove its bitterness.

Line cook: A line cook is a professional cook, or journeyman cook, who works a station on the hot or cold line during service. Line cook is generally one of the most stressful and physically demanding (and least well paid) positions in a restaurant, so much so that it's got its own distinct ethos and subculture. Line cooks are the rockers and the backbone of the American restaurant kitchen, and the best are a special breed, in a league of their own.

Liver: Liver is unusual in that it's a meat that can be cooked and served on its own, hot or cold, whole or chopped, or used as a seasoning device and even to thicken sauces. Chicken liver is most common. Liver is excellent sautéed, but it should be cooked briefly so that it remains moist. Types of liver commonly include that of calves, ducks, chickens, and some fish, notably monkfish. (See also foie gras, the fattened liver of duck and geese.)

Lobster: Lobsters are prized for the texture and flavor of their meat, which is really unlike that of any other creature. American lobsters from cold Atlantic waters are considered the best. They're best prepared fresh from their home waters, and they should be killed immediately before cooking or by the act of cooking. They behave best in the gentle heat of water, and over-cooking can make them tough and rubbery, but the lobster can be cooked in virtually any kind of heat, from the dry heat of a grill to the gentle heat of *beurre monté*. Their tails provide an abundance of meat but their knuckles or arms yield excellent morsels; the claw meat is of a different composition and because of the thick shell surrounding it, can take more heat. Some lobsters will have a green, liverlike gland called the tomalley, which can be used as a seasoning; some females carry eggs, or coral, which turn bright red and can be a vivid, if bland, garnish or sauce component. Lobster can be cooked and eaten immediately, but it is also excellent cooked and chilled. Spiny lobsters, a distant relative of the American lobster, live in warm waters and have a dense, sweet flesh; they are less commonly available fresh.

Loin: Loin is the muscle that runs along either side of the spine of the animal, the outer side or back (the tenderloin is on the interior of the rib cage); loin tends to be lean and tender and should be cooked fairly quickly or it will become dry, tough, and flavorless.

Lowboy: Lowboy is the slang term for an under-counter refrigerator.

"Low temperature long time": See LTLT.

Lox: Lox is salmon cured in brine, often smoked.

LTLT: an abbreviation for an approach to cooking: "low temperature long time" or simply "low and slow." Braised dishes or dishes cooked at temperatures under 300°F, often quite a bit under, as low as 120°F, fall into this category. Typically, meats requiring the tenderizing effects of long slow cooking, anywhere from 2 to 72 hours depending on the temperature, benefit from LTLT cooking, but anything from an egg to fish to vegetables and meats *can* be cooked this way with varying results, most notably in sous vide cooking.

M

Macerate: Macerate means to soak food in order to break it down or alter it in some way. Shallots may be macerated in vinegar to soften their sharp flavor. Ripe berries may be tossed with sugar (which will draw out their juice) and left to macerate in that juice to soften and sweeten them and intensify their flavor.

Maillard reaction: Maillard reaction refers to the browning of food, mainly protein and carbohydrates, other than that caused by caramelization, the browning of sugar. Maillard reactions can begin to occur at about 230°F, about 100 degrees lower than that of sugar caramelization. Maillard reactions are many and result in a range of great and complex flavors, from the seared exterior of a steak to the crust of bread to the golden brown skin of a roasted chicken to the roasting of beans for making chocolate and coffee. Often chefs use the word caramelization and caramelize when referring to Maillard reactions despite the fact that technically they're different reactions. See McGee for a complete chemical description of Maillard transformations.

Maître d' butter: See *beurre maître d'hôtel.*

Mandoline: a slicing and cutting contraption, sometimes referred to as a French mandoline, used to make uniform slices, juliennes, and *gaufrettes.* They're sturdy and perform a variety of tasks but they're expensive and somewhat more complex to set up and use than a Japanese mandoline, a simplified, plastic version of the same thing and, for slicing and julienning, just as good.

Marble: Marble is a kitchen countertop material prized by pastry chefs for its ability to maintain coldness, which makes it a good surface on which to roll butter-rich doughs. Its drawback is that it's porous and so is easily stained. Also, it reacts to acid, which can pit marble; thus, companies selling marble counters often coat or seal the marble. A small marble slab is convenient to keep at home, stored with sheet pans, and refrigerated before using for pastries and confections.

Marbling: Marbling refers to the quantity and quality of intramuscular fat in a muscle. A cook loves a well-marbled cut of meat, knowing that striations of fat will enhance a meat's flavor and succulence.

Margarine: a butter substitute once made from animal fat, now routinely made from vegetable oils. While margarine is cheaper than butter, it's not recommended for cooking or eating given that butter is plentiful and superior in terms of cooking and of flavor. If you insist on using margarine, be sure that it does not contain trans fats, which can result from hydrogenization (one method of turning a liquid fat to a solid one) and have been shown to increase blood cholesterol.

Marinade, marinate, marinating: Marinades are preparations intended to flavor meat or vegetables before they are cooked. Marinades can be dry (sometimes referred to as a dry rub) or wet, and can include a range of aromatics, oils, liquids, and acids. The literature on marinades is muddy and often inaccurate. Acids as a rule do not tenderize tough meats, as is commonly believed, nor does alcohol. Acids and alcohol denature the exterior protein, making it somewhat mushy (though some fruits such as papaya and pineapple contain protein- and gelatin-digesting enzymes that can ruin meats). Wines can flavor meats well, but they are most effective if some of the alcohol is first cooked out of them, and if aromatics are infused into them and salt is dissolved in it (for its osmotic as well as seasoning effects), before being chilled and poured over the meat. Flavor takes time to penetrate meat. Perhaps the most effective marinades are dry rubs that include salt and aromatics, and brines flavored with aromatics; osmosis due to the salt can carry flavors into meats. Oils become infused with the aromatics, but they don't really penetrate the meat and may prevent flavors from doing so. Other marinades act mainly to season the exterior of the meat. McGee notes that vacuum pressure can enhance the effect of marination not while the meat is being marinated, but rather when the vacuum is released and marinade rushes into the spaces where gas had been drawn out. Marinades likely were first used to preserve meat before refrigeration, which the acid and salt would have accomplished; we use them now exclusively for flavor. Pay attention to how various marinades affect your meat and fish, how time in the marinade affects the meat (longer is not always better), and marinate according to your tastes.

Marmite: a pot, usually one that's taller than it is wide, and thus is good to use for a consommé or for stocks and stews that require long cooking with less evaporation.

Marrow: The fatty connective tissue within bones can be a delicious garnish on or with a dish or a flavorful enrichment to numerous preparations—it is usually roasted or poached. Bones filled with marrow are commonly available in grocery stores. It's a good idea, after removing the marrow from the bone, to soak the marrow in salted water before cooking to leach out some of the blood. It can be diced and added to sauces, used to flavor a custard, or served on top of a main item as a flavorful garnish.

Marrow bones: Bones filled with marrow are the best source of large pieces of marrow. They should be soaked in salted water to leach out some of the blood. The marrow can be pushed out of the bone (this can be easy or difficult, depending on the shape of the bone) and poached or it can be roasted within the bone until it is molten. Marrow bones can be used for stock but aren't the best choice, since there is little meat on them and the marrow is mainly fat, which can cloud the stock.

Matignon [*mah-ti-NYOHN*]: *Matignon* means mirepoix, or aromatic vegetables, that are intended both to flavor a dish and to be served with the dish. Often poultry is roasted on a bed of mirepoix; if this mirepoix is to be served as a garnish, it's called *matignon*. In addition to onions, carrots, and celery, mushrooms and bacon are often included for additional flavor in *matignon*.

Mayonnaise: Mayonnaise is an all-purpose, fat-based sauce (see emulsified sauce) that's easy to make fresh and is most delicious this way. Store-bought mayonnaise, such as Hellmann's, can be quite good and is fine for everyday use; indeed, with the addition of spices, acids, aromatic vegetables such as onions or shallots, mayonnaise from a jar can be transformed into a great sauce to use at the last minute, for pork, chicken, or fish—a convenient shortcut for a small portion of an impromptu emulsified sauce.

McGee: Harold McGee is the author of the landmark book *On Food and Cooking,* an unparalleled work, one of the main references for this text, and a book cherished by home cooks and professional chefs alike for its explanations for why food behaves as it does. (See the essay Sources and Acknowledgments, page 40.)

Measure, measuring: Measuring food is sometimes critical (especially in baking) to the success of a preparation and sometimes not. When exact measurements are important, measure well. That is, rather than measuring by volume, weigh solid ingredients on a scale, which is the most accurate form of measuring. Use liquid measures for liquid ingredients. Avoid boutique measuring devices such as porcelain tablespoons or gimmicky cups whose volume can vary; stick with sturdy steel measuring devices. And when you're measuring, pay attention to the quantity you're adding. What do two tablespoons of oil look like going into the pan? When measuring a teaspoon of salt, put it in your palm first, see what it looks like, how much space it takes up; soon you'll be able to measure fairly accurately by eye.

Measuring cups: Measuring cups are divided into two categories, those for dry ingredients (specifically ¼, ⅓, ½, and 1 cup containers) and those for liquids (clear containers denoting various measurements on their sides). For convenience, it's good to have a variety of each kind.

Meat: Meat usually refers to animal muscle. For general information on the cooking of animal protein, see beef, chicken, lamb, and pork. Meat can also refer to the flesh, what is to be eaten, of fruits, vegetables, and nuts.

Meat grinder: While grinders aren't strictly necessary in the home kitchen—meat can be finely chopped by hand or cut in a food processor—they do create a distinctive and useful texture for sausages and burgers. They're available as stand-alone appliances and as attachments to standing mixers. Not only are they handy for making sausages, dumpling filling, and burgers, they can be used for other purposes, such as grinding bacon to use it as a seasoning, grinding greens to extract chlorophyll, or as a kind of tenderizer: if you have a tough cut of meat but only a short time to to cook it, the meat can be ground and seasoned and cooked, either loose or wrapped in some sort of casing.

Meat temperatures: Generally speaking, rare means between 120° and 130°F, medium-rare up to 140°F, medium up to 150°F, and well-done beyond that. Books differ on these definitions and the ones here are lower than those in most general cookbooks. The USDA has specific temperature recommendations regarding meat safety which err on the side of safety rather than flavor or nutrition (go to www.usda.gov). If you have concerns about safety, follow its recommendations. While we associate color with doneness, doneness—medium-rare, well-done, et cetera—refers to actual temperatures, not colors. (See specific meats for additional temperature considerations.)

Medium and medium-rare: See meat temperatures.

Meringue: Meringue is egg white mixed till it's fluffy and often sweetened with sugar. Meringue is a versatile preparation that's used as a leavener in cakes, the base for soufflés, to lighten mousses, or as decoration. Meringue can be baked to varying consistencies or it can be poached. It can be flavored with almonds and baked, a preparation called dacquoise. The ratio for a meringue is commonly from one to two parts sugar to one part egg white by weight. Sugar can be added in different ways that can affect the texture of the meringue and determine its uses. Granulated sugar can be added once the whites have gotten fluffy for a basic meringue. The egg white and sugar can be heated and then whipped (called Swiss meringue) or the sugar can be dissolved in a small amount of water and cooked till it's very hot, then added to the egg whites toward the end of mixing (called Italian meringue). If the meringue will not be cooked after it's made (if it's being used in a mousse, for instance), it's prudent to use one of the methods in which the egg white is cooked in the process of making it (Swiss or Italian). For crisp meringues, the mixture should be piped into the desired shape and baked in a very low oven, 200°F or lower, to thoroughly dehydrate them without browning them. Moist meringues, ones cooked for a meringue pie, can be tricky—undissolved sugar, under- or overbeating, under- and overcooking can result in graininess and "weeping," water leaching out of the meringue—so pay attention to small variations in how you prepare meringues and note the effects.

Metric measurements: Metrics are by far the most practical form of measuring in the kitchen and are often used in *haute* American restaurants. Ratios are more quickly recognized and recipes are easier to remember when using metric measurements. A perfect example of metric efficiency is that a good all-purpose brine combines 50 grams of salt with one liter (1,000 milliliters or 1,000 grams) of water, 5 percent salt by weight represented clearly in the numbers. Compare American equivalents: 5 percent by weight of a quart, or 32 ounces, is 1.6 ounces of salt. Basic rounded off conversions are: 25 grams equal an ounce, 450 grams equal a pound, and a cup equals 250 milliliters. But be aware when doubling or tripling recipes that small variations in conversions, when multiplied, can become big ones and can throw recipes off.

Meunière, à la [*MYOO-nyair*]: *Meunière* is an excellent, easy, all-purpose brown butter sauce, seasoned only by lemon juice and parsley, commonly used with white fish such as trout, but which works well on many mild-flavored items, which are first dusted with flour and sautéed. Butter is brought to the desired color and aroma, the lemon juice is added (to cool the butter and prevent the solids from burning), followed by parsley.

Microwave oven: While the microwave oven is rarely a good choice for cooking something through from raw to cooked, it's an excellent tool for reheating. Because so much of what professional kitchens do is cook food ahead of time and then reheat it at service, microwaves are not unusual to see there. When properly used they can be invaluable to home cooks for the same reason, reheating braises, starches, meat that's been grilled and chilled, even green vegetables that have been cooked and shocked, whether for speeding up the preparation of weekday dinners or finishing the food for a dinner party. And with some trial and error, green vegetables and root vegetables can in a pinch be cooked completely in a microwave with fairly good results.

Microplane: a registered name that has become the generic term for a very fine grater. They are inexpensive and convenient for any number of jobs—from zesting citrus to grating parmesan, chocolate, or nutmeg.

Milk: Milk can be a useful ingredient in the kitchen, primarily for diluting ingredients. It thins cream that would make a custard too fatty, a cream soup that's too thick; it loosens mashed root vegetables; it's the primary ingredient for a béchamel sauce, and it can be beneficial in batters. It's occasionally used in some doughs and pastries because it may give them a better brown color when baked.

Mill: To mill means to pass through a food mill. A food mill is used to create a smooth puree, usually of a starch or starchy vegetable (see food mill). Attachments to mill dry grains are also available but usually when chefs refer to passing food through a food mill, it's the first usage mentioned here.

Mince: Mince means to finely chop. A true mince is very, very small—till the food is reduced to pieces that are almost unidentifiable as such, and most important, in uniform tiny pieces. The fewer cuts you use to achieve the mince, the better. A mince is not chunky; chunky indicates chopped. If you were to smear properly minced garlic or shallot on a piece of toast, it would look like a uniform spread.

Minute, à la: See *à la minute.*

Mirepoix [*MEER-pwah*]: Mirepoix is a mixture of aromatic vegetables used to flavor stocks and sauces that will be strained out before the stock or sauce is used. Traditionally mirepoix means two parts onion, one part carrot, and one part celery, roughly chopped, a mixture that adds sweetness and aroma to a stock or sauce. Mirepoix can be used generally for a variety of aromatics that may be common to specific cuisines. Ginger, garlic, and scallions might be called Asian mirepoix; Cajun mirepoix would include green peppers. In kitchens where these looser terms for mirepoix are used, the onion-carrot-celery mixture would be called standard mirepoix.

Mise en place: Literally "put in place," *mise en place* is the kitchen term for your setup, the gathering and preparation of all the tools and food you need to complete the task at hand. *Mise en place* can refer to a cook's organization on the line before the evening's service (line cooks often refer to it simply as "meez" and can be extremely territorial about their own); *mise en place* can refer to the wooden spoon, wine, stock, rice, and salt you gather before starting a risotto. Because it's such an important part of the chef's life, so critical to efficiency of action and the use of time, the term often carries broader connotations of being ready. Excellent *mise* represents the ultimate state of preparedness, whether the physical *mise en place* of food and tools or the mental *mise en place* of having thought a task through to the end and being ready for each step of it.

Miso: Fermented soybean paste from Japan, miso is a staple ingredient finding increasingly wide use in America. It comes in many varieties, and, like many fermented foods, is used for the salty depth of flavor, often referred to as umami, it gives to a dish, from a soup to a sauce to stews and vinaigrettes.

Mix (verb): a seemingly pedestrian or perhaps obvious verb that is in fact one of the most important actions in cooking and can have an extraordinary impact on a preparation and sometimes even define it. Cakes, for instance, are sometimes categorized by the mixing method, the order in which the fat, egg, sugar, and starch are combined. Ground meat for sausage is mixed to incorporate seasonings and liquid, but also to encourage a meat protein called myosin to become sticky and thus help hold the sausage together, to give it a good bind. The proper mixing of dough is critical to the success of the bread—too little and it won't have the elasticity to contain the gas bubbles that make it rise, too much and it will lose its elasticity and become flabby, and the bread may likewise be flat. The method of mixing, whether by machine or by hand, the duration, the temperature of what is being mixed, even the path your spoon or whisk makes through what is being whisked—elliptical or figure-eight, for instance—impacts the food. Proper mix method should always be observed.

Moist heat (cooking): Heat defined primarily by the fact that it is at or below water's boiling point, 212°F, is one of our primary cooking methods. Braising, poaching, and steaming are methods of moist-heat cooking, used either for tough cuts cooked for a long period or very tender kinds of meat cooked quickly, as well as vegetables; we braise tough lamb and veal shank for a long time in liquid to break down its connective tissue and tenderize the meat in a way that won't dry it out; we poach and steam fish. Compare with dry-heat cooking. Moist heat can be used in conjunction with dry-heat cooking, as with a braise in which the meat is seared before going into the liquid, called combination cooking in cooking school.

Molasses: The syrupy by-product of extracting sugar crystals from the juice of sugar cane, molasses is one of many sweetening options in the kitchen. It brings complex caramel flavors along with the sweetness, as well as acidity and bitterness (the darker it is the more powerful the flavor). Because of this complexity, molasses can be a good option when sweetening savory dishes such as barbecue sauce and marinades, in addition to its more common use in cakes and cookies.

Mold: 1) A verb and noun concerning our efforts to give specific shape to food. All manner of molds are available from kitchen supply stores, from terrine molds to small silicone molds to ring molds. But common kitchen items such as plastic wrap, aluminum foil, parchment paper, cheesecloth, or a dish towel can make effective molds as well. 2) Mold on food can be beneficial, adding flavor to cheese or protecting the exterior of some dry-cured meats. Some molds are harmful; as a rule, fuzzy molds, green molds, or other brightly colored molds not typically found on the food should be removed from the food or the food should be discarded altogether.

Molecular gastronomy: This term was coined in 1969 by French scientist Hervé This (he subsequently published a book with that title) and denotes an approach to cooking that seeks to understand the reason food behaves as it does. In the 1990s it became attached to the work of Spanish chef Ferran Adrià, renowned for his use of unconventional leavening and gelling devices and chemicals, and to those chefs who followed in Adrià's footsteps.

Adrià and others, frustrated that the term did not describe their work, disavowed the term. It continues to be used to describe the cooking of chefs who employ unconventional techniques to create uncommon textures and unusual methods of serving food.

Monosodium glutamate: Better known as MSG, monosodium glutamate is a form of glutamic acid, a primary amino acid responsible for a flavor sensation we call umami, a deepening of savory, brothy flavors. Studies have shown that MSG, originally derived from seaweed, is not harmful even in large quantities. While judicious use of it can enhance the flavor of any number of preparations, chefs recommend using other foods that have the same effect on our palate but also offer other benevolent complexities such as fish sauce, parmesan cheese, shiitake mushrooms, and tomatoes, which contain glutamic acid or glutamates along with other flavor-enhancing amino acids. (See also umami.)

Monté au beurre [*MOHN-tay oh bur*]: *Monté au beurre* means to incorporate whole butter into another liquid, usually a sauce. Many sauces are finished this way because butter adds great flavor, a smooth texture, and a satisfying richness. To mount butter into a sauce, the sauce must be hot and you must continuously stir or swirl the cold butter into the sauce until all of it is incorporated to ensure it remains emulsified in the sauce. (See also a related term, *beurre monté*.)

Mortar and pestle: An ancient culinary tool that can still be a valuable part of any cook's kitchen, mortar and pestle—they can be large or small, and made out of anything from stone to porcelain to wood—are used today for grinding everything from dried spices to fresh vegetables and creating unique versions of salsas and aïolis. While a grinder may be preferable to a mortar and pestle when pulverizing spices or other dried ingredients, soft or moist ingredients (as with a traditional salsa) ground with a mortar and pestle will produce a distinctly different result than those same ingredients pureed in a food processor.

Mother: Mother can refer to a gelatinous substance that develops on the surface of vinegars generated by the bacteria and the acetic fermentation that transforms the alcohol in wine to acid. Mothers can be added to wine and if handled properly, the wine will develop into vinegar. It's as simple as emptying wine into a large jar, making sure to aerate it well if it's

THE ELEMENTS OF COOKING A TO Z   171

freshly out of the bottle (certain volatile compounds can kill the bacteria if the wine is combined with the mother straight from the bottle), adding the mother, covering with cheesecloth to allow it to breathe, and letting it sit for two to four months. The results can be far more fruity and flavorful than what you can find at the store. More wine is simply added to the mother to start the next batch.

Mother sauces: Mother sauces were the backbone of the *saucier*'s station, providing a way that one person might create numerous sauces *à la minute* using a few base sauces. While classical mother sauces, stock thickened with roux, may be uncommon in today's restaurants, most kitchens do make a few stocks that serve as the base for numerous sauces. A mother sauce is one that can be made and held, and then any number of aromatics and seasoning can be added to it for countless variations. The main mother sauces are béchamel (milk based), velouté (white-stock based, chicken, or fish), and *espagnole* sauce (based on brown veal stock). Tomato sauce, the French sauce *tomate,* not marinara sauce, is considered by some to be a mother sauce, as is hollandaise, but hollandaise differs from mother sauces in that you don't typically make numerous derivative sauces from hollandaise; rather many sauces use the emulsified butter sauce method—a reduction of aromatics and acid, with butter emulsified into the reduction and whipped egg yolks—a method of which hollandaise has become the emblem. Mother sauces are sauce bases but should not to be confused with "base," the name for commercially prepared sauce bases, which are typically so inferior to the mother sauces you can make yourself as to be unrecognizable as good food and not worth the money. Home cooks won't make use of mother sauces the way Escoffier's *brigade* did or the way restaurants today handle sauces, but the notion that many of the great sauces derive from only a few fundamental sauces is a useful one to understand and to put to use when making stocks and sauces at home. (See the essay Sauce, page 12.)

Mount: To mount means to incorporate fat into a sauce or some other preparation, usually butter into a sauce to finish it (see *monté au beurre*).

Mousse: from the French word for foam, a light airy preparation, usually sweet (but a word occasionally applied to savory dishes). Anything that's light and airy, a solid foam, can be generically described as a mousse. Dessert mousses are most common. The traditional method is to whip egg yolks and sugar till the yolks fall in ribbons (often today this is done over a water bath to cook the yolks and help to melt the sugar). A basic meringue is folded into the yolks, the flavoring (melted chocolate, for instance, or a strained fruit puree) is folded into this, and finally, whipped cream is folded in to finish the preparation.

Mousseline: Mousseline is a delicate forcemeat of fish or white meat, pureed with egg white and cream (the basic ratio is one pound of meat, one egg white, one cup of cream) then shaped (whether in a terrine mold, into quenelles, in a sausage casing, or used as a stuffing) and gently cooked. It's a delicate and refined preparation. The word has a second meaning: emulsified butter sauces that are lightened by the addition of whipped cream can be referred to as mousselines.

MSG: See monosodium glutamate.

Muscle: What we call meat is the muscle of the animal or fish; it's composed primarily of protein fibers bundled up by connective tissue. The more heavily worked that muscle is, the more connective tissue it needs and therefore the tougher it is. Sometimes chefs will refer to a piece of meat as a whole muscle to designate that it hasn't been cut into pieces or ground.

Mushrooms: A variety of mushrooms such as morels and chanterelles are now commonly available in grocery stores in addition to the white and brown staples offering more textures and better flavors from mushrooms. Mushrooms can be cooked in numerous ways and usually benefit from "dry-heat" techniques that help them develop flavor—sauté, roast, even grill. Their savory, meaty flavor spreads well through fat, which is why they work so well in cream soups and sauces. When sautéing mushrooms (especially the bland white button mushrooms), it's best to get your pan as hot as possible so that you can achieve the complex flavors from browning before they begin to release their moisture (making further browning impossible).

Mussel: Mussels are perhaps one of the easiest creatures to cook, so if you can find a good source for them, they're a great item to serve at home. And if they're really good, the simpler the preparation, the better—steamed until they're open in a little white wine with thyme and garlic. Because this mollusc is a filter-feeder, mussels can contain toxins, so the source and how they've been handled after being taken from the water matter; also, they must be very fresh because they are alive until they are cooked and once out of the water they are, like oysters, in effect feeding on themselves. Some chefs will only order mussels at a restaurant if they know the chef personally.

Mustard: Not only a great condiment for a charcuterie platter or a hot dog, mustard is an all-purpose seasoning for sauces, if not a sauce itself—combining pungency with acid and aromatics. Roast chicken with some good mustard is excellent, for instance. Moreover, mustard added to the liquid ingredients into which fat will be emulsified—when making a vinaigrette or a mayonnaise—strengthens the emulsion. Mustard powders are ground seeds. Coleman's mustard is a seed blend that's very pungent. Dijon is a blend of mustard powder and acid and aromatics. They're all very different. Taste them as you would any seasoning and evaluate them; use them to your own taste. Basic mustards can be made simply by adding cool water to dry mustard powder, seasoning with salt and sugar (and perhaps a vinegar, a spice such as mustard seed, caraway, cumin, or other aromats), and allowing it to bloom for 30 minutes (served right away or heated it can be bitter).

Myoglobin: Myoglobin is the oxygen-carrying protein in muscle responsible for the red color in meat and fish. Some salts, such as sodium nitrite, cause oxygen to bind with the myoglobin and so will cause the meat to remain reddish even after cooking (as in bacon and ham).

Myosin: Myosin is a main protein in meats, one that composes the fibers that make up muscle. It becomes sticky when kneaded or mixed and helps to give a pâté, sausage, or hamburger a good bind and texture (especially when salted well in advance, given that myosin is salt soluble).

N

Nage [*nahj*]: A *nage* is like a court bouillon or a *cuisson*—an aromatic liquid in which an item, usually fish, is cooked. The term *nage* (or *à la nage*, literally, in the swim) is typically used when the item is also served in this cooking liquid (the liquid—a vegetable, fish, or meat stock—is not reduced like a *cuisson* sauce or discarded like a court bouillon). It's an easy, flavorful, efficient form of cooking and serving fish and shellfish.

Nam pla: See fish sauce.

Napolean: A traditional dessert based on the idea of layering pastry cream and puff pastry has given rise to the use of the word as an all-purpose descriptor for any hard or crispy ingredient layered with anything soft. It's a useful idea when thinking about different ways of combining ingredients with such qualities, savory or sweet.

Nappage, nappé, **nap:** *Nappage* is French for tablecloth or cover, and in the kitchen, the word refers to sauce, a covering for the food. *Nappé* refers to a specific consistency, a sauce with good body and texture, not thin like a *jus,* or thick like a hollandaise. To nap food is to coat it with a sauce of such consistency.

Neck: Necks don't have a lot of edible meat on them; they are composed mainly of bone and other connective tissue, so they give stocks good body, especially poultry necks. Poultry necks (duck and goose, for example) also have the diameter of sausage and so the skin can be used for stuffing.

Nitrates and nitrites: Nitrates and nitrites are naturally occurring chemicals that, when carried on sodium in the form of sodium nitrate and sodium nitrite, are used in the curing of meat. (See sodium nitrate, sodium nitrite, and potassium nitrate.)

Noisette: See *beurre noisette.*

Nonreactive: Nonreactive refers to the material cookware is made of and means that it will not react to acid and salt. Practically speaking, it means not made of metal. The cast iron skillet reacts to acid and can affect a tomato sauce, for instance, and long-term curing with salt should not be done in a metal container. Typical nonreactive materials are glass, enamel, and plastic.

Nonstick pans: Nonstick pans are good for specific kinds of cooking; they should not be your default pan, should not be the first pan you grab. Nonstick pans are optimal for foods that need to be cooked over moderate heat but that also might stick if placed into a pan that's not screaming hot, fish and eggs for instance. But for most cooking, a plain metal surface— steel, iron, enameled iron—is best because food browns in such pans, and more complex flavors and textures are developed both on the item being cooked and in the pan itself. A well-stocked kitchen will have one or two meticulously cared for but infrequently used nonstick pans.

Noodles: Noodles are one of the great pleasures of the table and also one of the great pleasures for the cook because of their many forms and versatility. The forms are what's key to the cook—they can be long strands, wide strips, tubes, or broad sheets, either extruded through a die or rolled and cut. The main consideration in choosing a pasta is its thickness (which will determine the quality of its bite) and the way its shape carries a sauce (generally, the finer the sauce, the finer your noodle can be). Noodles in the West are typically wheat-flour based, often made with egg, but noodles made from rice flour dominate Southeast Asian cuisine (these are cooked, then dried and simply rehydrated to serve), noodles from sweet potato starch are popular in Korea, and Japan is famous for its buckwheat noodles called soba. So don't always think you're limited to Italian pasta when you think of noodles.

Nouvelle cuisine [*noo-VEL kwee-ZEEN*]: Nouvelle cuisine was coined in the mid-1970s by the critics Henri Gault and Christian Millau (and elaborated on in a 1976 book) to describe an approach to cooking advocated by a handful of innovative French chefs, one defined by their reevaluation of the dictates of traditional French *haute cuisine*. Nouvelle cuisine stressed reduced cooking times for fish and vegetables, lighter sauces, smaller portions, an overarching attention to the quality of ingredients themselves, and an artful presentation. America made nouvelle cuisine a trend and it quickly became a term of ridicule, denoting bizarre pairings and miniscule portions at exorbitant prices. But its meaningful command that chefs appreciate and elevate the ingredients themselves to serve food of very high quality in a dynamic and healthful way is arguably still the main guiding force in the best restaurant kitchens in America.

Nuts: The edible seeds, one-seeded fruit of various trees and shrubs with hard shells, roasted and salted, are of course very good to snack on, but they are a boon companion to the cook, adding flavor, crunch, and sometimes sweetness to innumerable dishes from savory to sweet, simply as a garnish, whether almonds on green beans or cookies, cashews on salads, or peanuts on chicken, or as a fundamental component of a dish. They are almost always toasted to develop their flavor and harden their texture. They can be candied and/or spiced for additional flavor. Nuts are also an excellent way to thicken and flavor sauces, almonds in a romesco sauce or cashews blended with cream for an Indian sauce base.

O

Oblique cut: a cut used on long vegetables for the visual appeal of an irregular, angled shape. Carrots, if they are to be cooked and served on their own, can be given an oblique cut for visual complexity, for instance. The vegetable is sliced on a diagonal, and then rolled a quarter turn, cut on a diagonal and rolled again, et cetera.

Offal: The innards and extremities of animals, also called variety meats, offer an enticing range of flavors, textures, and preparations that exceed in number and satisfaction those that can be achieved with standard muscle cuts. What was once common in an agrarian society as a matter of practicality is considerably less so today, except, ironically, at high end restaurants. But as farmers' and specialty markets proliferate and more restaurants cook with them, innards and extremities are increasingly available. Offal can be divided into four overlapping categories: tender or tough (kidney, for example, requiring quick cooking, and tongue or tail, requiring low and slow cooking to tenderize them), and red or white (liver or heart, for instance, and sweetbreads or brains). Other categories of offal include ears, feet, intestine, cheeks, head, spleen, stomach, coxcomb, and testicles. They tend to be especially high in cholesterol, iron, and vitamins. (The most comprehensive and best book devoted to cooking offal comes from the Time-Life *The Good Cook* series, *Variety Meats,* published in 1982, edited by Richard Olney.)

Offset spatula: Offset spatulas have an angled blade so that when it is flat, the handle is raised, often at a 45 degree angle or so, a design that makes them unusually versatile for flipping food or for precise placing. They're made in all kinds of sizes and while not strictly necessary are highly recommended for those who cook a lot.

Oignon brûlée [*ohn-NYON BREW-lay*]: Literally burnt onion, *oignon brûlée* is an onion that has been halved and then cooked on that cut face until the onion is black. It will add additional color along with the sweetness of the onion to stocks and soups. It's not a common technique, and many chefs don't want anything burned in their food and so don't use it for this reason, but onion that's deeply caramelized, almost black but not charred dry, will add a depth of flavor and color to a stock.

Oignon piqué [*ohn-NYOHN pee-KAY*]: *Oignon piqué* is an onion onto which a bay leaf has been affixed by cloves (though sometimes the bay leaf is inserted into a slit and the cloves inserted straight into the onion), an aromatic preparation often used for white sauces. The reason for the "pricked" onion is simply to make the aromatics easy to remove once they've done their work.

Oil: See cooking oil, fat.

Olive oil: Olive oil is distinguished from other oils by its rich flavor and the fact that it mostly monounsaturated fat and low in saturated fat. Olive oil can be used as a flavoring device or a cooking medium. Very good olive oils, those from the first pressing of the olives that aren't cooked or filtered, are best used for flavoring. Refined olive oils are best for cooking, but they're more expensive than other cooking oils and so should be used specifically when you want their particular flavor.

Olives: Once sold primarily in two varieties in the United States, green and black (and relegated respectively to the martini and the pizza), many varieties of olives are now commonly available in grocery stores. While good to eat on their own, olives meant for hors d'oeuvres can be further enhanced by creating your own marinade with herbs and aromats, citrus zest, spices to your own taste. To the cook, the salty, acidic, flavorful olive is an excellent all-purpose ingredient as a garnish with umami effects, whole, sliced, minced, or pureed, which can function much like a sauce; olives add excellent depth and complexity to stews and braises, as well.

Omega-3 fatty acids: specific types of fatty acids that appear to have numerous health benefits for the brain, eyes, heart, immune system, and body metabolism generally. They are contained in the fat of cold-water ocean fish (animal fat that must remain fluid at near freezing temperatures, explains McGee), green leafy vegetables, and some seed oils.

Omelet: The omelet is one of the great traditional egg preparations for a reason: it's simple, elegant, inexpensive, and delicious. It's such a basic preparation that some chefs, when trying out a potential hire, ask them to make an omelet. Proper omelet technique includes whisking or stirring the eggs until they are uniformly combined, with no white visible; the eggs are added to a very hot pan and stirred quickly for a fine, elegant curd, until just set, then rolled out of the pan onto a warm plate. There are any number of variations depending on the chef: cream or bits of butter can be added to the raw eggs (some chefs believe adding milk makes them heavy and adding a small amount of water can make then lighter from the steam created; others may add a little lemon juice or acid to make the curd more delicate); they can be flavored with *fines herbes*; they can enclose cooked vegetables or cheese; a small pat of soft butter can finish the cooked omelet with an inviting sheen. Omelets are an important part of a cook's repertoire. (See the essay Egg, page 22.)

Omelet pan: An omelet pan is a circular iron pan with very low, wide-angled sides that is carefully seasoned, never washed with soap, and used only for omelets to ensure that a natural nonstick surface is created and maintained.

Onion: One of the most important ingredients in the savory kitchen, perhaps even the most important food ingredient from an aromatic standpoint (*the* most important ingredients are water and salt, but they are not, strictly speaking, food). Onions are used continually in the cooking process—their importance to stock is fundamental, they flavor food throughout the cooking, and they are delicious cooked and served on their own or accompanying another dish. They provide a range of flavors depending on how they're cut and cooked, from sharp and sulfurish to deeply sweet. Their aromatic sweetness is the key to their versatility. Spanish onions are the best all-purpose onions because they're inexpensive, large, and always available. But don't neglect red onions—they are excellent and can be used as your all-purpose onion as well. Sweet onions such as Vidalia and Wala Wala are fine for cooking but they're more expensive and so should be used for raw preparations that take advantage of their containing fewer of the sulfur compounds that make other onions harsh. Raw onions for salads can be soaked in salted water or macerated in an acid to substantially reduce their harsher qualities. (See also leeks, shallots.)

Organic: The term organic means, according to the FDA, that food so labeled has not been grown using pesticides, hormones, or anything synthetic, genetically engineered, or irradiated. But many in the industry believe that agribusiness, through lobbying efforts as well as the capitulation of several organic farms to the life-preserving business techniques of agribusiness, has so watered down the legal definition of organic that "certified organic" is no longer a meaningful term. More important, they say, are indications that the food is being naturally or sustainably raised—beef from cows that grazed on grass rather than on corn in a concentrated feedlot, pork from pigs raised on farms, not in overcrowded barracks, fruits and vegetables from the area where they're being sold and not trucked in from across the country or another hemisphere.

Organ meat: See offal.

Osmosis: liquids and solids crossing a cell's semipermeable membrane, fundamental to our body's existance, is also a great asset to the cook, primarily in conjunction with the powerful effects of salt, whose concentrations on one side of a cell wall force the liquids on either side of the cell to equalize salt concentration. This is how a brine (and some of the flavors in that brine) penetrate to the interior of a muscle or a vegetable.

Ounce: As with all weight/volume measures, distinguishing between liquid volume or dry weight is important. An ounce is equal to $\frac{1}{16}$ of a pound or about 28 grams; a fluid ounce is $\frac{1}{8}$ of a cup or 2 tablespoons (or about 30 milliliters).

Oven: The oven is one of the cook's major tools, so it's important to have a good one with reliable temperature controls. Use an oven thermometer every now and then to ensure the oven temperature is what you've set it to. Whether your oven is gas or electric matters less than how high a temperature can be reached and how low a temperature can be sustained, the two main criteria defining the quality of this appliance. It's important to remember when you're cooking in an oven that it has hot spots and cool spots, so many items benefit from being rotated during cooking. A convection oven, an oven with a fan to circulate heat has fewer hot spot/cool spot problems, also cooks food more quickly.

Oven spring: Oven spring is the term bread bakers use to describe the sudden rise of bread during the first few minutes of baking a yeast dough. The elevated temperatures make the yeast especially active, releasing increasingly more gas, before they die from the heat; this, in addition to the heat's expanding the gas already released within the dough causes oven spring. Oven spring indicates a good yeast culture and good elasticity in the dough. Oven spring will carry on until the interior of the dough reaches 138°F, yeast's thermal death point.

Oven thermometer: a useful tool for ensuring the temperature inside your oven is what you think it is. Place it in various parts of your oven, back and front, top rack and bottom, to get a sense not only of what the temperature is when you set your oven to, say 425°F, but also of how uniform the heat in your oven is, which should help you to use your oven better.

Oxidation: Oxidation—literally, an oxygen molecule taking an electron from another molecule—is happening all the time, within our bodies and without, for good and for ill, to fats that sit too long, to poorly wrapped meat in the fridge, to the wine poured into your glass. In the kitchen we use the word oxidation almost exclusively to describe the browning of the cut surfaces of fruits and vegetables. A cut potato will turn brown if exposed to air; putting potatoes in water prevents oxidation by keeping oxygen from contacting the surface. Lemon juice, or almost any acidic ingredient will slow the browning of an apple by interfering with the enzymes that speed up oxidation.

Oyster: The oyster is one of the few animals that we eat while it's alive. When this bivalve is out of the water it more or less feeds on itself; thus the sooner an oyster is eaten after it's removed from the water, the better tasting it's likely to be. It should be stored as cold as possible, preferably on ice, and used as soon as possible. Their texture and flavor depend in many respects on the qualities and temperature of the water in which they grow; generally oysters from colder saltier water are most valued. Exquisite raw, they can be eaten with no seasoning, a little lemon juice or for more flavor, a mignonette sauce (shallots and wine vinegar), or even cocktail sauce, though if the oysters are very good, the less done to their flavor the better. Oysters are also excellent cooked, deep-fried, in a stew, or roasted or grilled in their shell.

P

Paddle (noun): a broad mixer attachment, sometimes called a beater, used to mix doughs and batters such as *pâte a choux* or a pâté forcemeat; distinguished from dough hook and whip, the two other common mixer attachments.

Paddle (verb): To paddle means to mix a dough or batter using the paddle attachment.

Paillard: Traditionally, this refers to a lean cut of veal or beef—loin, top round—that has been pounded thin and broiled or grilled, but the word can be used generally to describe a lean cut of meat, pounded thin, and cooked.

Pain de mie: Literally the crumb of the bread, or interior, pain de mie refers to plain white loaves (sometimes called Pullman loaves), used to make plain slices of toast, croutons, or bread crumbs.

Painters' tape: Painters' tape, valuable because it doesn't leave a trace of itself when removed, is a good tool in the kitchen for labeling plastic containers.

Palette knife: A palette knife is a long, narrow, metal spatula with a rounded tip that is handy in the kitchen for flipping food as well as for frosting cakes (it's often referred to as a cake froster), spreading tuile batter, et cetera. Palette knives also come in a variety of sizes, as well as offset versions, which can be especially useful.

Pan: A shallow pan is one of your primary cooking tools, so buy at least two good ones, one small, one large, the heavier the gauge the better, preferably steel though cast iron is excellent as well. The heavier the pan, the more heat it will retain when cold food is added to it, and it will cook the food more evenly. Avoid nonstick pans except for cooking delicate food requiring lower heat, such as for fish and eggs. Once you have two good pans, then it's helpful to acquire more—yes, a nonstick for specific items but otherwise kept immaculately clean and properly stored, a pan with sloping sides (*sauteuse*), a pan with sides at right angles (*sautoire*), a pan with a lid, et cetera. Quality pans well maintained will last forever and make a difference in the taste and texture of the food you cook. Many pans are available in many materials, from inexpensive aluminum to pricey and beautiful lined copper. For the cook, a heavy-gauge steel pan or cast iron remain the best choice for reasons of both cost and effectiveness. (See the essay Tools, page 35.)

Panade: A panade is a mixture of starch and liquid used as a binder. Panades are often included in forcemeats such as a pâté, not only to bind but also to improve texture and enrich the mixture. A panade could be as simple as flour and water, but more often bread is the starch; the liquid is often milk or cream; eggs can be included as can other seasonings such as a brandy; *pâte à choux* is sometimes used as a panade.

Pan-fry: Pan-frying is the shallow version of deep-frying, a so-called "dry-heat" cooking method. Whereas sauté requires a thin layer of fat in which to cook an item, pan-frying uses enough fat to come up the sides of the item being fried, as much as halfway up, but not so much as to cover the item. We often pan-fry thicker cuts, such as pork chops, to ensure that their entire surface is cooked crisp in the hot fat. You do need to keep an eye on the temperature of the fat; allow it to get too hot and the fumes will ignite (if this happens, cover the pan, turn off the heat, and let it cool).

Pan gravy: one of a number of names for a sauce that's made in the pan the meat was cooked in, it's not necessarily different from a *jus* or an *à la minute* sauce, but it does connote a more rustic and hearty preparation rather than a highly refined one. Some consider that pan gravy is defined by the fact of flour being added directly to the fat in the pan to create a roux that will thicken additional juices and stock (if no flour is added, then it would be called a *jus*).

Pan grilling: Cast iron pans with ridged surfaces will become hot enough to create grill marks on meat. These pans are used primarily for the aesthetic appeal of grill marks; they don't impart the flavors of cooking on a grill over charcoal or wood. They are best for very tender cuts of meat that need only brief cooking, fish or tender meat—tuna or beef, for instance—that is to be served very rare.

Panko: Sometimes called Japanese bread crumbs, which is what these bread crumbs are, they are especially coarse and hard and so, used as a breading, result in a very crunchy crust when fried.

Pan-roast: a "dry-heat" technique common in restaurants but which is equally advantageous in the home. An item, often a larger muscle such as a tenderloin rather than an individual item, is sautéed in a hot pan to sear the surface for flavor, and then placed in a hot oven; it will finish cooking more uniformly and more quickly in a hot oven.

Pan-smoke: Given a good exhaust hood, it's possible to smoke foods on your stovetop using a stovetop smoker. They're available at most cookware stores or can be improvised using a small roasting pan and a rack. Pan-smoking works best for items that don't need lots of smoke, mild tasting items such as fish rather than bacon; on the other hand smoke is strong, so a little bit goes a long way on a pork roast. Also, because the heat is direct (the burner heats the wood chips or dust), the interior can get very hot and cook the item, so pan-smoking must be done carefully; too much smoke and too much heat can ruin a dish.

Pan-steam: Pan-steaming is a method of cooking vegetables rapidly in a covered pan. The technique is to get a pan smoking hot, then to add the vegetables and just enough water to steam them, and cover the pan tightly. Use the technique with vegetables (usually green ones) that are already very tender and so need very little cooking, young green beans and peas, for instance. A small amount of butter can be added while the water is steaming to form a kind of quick glaze for the vegetable.

Pantry: 1) Your collection of nonperishable food items is a critical facet of your kitchen and your ability to cook well, especially instinctively. A good pantry will include a range of dry starches and legumes, basic vinegars, oils, condiments, canned tomato in various forms, fresh spices, dried herbs, et cetera. 2) Pantry can also refer to the garde manger or cold-food station of a restaurant kitchen from which salads, sandwiches, and other items that don't need to be heated are served.

Papillote [*pah-pee-OHT*]: *En papillote* means in paper, usually oiled parchment paper. Food cooked *en papillote,* often fish or other delicate meat, is steamed, so the flavors of high heat aren't associated with it; thus other flavors should be introduced within the package, such as aromatic vegetables; additional herbs, spices, or even marinades can be used and sometimes the item can be seared before being sealed in the paper pouch. The benefits are that it's a fat-free method of cooking (though some compound butter can be added for flavor), all the flavors remain in the packet until the packet is cut open, and serving an item *en papillote* creates a dramatic preparation. The tricky part is knowing when the item is done, so it's best to follow a tested recipe to get a sense of timing for the specific kind of item you're cooking. Also it's important to serve *en papillote* items properly—so that the one who's being served can enjoy the intense aromatic steam as it's released from the packet. It should either presented by a server and plated or it can be presented on the plate for the diner to open; in this instance it should contain all the components of the dish rather than be served with other components on the plate.

Parboil: To parboil means to partially cook a fruit or vegetable in water that's at a heavy boil, then shocking the item, in order to finish cooking it later. The reason we parboil food is to make it easy and quick to finish cooking *à la minute,* or as a pre-cooking stage, for instance to begin rendering bacon fat or poultry skin.

Parchment paper: paper treated with silicone, rendering it heat, fat, and moisture resistant. It's commonly used in baking; cookies and cakes won't stick to it. It can also be used for numerous other purposes, such as an all-purpose lining for any cooking vessel. Also, braises that need to reduce as they're cooking in the oven can develop a skin—to prevent the skin but allow some evaporation, a parchment lid can be pressed down onto the braise. And the paper can be folded to make waterproof packages, whether for cooking *en papillote* or piping chocolate ganache onto a cake or petit fours; maître d' butter or cookie dough can be rolled in it; dough can be rolled out between sheets of it; it can be shaped into virtually any shape of funnel, it can be tied around a ramekin to support a rising soufflé. Parchment paper is an excellent cook's tool.

Parcook: To parcook means to partially cook food; almost always used in order to make its final cooking quick and easy.

Pare, paring knife: To pare, deriving from the word for prepare, means to trim away. A paring knife, a knife with a short blade (about 3 inches) is one of two of the essential knives in the kitchen.

Parisienne scoop: Known more commonly in America as a melon baller, this is a specialty tool for shaping food into spheres. It's not an essential tool, though you see them in many chefs' tool boxes; they come in various sizes and are often used on vegetables to make appealing uniform shapes out of carrots or zucchini, for instance.

Parsley: Once the default garnish on an otherwise greenless plate at restaurants, parsley in fact is an herb of extraordinary versatility in cooking, used as an aromat in stocks, soups, and stews, or finely chopped in order to finish numerous sauces, added to maître d' butter, a fundamental ingredient in gremolata or tabbouleh. Two types are widely available, curly and flat leaf, which is sometimes called Italian; most chefs prefer the flat leaf parsley because it has a less assertive flavor and a more delicate texture than curly.

Pasta: Pasta, Italian for paste, refers to the range of wheat-flour-based preparations resulting in noodles and dumplings; some people even consider polenta to be in the pasta category along with Parisian gnocchi (*pâte à choux*–based lump). The varieties and preparations and shapes of pasta are countless. Dumplings can be little lumps such as spaetzle, or even couscous, or they can be stuffed pasta. Pasta dough can be flour, water, and salt, or it can include egg or other starches such as potato, or pureed vegetable, or aromatic herbs. Pasta can be bought dried and fresh, and while there are quality differences among brands, one can't argue that fresh is better than dried or the reverse. They are different—fresh tends to be more tender and requires less cooking. Making your own pasta is not difficult and results in still another set of qualities.

Most pasta should be cooked in water salted to taste until it is tender but firm, or even al dente, but never so sodden that it's falling apart. It should then be strained and oiled and served; some preparations suggest adding partially cooked pasta to its sauce so that it will absorb some of the flavorful liquid and help to thicken the sauce. If you're not serving it right away, it should be shocked in an ice bath, drained, then oiled and kept cold till you're ready to reheat it. Pasta can be reheated in boiling water, in sauce, in a microwave, or by sautéing.

Pasta machine: A pasta machine is one of those specialty appliances or attachments that comes in handy if the urge to make pasta strikes. Strictly speaking, it's not essential, but it will allow you to roll the dough much thinner and more easily than you'd be able to do with a rolling pin and to cut it finer and more uniformly than you'd be able to do by hand. Because of the gradual development of the gluten, machine rolled pasta can be both thinner and more durable than pasta flattened by a rolling pin. There are two basic types of machines, those that extrude pasta through a die, and those that roll and cut pasta. Extruded pasta usually uses the high-protein semolina flour and water and is often dried after being extruded. Hand crank pasta machines can also be used to roll sheets of caramel or stiff chocolate ganache to make sheets or to laminate two such malleable sheets together.

Pasteurize, pasteurization: Pasteurization is the process of heating a liquid—such as milk or fruit juices—to specific minimum temperatures for specific durations in order to kill pathogens. The process not only ensures that liquid doesn't make anyone sick, it also serves as a preservative by killing those microbes responsible for a food's deterioration. The reason cooked meat will keep longer than raw is because it's been, in a manner of speaking, pasteurized.

Pastry: Pastry is a mixture of flour, fat, and liquid that's cooked; in other words, a bread dough with a substantial amount of solid fat (lard, butter). The fat shortens or weakens the gluten network that makes bread dough elastic; pastry is not elastic largely because of the fat. Its tenderness is also determined by factors such as the type of flour used, how much the dough is worked, and its pH or acidity. Pastry can be savory or sweet, crumbly or smooth, flaky or dense, straight or seasoned. The behavior of pastry is determined in large measure by the way the fat is handled. If it's layered it can create anything from a flaky pie crust to an elegant puff pastry. Like other starch preparations—doughs, noodles, potatoes—pastry can perform any number of jobs, from framing or containing food to being the centerpiece of a dish.

Pastry bag: conical bags commonly made from cotton coated with polyurethane are used for piping everything from pastry cream to mashed potatoes to *pâte à choux* dough. You can even stuff sausage casing with them. They're not one of the home kitchen essentials, but they have many uses. Plastic disposable pastry bags are also available and a good option; cloth bags take some time to clean, but they're stronger and less expensive than plastic. Disposable plastic bags have the advantage of ease and convenience, and they won't transfer flavors that a canvas bag might.

Pastry brush: A brush like a small trim paint brush, 1½ inches wide, is used for any number of tasks, from brushing egg wash onto pastry to basting meats, to brushing down the sides of a pot with water to keep sugar or caramel from burning.

Pastry cream: See *crème pâtissière*.

Pastry flour: See flour.

Pastry wheel: Cutters used for long pieces of dough come in a variety of sizes. The wheel can be straight or, for decorative edges, fluted.

Pâte [*paht*]: French for paste or dough, as in *pâte à choux, pâte brisée*.

Pâté [*pah-TAY*]: a mixture of meat (or fish or shellfish or liver), and fat and seasonings that's cooked in a mold or a crust, cooled, and served cold.

Pâte à choux [*paht ah shoo*]: a versatile dough of flour, water, butter, and eggs distinguished by the fact that the flour is combined with the butter and water and partially cooked before the eggs are added to it. The resulting dough, which can be sweet or savory, puffs when it bakes and so has a light and elegant texture in and of itself and a neutral, eggy flavor that carries more assertive savory and sweet flavors well. Gougères, cheese puffs, are made by seasoning *pâte à choux* with parmesan or other cheeses and are served warm from the oven or cooled and filled with a savory *farce*. But these puffs can also be filled to make such sweet preparations as éclairs (cream puffs) and profiteroles, sweet puffs filled with ice cream and covered in chocolate sauce. *Pâte à choux* is sometimes added to forcemeats as the panade, something that binds, enriches, and flavors. *Pâte à choux* can be poached, a form of pasta sometimes called Parisian gnocchi. *Pâte à choux*— a basic ratio is equal parts flour and water by volume and ½ part each butter and egg (1 whole for 2 ounces water)—is made by bringing water and butter to a simmer, stirring in the flour, and cooking the mixture till it pulls away from the sides of the pot and dries out somewhat. Eggs are then beaten into it one by one. The mixture is typically piped onto a sheet pan and baked. *Pâte à choux* is a fundamental part of the cook's repertoire.

Pâte brisée [*paht bree-ZAY*]: *Pâte brisée* is basic pastry dough for crusts, pie dough. A basic ratio is three parts flour, two parts fat, one part water. (If sugar is added, it's called *pâte sucré*.)

Pâté en croute [*pah-TAY ohn kroot*]: *Pâté en croute* is pâté baked in a pastry dough. It can take many forms, from the unrefined English pork pie to the highly refined *pâté en croute* with inlay and interior garnish.

Pâte feuilletée [*paht foy-TAY*]: See puff pastry.

Pâte sucré: *Pâte sucré* is sweetened pastry dough, or pie dough; see also *pâte brisée.*

Peasant style: The term peasant, when applied to food, is meant to suggest either simplicity or coarseness of texture of ingredients; some consider the word to connote rusticity, authenticity; others feel the word is hopelessly vague, even demeaning in its suggestion of lesser quality ingredients, or requiring less effort in its preparation, and so should be avoided. Better to use the descriptor country or *campagne,* if necessary.

Pectin: a substance found in fruits and vegetables that's used as a gelling agent in fruit preserves and jellies.

Peel (noun): 1) Rarely are the peels of fruits and vegetables used in cooking because they tend to be tough and flavorless. Part of the peel of citrus fruits, called zest, is often used for its vivid, refreshing flavor. 2) A flat, broad wooden paddle used for transferring heavy pieces of dough to and from the oven, especially handy in home kitchens for pizza.

Peel (verb): As a rule, peel your fruits and vegetables to achieve the best flavor and appearance in whatever preparation is at hand. This is de rigueur in restaurant kitchens but less so at home. Fruit peels are tough and have little flavor; vegetable peels, while nutritious, are often dirty. At home, use your judgment; ask yourself if the food will look or taste worse if you decide not to peel a fruit or vegetable. For fruits and vegetables that will be eaten raw, sanitation can be an issue but it's not something to be paranoid about. Always wash fruits and vegetables to remove potential bacteria even if the item is to be peeled (the act of peeling can leave bacteria on the flesh of the fruit).

Peeler: A good vegetable peeler is an important tool in the kitchen; avoid the very cheap and the newfangled. Be observant of the depth of the peel; some peelers cut so deep that you end up wasting more of the vegetable than necessary.

Pellicle: In the kitchen, pellicle refers to the tacky surface meat will develop after being cured and allowed to air dry, usually refrigerated. Smoke compounds collect more efficiently on the tacky surface than on a moist surface, so many items bound for the smokehouse are first allowed to develop a pellicle.

Pepper: Pepper—ground peppercorns—comes in three colors, black, white, and green, but usually pepper refers to black pepper. Pepper is often used as a default seasoning along with salt, but you should always ask yourself if what you're seasoning will benefit from the spiciness and heat of pepper. Pepper is best lightly toasted whole, then ground or finely chopped. Second best is freshly ground from a pepper mill. Avoid buying preground or cracked pepper because its flavor quickly pales. In dishes that benefit from pepper but whose appearance would be compromised by black specks, many chefs use white pepper.

The size of the cracked pepper grain will affect the dish; the finer the grind, the more evenly it will be distributed throughout the dish. In the rare instances you want pepper to have a bite, it's best to finely chop it to the desired size. When using peppercorns as an aromatic in a stock, it's best first to crack them using the bottom of a sauté pan; they release considerably more flavor this way than if they're added whole to a stock.

Black pepper is deeply aromatic and spicy; white can be astringent and acidic; green is less hot and very aromatic. White and black are sold dried; green is sold dried and also packed in brine (brine packed peppercorns are soft and usually used in sauces whole or chopped).

Pepper mill: An important tool for the cook, a pepper mill makes freshly ground pepper easily accessible for seasoning food while cooking and for finishing dishes. The primary factor in choosing a pepper mill is the size of the grind. Peppercorns are tough and chewy, so a good pepper mill grinds the pepper finely enough that the pepper doesn't have a noticeable bite of its own.

Perfection: Much is said about perfection in the kitchen and seeking perfection. Perfection is a direction, not an end. Because perfection is an idea rather than an actual quality, its fundamental importance to the cook is as a motivator, a pusher—the idea pushes you to work harder and to take better care in each step of your work.

Perforated spoon: A perforated spoon is one that has holes to allow liquid to drain from it. A perforated or a slotted spoon is an essential cooking utensil.

Persillade [*PEHR-see-yahd*]: *Persillade* is a mixture of parsley and garlic, finely chopped, used as flavorful garnish for meats and fish, either during cooking or immediately after cooking while the meat is still hot. It's a powerful pairing of two common aromatics. (See also gremolata.)

Pesto: Traditionally pesto is made by grinding basil, olive oil, garlic, pine nuts, and Pecorino Romano or Parmigiano-Reggiano cheese in a mortar with a pestle, though it's more commonly made today in a food processor, which is fine. Also, the technique can be used for other strongly flavored leaves such as sorrel and arugula and make use of different nuts, such as walnuts.

pH: pH is the level of acidity or alkalinity in food, measured from 0 to 14; 7 is considered neutral and numbers descending from 7 describe increasing acidity. While it's not common to need to know a food's pH level, it can be important; a dry curing sausage, for instance, must have a low enough pH (that is, enough acidity) to protect it from bacteria. And from a general standpoint, it's useful to understand how the acidity or the alkalinity of a mixture affects the finished product. Dough to which a base has been added, making it the opposite of acidic, will be noticeably softer. Leavening is often a result of the interaction between a base and an acid.

Phyllo dough: Phyllo is leaf-thin sheets of dough often used in Middle Eastern and Mediterranean desserts (baklava, for example), valued for its delicacy and crispness. But phyllo, which is commonly available frozen in grocery stores, is also a valuable all-purpose pastry with many applications. It can be used to make a tart shell, it can enclose a savory filling, or be layered, seasoned, and baked and used as a crisp garnish. Phyllo is very delicate, dries out quickly, and can be brittle and difficult to work with. It's commonly brushed with melted butter before being used to keep it pliable and enhance its flavor and capacity to brown when cooked; sheets that are out but not being worked on should be covered with a damp towel. Because it's so fine and delicate, it's almost always used in layers.

Pickle: To pickle means to cure in a brine and can refer to vegetables, meat, or fish. Often a pickle denotes some sort of acidity in the ingredient being pickled, most commonly with cucumbers. A natural pickle is one in which acid is developed through fermentation, bacteria feeding on the sugars of the vegetable and generating lactic acid, a preservative in addition to the salt. A good brine for pickling vegetables combines 50 grams of salt per liter of water for a 5 percent salt solution. The term can also mean cooked or marinated in vinegar without preservative techniques.

Picnic shoulder (pork): The picnic shoulder is a cut of the pig from the middle of the front leg, above the hock and below the shoulder butt, is relatively tough, and is best slow-roasted or braised. When it's cured (and sometimes when it's not) it's called a picnic ham.

Pie: Pie can be used to refer to virtually anything that combines a crust and a filling and can range from savory to sweet. (See tart.)

Pie dough: a dough combining flour, fat, and water; a common ratio is three parts flour to two parts fat to one part water, called a 3-2-1 dough, though the choice of fat can affect the amount needed not to mention flavor and even the behavior of the dough (lard, in which all the water has been cooked out, affects the dough differently from whole butter, which contains water; it's a much more powerful shortener than butter or vegetable shortening and also adds a more savory dimension to the flavor).

Pie weights: weights specifically made to rest on pie or tart dough to maintain the dough's shape when it's blind baked (baked without its filling). They're convenient but dried beans poured into the shell on top of foil or parchment paper serve the same function.

Pig: See hog, pork.

Pigs' feet: Though they are renowned as a bistro staple, pigs' feet, also referred to as trotters, have very little meat and lots of bones and connective tissue, which makes them best for pork stock or dishes to which you want to add body. When making any version of trotters, it's a good idea to supplement them with meat from the hock, the joint above the trotter. Some preparations remove the interior above the hoof, wrap the skin around a forcemeat, cook it, and serve it sliced like a sausage or even dry cure it.

Pigskin: Pigskin is loaded with gelatin and can be added to stocks and stews for body. It can also be confited or slowly cooked in liquid until completely tender, scraped of its fat, and added to sausage or forcemeats, or roasted or fried or rendered and deep-fried for cracklings.

Pilaf: Pilaf denotes a cooking method used for grains. A common preparation for regular long grain rice, rice pilaf, is to sauté diced onion in oil or butter, add one part rice and briefly sauté this, then add two parts stock and any additional aromats and seasonings (bay leaf and salt, for instance), bring the mixture to a simmer, cover, and place in a medium-hot oven for 20 minutes. Pilaf is a technique, not a recipe, meaning that it can be used with many grains. The proper ratio of grain to liquid depends on the grain.

Pinbones: Pinbones are the small bones that in "round" fish run along the top half of the fillet from behind the gills about three-quarters of the way along the length. They should be removed if possible before serving, especially those in larger fish such as salmon (needle-nosed pliers are well suited to the task but special fish bone tweezers are also available and work well).

Pincé, pinçage [*PEHN-say, PEHN-sazj*]: *Pincé* is an uncommon term that denotes tomato, usually tomato paste, that is sautéed until it's browned to intensify the flavor of the tomato, often used in brown stocks and sauces to deepen the color and flavor of the stock or sauce. Browned tomato used to flavor stocks and sauces is often referred to as *pinçage*.

Pinch: a purposefully vague quantity denoting a small amount, often to taste. Think about what a recipe is asking you to pinch. A pinch of nutmeg will go a long way. A pinch of salt usually won't, but a "three finger pinch" of it often will. Use your common sense.

Pink salt: Pink salt is the generic term for sodium nitrite, curing salt, salt with 6.25 percent nitrite added to it. (Pink salt is not the same as a product called sel rose, French for pink salt. Sel rose contains potassium nitrate, saltpeter.)

Plancha: a griddle or flattop used in place of a sauté pan. Foods cooked on a plancha are cooked directly on the iron surface; it's mainly used in restaurants where it can be a very convenient tool because it stays so hot and allows you to cook several portions at once.

Planks (cooking on): Food cooked on planks of flavorful wood can pick up smoky woody flavors. Salmon is often cooked on cedar planks. While this was apparently a traditional Native American technique common in the Pacific Northwest, and while it can be a good cooking technique (traditionally the fish was tacked to the board, which was then propped up close to the fire) beware of gimmicky packages of cedar sold at gourmet food stores.

Plate (verb): In restaurant parlance, this word means to put the food on the plate. Food that's ready to be served is ready to be "plated."

Pluche: A pluche denotes whole leaves of an herb connected by a bit of stem and is usually used as a finishing touch (a pluche of chervil, for instance).

Plump, plumping: Another term for rehydrating, plumping is usually done to dried fruit and usually calls for alcohol or a flavorful liquid rather than water (dried cherries plumped in brandy, for example).

Poach: A "moist-heat" method, poaching is among the most even and gentle forms of cooking because the cooking temperature can't rise above 212°F, the boiling point. Poaching, though, does not mean boiling; the agitation of the bubbles can damage delicate food, and raising the moisture in the item you're cooking to the boiling point can overcook it and dry it out; optimal poaching temperatures usually range from 160° to 180°F. Poaching can be divided into two categories, "deep-poach" and "shallow poach." In a shallow poach, the liquid the fish has poached in, the *cuisson,* often becomes part of the finished dish. With a deep-poach, the cooking medium, usually a *court bouillon,* is discarded, but it is usually distinguished by being robustly flavored with aromats or acids or other seasonings.

Poêlé: To poêlé means to roast something in its own juices, usually on a bed of mirepoix and butter in a covered pan, sometimes referred to as butter-braising or butter-roasting.

Pork: The muscle of hogs is abundant and flavorful and can be put to a remarkably wide range of culinary uses, from braises to sautés to cures; pork is unmatched in the animal world for versatility. Tender muscles such as the loin and tenderloin are best sautéed or quickly roasted and served juicy. The USDA recommends that pork be cooked to a temperature of 150°F to kill trichinosis, once common in pig but no longer so. Most chefs won't cook tender cuts past medium, if that, and this is perfectly acceptable (trichinosis is killed at 137°F, see McGee, and can also be eliminated by freezing), because the larvae is no longer an issue in commercial pork. The hard-working muscles, the legs, and the belly must be slow cooked to tenderize them. The shoulder butt of naturally raised hogs has about a 70:30 ratio of meat to fat, perfect for grinding into sausage.

Pork shoulder butt: A cut from the shoulder of the pig, sometimes called shoulder, sometimes called butt or Boston butt, shoulder butt is usually very well marbled with fat and so is excellent to grind into sausage or to braise or slow roast until it shreds easily. It takes the flavor of smoke very well and is the cut typically used for all manner of barbecue.

Pot: A fundamental cooking vessel, a pot's shape and size in part determines the cooking; it's thus important to have heavy pots of varying sizes and to use the appropriately sized pot (choosing a narrow deep pot rather than a wide pot to cook something longer with less reduction). While you can do most of your kitchen work with two pots, a big one and a little one, having a small variety of sizes is convenient. (See the essay Tools, page 35.)

Potassium nitrate: See saltpeter, curing salt.

Potato: While there are all kinds of varieties of potatoes, the main distinction between them is designated by their skin. Coarse, thick-skinned potatoes (russets or baking potatoes) have a high starch content relative to thin-, smooth-skinned potatoes (boiling potatoes). You can cook all potatoes any way you wish, though there will be differences. As a rule, high-starch russets are best cooked with dry heat (baking, frying) while thin-skinned, low-starch potatoes perform best in moist heat. Baking potatoes will be light

and fluffy while boiling potatoes will be denser when baked. Baking potatoes should be used for fried preparations. You can boil baking potatoes,
which are good for fluffy mashed potatoes, but they don't hold together as
well when sliced. So boiling potatoes are preferable for potatoes that will be
boiled but not mashed (sliced fingerlings, for instance, or other low-starch
potatoes for potato salad). If you mash these thin-skinned potatoes, they
will be gluey. It's best to "boil" baking potatoes with their skins on (started
in cold water); this prevents the exterior of the potato from overcooking
and flaking away before the potato is cooked through. Also, the water
should not be at a rolling boil, which can damage and overcook the potato;
a gentle simmer is sufficient.

Pot liquor: The liquid left in a pot after you've cooked meat and or vegetables is often an intensely flavorful, nutritional stock. The liquid your
beans or greens or pork cooked in can be added to the dish you're preparing for flavor and moisture; for even more refinement and power, some
pot liquors can be fortified by being strained into a smaller pot and
reduced.

Potted Meats: Potted meats typically refer to meats that are slowly cooked
until they're shreddably tender, then mixed with some of their fat, some of
the cooking liquid, some seasoning, and allowed to cool; they can be
eaten casually with bread and mustard and make a perfect hors d'oeuvre.
Rillettes—usually of pork, but duck, rabbit, and salmon are common as
well—are the most literal form of the potted meat preparations but confit
and even pâté falls into the potted meat category. Originally a method of
preserving food, potted meats remain a delicious way to transform tough
inexpensive meats into delicious food.

Poultry: See chicken, duck, and turkey.

Poultry shears: Strong kitchen scissors that can cut through smaller bones,
joints, and shell can come in handy. Given that most everything they can
do can also be done by a knife, or unless you break down a lot of birds,
consider them a convenience item rather than a kitchen essential.

Prep, prepped: 1) Kitchen shorthand for prepare and prepared. See the
essential concept *mise en place*. 2) Prep cook is traditionally the bottom
rank in the kitchen *brigade*.

Preserve, preserved: Food treated with salt or other protein-changing techniques (such as drying and cooking) is preserved, also called cured. Once a set of food skills fundamental to the health of communities, food preservation is no longer a requisite in our age of easy refrigeration and freezing and an abundant food supply. And yet we still preserve food because these methods, developed over hundreds if not thousands of years, result in delicious food: bacon and ham, salumi, sauerkraut and kimchi, smoked salmon, duck confit. Because cooking kills the microrganisms that cause decay, cooking is in effect a form of preservation, and so even pâtés are a kind of preserved food and part of the charcutier's craft. Preserving food, from pork to lemons, should be a part of most cooks' repertoire.

Preserved lemon: See lemon confit.

Preserves: Preserves are fruit that's been cooked with sugar and often a gelling agent such as pectin; it's a great example of the fact that the act of preserving food, in this case an abundance of seasonal berries or fruit, can transform the food into something that is both durable and delicious.

Pressure cooker: a kitchen tool that allows you to cook food in water that's above the boiling point (at about 250°F, according to McGee). It's especially effective at cooking dried beans quickly and good for cooking at high altitudes where water boils at low temperatures.

Primal cuts: the main or large cuts of meat—the shoulder, the rack or the saddle, the leg, for instance—that will be broken down into smaller individual cuts called subprimal cuts.

Processed: Processed is vague term now associated with food that's been heavily worked over by agribusiness companies and includes undesirable additives such as excessive salts, sugars, and preservatives, food to be avoided. But the term can also mean pureed in a food processor, and can even realistically be attached to cured products such as bacon and smoked salmon.

Proof: Proof, a word apparently deriving from a baker's need to prove his yeast was alive, is a verb that refers to the dough's rising, often the final rise, after the dough has been shaped.

Prosciutto [*pro-SHOO-toh*]: Prosciutto is the Italian word for dry cured ham. The hind leg of the pig is packed in salt for about a day per pound depending on the maker, then it's rinsed and hung to dry for many months and up to a couple years. The most highly regarded prosciuttos are those from Parma, Italy, and what's called *jamon iberico* of Spain. Other names of prosciutto varieties include Bayonne and San Danielle. In France, dry cured ham is called jambon cru (raw ham). Prosciutto that has been smoked is called spec. Prosciutto is best sliced paper thin and includes a good amount of fat. It can also be used in cooking and will add an excellent dimension and depth to pastas, sauces, soups, et cetera, but it will also release copious amounts of salt, so be careful when seasoning a dish to which you've added prosciutto.

Protein: Of the four fundamental food molecules, proteins—combinations of amino acids—are the most mutable; the changes they undergo in the cooking process (whether by acid, by salt, by heat) result in the differences in texture and appearance between what we know as raw and cooked. When egg white goes from translucent to opaque, when chicken goes from pink and fleshy to white and stiff, when acid is added to hot milk to curdle it for cheese, when a strong stock cools and solidifies, when dense wet dough becomes moist airy bread, this is the result of protein coagulation. Proteins also tend to brown under high heat, giving us the crust on bread and the crispy sear on a piece of sautéed meat or roasted chicken skin. Protein provides many of the amino acids fundamental to our bodies. Many of the amino acids that compose proteins contribute great flavor (see umami) to our food. Because it is the building block of muscle, in professional kitchens, the word itself is shorthand, generally, for meat or fish. (See McGee for more complete descriptions as well as illustrations of proteins at the molecular level.)

Puff pastry: Dough into which a block of butter has been carefully layered puffs into a delicate flavorful pastry called puff pastry, or *pâte feuilletée,* that can be used variously in both the savory and the sweet kitchen. It's in a category called laminated dough, dough that has been layered with fat. When yeast is added it becomes especially soft and fluffy (as with croissants). The layers of dough are created by folding dough around a block of butter and rolling this out, then folding it in thirds, like a letter, and rolling it out again, refrigerating the dough for several hours each time until the butter has become firm. The folding process is usually repeated six times; the number of layers of butter multiplies exponentially. The process can be speeded up by giving the dough four folds and rolling it out this way three times with less time chilling in between; the result is acceptable but it isn't quite as uniform as traditional puff pastry. Puff pastry freezes well, and it can be found frozen in most grocery stores (beware the use of trans fats in these). When making your own puff pastry, consider flavoring the butter for interesting variations.

Puree: to turn something solid into a loose uniform mass. Depending on how sturdy the item is, purees can be made in several different ways: in a food processor, in a blender, by passing it through a food mill or through a tamis (drum sieve); purees made with a food mill or tamis tend to have the most uniform texture, which is one of the critical qualities of a good puree. Blenders can also make excellent purees. Food pureed in a processor can have chunks, and starchy food can become gluey, and so this should be your last choice as to how you make your puree.

Pure starch: Starch from which the proteins and other components have been removed is called a pure starch. Pure starches, such as cornstarch, make good thickeners (see slurry); compared with sauces thickened with roux, made from flour, which require cooking and skimming, thickening with a pure-starch slurry is easy and quick, but the slurry will break down with repeated or extended heating.

Pyrex: Pyrex is the trademarked name for heat resistant glass, a good material in which to bake; it's used to refer to any glassware suitable for cooking.

Q

Quatre épices: Literally "four spices," this French blend combines black pepper, nutmeg, cinnamon, and cloves, and is often used in pâtés and some sausages. It's best to blend your own for the sake of freshness and personal taste. A working ratio is three parts pepper to one part nutmeg, cinnamon, and clove. Some recipes may call for additional sweet spices such as allspice and ginger.

Quenelle: Quenelle refers to an egg shaped portion of any given preparation. Quenelles are made either by scraping a mixture—often a forcemeat to be poached—between two spoons for the traditional three-sided quenelle or, for a more elegant shape of soft material such as ice cream, by dragging a spoon over top of the material so that it curves with the bowl of the spoon.

Quick bread: Soft, cakelike breads, often sweet, that don't require kneading and typically use some sort of chemical leavening such as baking powder are called quick breads—cornbread and popovers, for example.

R

Rabbit: Rabbit can be a very tasty meat, especially if it's grown well on a diverse diet (commercially raised rabbit can be bland). The loin is tender and should be briefly cooked. But some farm raised rabbit is tender enough to grill the hind legs as well. The forequarters and hind legs are customarily braised; though they can also be boned and the meat used for sausage or a *farce* to be cooked with the rabbit. Rabbit offal—liver, heart, kidney—are excellent for grilling, sautéing, and confiting as well.

Rack: 1) Racks—raised metal grates—are useful for cooling food and for food that benefits from having all sides exposed to the air—food that needs to dry, for instance, or food that is breaded and might become soggy on the bottom—and for food that benefits from having all sides exposed to the dry heat of the oven. Racks can also be used in the bottom of *bains-marie* to make the cooking of custards and pâtés more uniform. They can elevate a roast so that the roast doesn't sit in the rendering fat and juices. 2) A primal cut of meat taken from the back of land animals that includes part of the spine, the back ribs, and the loin.

Raft: The mass of coagulated egg white (and often meat and aromats) that rises to the top of the pot, filtering cloudy stock into clear consommé. When it's liquid, the egg white mixture is called a clarification. (See clarification for the technique.)

Ramekin: a small dish, usually porcelain with straight sides, that can be used for holding ingredients, for cooking (often in a water bath), and for serving. A set of them is a useful tool to have in the kitchen not only for *mise en place* but for cooking and serving as well.

Rare: See meat temperatures.

Reach-in: Reach-in is shorthand for reach-in cooler, to distinguish it from the walk-in cooler.

Recipes: Recipes are not assembly manuals. You can't use them the way you use instructions to put together your grill or the rec room Ping-Pong table. Recipes are guides and suggestions for a process that is infinitely nuanced. Recipes are sheet music. A Bach cello suite can be performed at a beginner's level or given extraordinary interpretation by Yo-Yo Ma—same notes/ingredients, vastly different outcomes.

How to use a good recipe: First read it and think about it. Cook it in your mind. Envision what it will look like when you serve it. Try to know the outcome before you begin. Read a recipe all the way through not only to understand it generally, but to make your work more efficient and to avoid making errors or taking unnecessary steps. Perhaps a dough needs to chill for an hour in the middle of a preparation, perhaps meat needs to be salted for twenty-four hours, or a liquid must be simmered, then cooled. The recipe suggests adding the flour, baking powder, and salt one at a time, but perhaps you can combine all the dry ingredients ahead of time while you're waiting for the butter to get to room temperature so you can cream it with the eggs. Taking a few minutes to read a recipe, acting out each step in your mind as you do, will save you time and prevent errors.

Measure out or prep all your ingredients before you begin. Don't mince your onion just before you need to put it in the pan, have it minced and in a container ready to go, have that cup of milk and half cup of sugar set out before you. Good *mise en place* makes the process easier and more pleasurable and the result tastier than preparing a recipe with no *mise en place*.

If you're unsure about an instruction, use your common sense. You've already imagined in your head what the goal is. Work toward that goal using all your senses.

How to perfect a good recipe: Do it over again. And again. Pay attention. Do it again. That's what chefs do. Often great cooking is simply the result of having done it over and over and over while paying attention.

Great cooking is as much about sheer repetition as it is about natural skill or culinary knowledge.

Reduce, reduction: To reduce means to simmer gently to diminish the quantity of water in a mixture and thus concentrate the liquid's flavor and to thicken it. Stocks and sauces, wines and vinegars are reduced for these reasons. When a liquid is defined by its concentration and intensity of flavor, it is called a reduction. When reducing stocks and sauces, it's helpful to pull the pot partially off the flame; protein and impurities will collect on the cool side of the pot where they can be easily skimmed off and discarded. Be careful of overreducing meat-based stocks and sauces; they can become gluey. If you've overreduced a sauce, do not add stock, add water (which is what has been lost). Wines and vinegars should be reduced very slowly, not simmered away but rather kept at what might be thought of as a speeded-up-evaporation temperature to preserve the liquid's flavor and prevent the liquid's sticking to the sides of the pot, burning and adding a bitterness to the reduction.

Refresh: 1) To rejuvenate a dish or a sauce by adding fresh ingredients. Stock based sauces can be refreshed, for instance, by adding more stock and fresh herbs. 2) Some cookbooks and recipes use "refresh" as a synonym for "shock," plunging cooked food into an ice bath to stop it from cooking. Avoid this illogical term; use shock, which is more accurately descriptive.

Refrigerate, refrigerator: A refrigerator is not only a ubiquitous storage device that preserves food, it can also be thought of as a tool. Food that must be cooked and then cooled for service later—risotto, mushrooms, sautéed greens, what have you—will be better the faster they're cooled. And it's the safest place to thaw frozen foods. Your refrigerator should be kept at or below 37°F; keep in mind also that a refrigerator has hot and cool spots, just like an oven. Use your refrigerator thoughtfully by keeping food well wrapped to prevent its picking up other aromas; keep wrapped food well marked so that it's easily identified (and not ignored and forgotten); keep food well organized; and be careful about cross contamination (don't put a shallow pan or plate of raw meat over dairy or vegetables that won't be cooked before being eaten).

Rehydrate: to soak dried food in a water-based liquid; usually the more gradually food is rehydrated, the better it is for the food, especially with legumes. When fruits are rehydrated, often in alcohol, the word plumped is often used. When some items are hydrated, notably dried mushrooms, the liquid used to rehydrate them becomes a flavor tool as well (strained through cloth or a coffee filter).

Remouillage: a second stock, usually made in restaurant kitchens, from bones that have been used once for a primary stock in order to make complete use of the bones. It's a weaker stock, of course, and is often added to the primary stock and reduced.

Render: Rendering means to melt solid animal fat with gentle heat, commonly pork fat or duck fat. To render fat, place it in a pan with a few tablespoons of water and cook over low heat or in a low oven until all the fat has rendered out and all the water has evaporated; the smaller its cut (grinding it is best), the more efficiently it renders. Strain the fat and allow it to cool. Rendering should be done as gently as possible; if, after the water is gone, it gets too hot, it can brown and overcook, taking on roasted flavors, and ultimately begin to break down and taste bitter. Rendered fat is an important cooking material and ingredient. Confits are made by poaching tough meat in fat, rendered fat is excellent for sautéing, pan-frying, and deep-frying, and rendered pork fat (lard) is used abundantly in pastry as a shortening.

Rennet: Rennet is the general term for enzymes found in the stomach of ruminant animals and some vegetables, used to curdle milk for cheese making. The enzyme (chymosin) is now typically genetically engineered.

Rest: to allow a period of time between removing food, usually meat, from the heat and cutting and serving it. Resting cooked meat is important in that it allows temperatures to equalize and the juices to redistribute themselves throughout the muscle (see also carryover cooking). Some chefs have suggested that cooking time and resting time should be the same; while this might be more true of a small piece of meat rather than, say, a chicken, it does underscore the great importance of resting, that it can be just as important as cooking, and reinforces the fact that the larger the cut of meat, the more time you should allow it to rest. With few exceptions, fish does not benefit from resting; it tends to dry out. Bread and pasta doughs are often rested, that is, given a period of time to allow the gluten to relax so that the dough can more easily be shaped. Pastry doughs are often rested in a refrigerator or cooler to allow the gluten to relax and for the shortening to firm up.

Retard: a baker's term for slowing the growth of yeast in doughs in order to lengthen the fermentation time and develop flavor, usually done by placing the dough in a retarder, an actual box made for this purpose or some sort of enclosed, controlled, cool environment.

Ribbon: Ribbon refers to the consistency of a yolk-based mixture—sabayon, lemon curd—being whipped as it's being cooked, usually over hot water. As the yolks and other ingredients cook and air is incorporated into them, the mixture will become so thick that it will fall in slow ribbons from the whisk.

Rice: Rices, whether short grain or long grain, are all the same in that their cooking is mainly a matter of hydration generally and a gelatinization of their starches. Rices generally require two parts water to one part rice; some, aromatic rices such as jasmine and basmati, require 25 percent less water and sticky rice requires less than that (it's soaked and then simply steamed). Others such as brown rices, which retain their husk, require more. Rice can be done on the stovetop or in the oven. A special variety of short grained rice—Arborio, Carnaroli—is used for risotto, rice to which liquid is added incrementally while the cook stirs continuously, creating a thick, creamy sauce as starch leaves the rice. Rice is a remarkably versatile starch that can be used in both the savory and sweet kitchens. Rice flour is used to make noodles and wrappers in Asian cuisines.

Ricer: A tool for pureeing soft root vegetables, a ricer performs the same function as a food mill and, for small quantities of very soft starches, is more convenient.

Rillettes [*ree-ETS*]: Tough cuts of meat that are cooked until shreddable, mixed with seasonings and fat and cooled, are rillettes, which are often spread on crusty bread or a crouton. They are usually served in the beginning of a meal and make a great hors d'oeuvres. Pork is the most common meat used for rillettes, but duck, goose, rabbit, and many fish make excellent rillettes as well. Rillettes likely originated due to the need to preserve and make use of the abundant meat and fat trim from the hog.

Ring molds: Metal bands of varying widths fastened into rings can be used for shaping food into discs, cutting food into uniform shapes, and as molds for cooking (quiche, small tarts, for example), and as a plating device used to give loose food, such as salad greens, more height. A specialty cooking tool. PCB pipe can be cut to the desired depth and used as rings for molding food.

Rise: To rise means to allow the yeast in doughs to feed and thus release gas in order to leaven and flavor bread.

Risotto: Risotto is a rice preparation featuring a short grained rice (such as Arborio, Carnaroli, or Vialone Nano), wine, aromatic vegetables and seasonings, and fat, and is distinguished by its method of continuous stirring as flavorful liquid is added incrementally, resulting in a dish of great creaminess and richness in the pantheon of rice preparations. A good working method for preparing risotto is this. Sauté diced onion until translucent, turn up the heat to high, add a small handful of rice per portion, and sauté the rice to toast and coat it with oil, then add white wine. Cook it, stirring, until the wine is gone and until no harsh aromas from the alcohol remain. Begin adding a flavorful chicken or vegetable stock, just barely to cover the rice, and cook this stock down (fresh stock makes a world of difference here), stirring all but continuously. Add more stock when the first stock is almost gone, season with salt, and continue this process until the grains are tender. Remove the rice from the heat and stir in the fat (cream and butter are best), finish with some freshly grated Parmigiano-Reggiano, and serve immediately. Note that risotto can be prepared well in advance of serving it; cook the rice till it is two-thirds completed, pour it out onto a plate or a tray, and chill it; it can then be finished as needed, though it should always be finished as close to serving it as possible. Variations—savory or sweet, red wine versus white, the addition of other vegetables or meat, or finishing with a vegetable puree in place of some of the butter and cream for a cleaner, brighter vegetable dish—are countless.

Roast: a "dry-heat" method of cooking, usually done in a hot to very hot oven and usually uncovered (to avoid steaming the item), resulting in so-called "brown" flavors, the deep rich flavors of browned meats and caramelized vegetables. We usually use this technique and this term for larger cuts of meat and whole birds.

Roasting pan: A small and large pan for roasting are good items to have in your kitchen, but remember that you can roast in sauté pans, cast iron skillets, and pots. The size of the roasting vessel can be important, depending on what you're roasting, whether you need aromatic vegetables to be bunched up around what's being roasted, how the released juices and fat will be affected by the size of the pan; roasting something in a deep pot would not be a good idea—it would steam rather than roast. Racks can be put in the bottom of pans used for roasting to prevent the bottom of meat from frying.

Robot Coupe: Robot Coupe is a brand name food processor common in professional kitchens; often the name is used as a generic term for food processor or as a verb for processing food.

Rolling pin: A rolling pin is an essential cooking tool if you work with doughs and is a handy device as well for crushing or cracking food (pitting olives for tapenade, cracking peppercorns, for instance). The shape and type of material are a matter of personal preference dependent on how you use them (a marble pin that will maintain cold if you roll a lot of butter rich doughs; a rolling stick that is small and light if you travel with cooking gear).

Rondeau [*rohn-DOH*]: A rondeau is a round shallow pan with straight sides, made in varying sizes with a loop handle on either side and a lid.

Root vegetables: When we say root vegetables, we are usually referring to hard starchy roots, stems, and tubers—potatoes and yams, carrots, beets, and parsnips—rather than other moister softer bulbs and stems, such as onions, radishes, and water chestnuts. They're valued for their variety, versatility, economy, capacity for long storage, and ability to caramelize and add sweetness. They can be boiled, glazed, fried, grilled, and roasted with varying effects.

Rouille: an olive-oil-based sauce, seasoned with red chillis, garlic, and traditionally thickened with bread, usually served with bouillabaisse or fish stew. Mayonnaise or aïoli seasoned with red peppers and other spices is often served as rouille.

Roulade: Roulade can mean a flat piece of meat that is rolled around ingredients and cooked, or it can refer generally to any kind of meat or forcemeat shaped into a cylinder.

Roux: A roux is a paste of cooked flour and fat used to thicken sauces. Though any kind of powdered starch and fat can be used, roux is traditionally made by combining equal parts by weight of flour and butter and cooking the mixture at least until the raw flour taste has cooked out (the flour will begin to smell like pie crust). Roux can be cooked more for deeper levels of flavor and color, depending on the sauce being thickened, from pale to deep brown, though the darker it is the weaker its thickening powers. For even dispersion of the roux, roux is usually added cold to a hot sauce; conversely a hot roux can be added to a cold sauce, which will then thicken upon reheating. Once it has been added and has heated to the point that it's thickened its sauce, the sauce can be moved to the edge of the heat and gently simmered to allow impurities to collect at the cooler side of the pot and be removed for a very clean, smooth sauce. Roux-thickened sauces should have a *nappé* consistency and a smooth feel on the palate, they should not be heavy and starchy. A one to ten ratio (by weight) of roux to sauce will result in a good *nappé* consistency; for example, to thicken 40 ounces of stock, use 4 ounces of light or pale roux.

S

Sachet d'épices [*sah-SHAY day-PEES*]: A *sachet d'épices* is a variety of aromatics wrapped in cheesecloth used to flavor a stock or sauce that is afterward removed from the pot. A traditional mixture of aromatics includes stems of thyme and parsley, bay leaf, garlic, and peppercorns. The reason for the sachet is so that the aromats can be easily removed from the pot; if the stock or sauce is going to be strained, the aromats can be added directly to the pot.

Saddle: a cut, usually of lamb, venison, and rabbit, comprising both sides of the ribs and both loins, in effect the whole back of the animal. Saddles are typically roasted and were once served in restaurants whole to a table for the drama of its presentation and the elegance of the cuts, but this is rarely done anymore, given that tableside service is out of fashion.

Salad: Salads today can be broken down into three broad categories, served cold unless otherwise noted: green, non-green, and composed. Green salads are ones in which the predominant ingredient is tender tasty lettuces. Non-green salads include preparations in which fruit, legumes, a mixture of juli-enned root vegetables, a staple starch, egg, fish, or meat are the main ingredient. Composed salads are those which orchestrate several primary ingredients—meat, cheese, raw or blanched-and-shocked vegetables—in addition to greens (cobb salad, for example, is a traditional composed salad).

Green salad basics are simple: the fresher the lettuce the better the salad (this cannot be overstated); wash your greens and dry them carefully; tear them into convenient sizes and dress just before serving, either with a vinai-grette or simply oil and vinegar. When using oil and vinegar, order matters: salt the greens first, allow the salt to melt so that it will distribute evenly, coat the lettuce with oil, then season with the vinegar. The quality of a non-green salad—bean, potato, pasta, for example—is almost always determined by the sauce, seasoning, and texture (because they're usually soft, they benefit from ingredients that introduce some kind of crunchiness). Composed sal-ads, whether a classic such as niçoise, or Thai salads featuring hot meats or grilled meats served cold, or one simply combining cooked and chilled veg-etables (sometimes called *à la grecque* vegetables), are very likely underused in home kitchens and shouldn't be: they are quick to prepare, healthy, and satisfying.

Salamander: Salamanders are above-stove broilers used in restaurant kitchens, so named, apparently, because they are often used to change the color of food, to give an appealing browned color and texture to a *glaçage* or to finish a gratin.

Salami: the Italian word for dry-cured pork sausages, usually featuring a coarse grind of meat and fat that remain visually distinct.

Salmon: The most significant distinctions in the quality of salmon and how you will cook it are those between farm raised and wild. Wild salmon tends to have a more nuanced flavor, a more appealing texture, often a deeper color and, importantly for the cook, is usually leaner. Also it may be better for you, and is usually more expensive. Farm-raised salmon has a less var-ied flavor than the various species of wild salmon, which are found in the colder waters of the Pacific and Atlantic oceans. Farm-raised salmon also tends to be fattier than wild. Thus, wild salmon should be cooked very gen-tly and never cooked beyond medium rare or it will be dry and flavorless.

Farmed salmon is much more tolerant of heat. Evidence that farm-raising salmon may have a harmful environmental impact, not to mention a lesser flavor, suggests that it's better to purchase wild salmon when the choice is available and affordable. Salmon is served raw (though it's best to use only wild salmon for raw preparations), cured and cooked, and cooking methods are various—grilling, roasting, sautéing, poaching.

Salpicon [*sahl-pi-KOHN*]: *Salpicon* is a French term for diced meat or fish bound with a sauce (or with a syrup or cream in a fruit *salpicon*) and used as an *appareil* or a filling.

Salsa: the Italian and Spanish word for sauce. Here we usually use the term to denote the Mexican preparation of chopped tomatoes, aromatic vegetables, and piquant seasonings. It can be green (from tomatillos and green chillis) or red (from tomatoes and red chillis), cooked or raw, and is usually served cold, but the term salsa can be used for Italian, Spanish, and Mexican sauces in general.

Salt: Salt is arguably the most important and powerful ingredient in the kitchen, and many chefs consider the ability to use salt well to be the most important skill a cook can have. It's used in dishes across the board, from savory to sweet, on protein, vegetable, and grain. It is a preservative more powerful than any other, one that alters taste and texture of meats and vegetables. General rules for seasoning with salt are few: always use salt that has not been iodized, which gives the salt a harsh chemical flavor; kosher salt is the best all-purpose salt for cooking and seasoning, though sea salt is good, too. Countless special salts are marketed, from flavored salts to salts from specific rock formations and eras. Taste and evaluate unfamiliar salts before buying and using them.

Salt food far enough in advance of eating what's being salted for it to melt and distribute itself. Use salt earlier rather than later in the cooking process. Salt meat well in advance of cooking it; it is possible to oversalt meat, but it is not possible to salt meat too early; the larger the cut of meat, the earlier that meat should be salted. The delicate flesh of fish can be "burned" by salt if it's seasoned too early; fish should be seasoned very close to cooking it.

When salting cooking water for grains, pastas, and legumes, taste the water after you've salted it; however salted the water is, that's about how salted the finished food will be; the water should taste pleasantly sea-soned, not salty (see salted water).

Many people are concerned by salt warnings. While it's true that con-suming too much salt can be bad for you, the majority of the salt we eat today is hidden in processed foods; unless you have hypertension, high blood pressure, or water retention, salting foods properly is not a health issue in a diet composed of natural and nonprocessed food. (See the essay Salt, page 18.)

"Salt and pepper to taste": See "to taste."

Salt cod: Cod is one of the most important foods in the history of Western civilization because its meat preserved so well, most commonly with salt. Cod that has been salted, then dried, is a versatile ingredient in contempo-rary kitchens. One of the oldest commonly preserved foods, salt cod, cod that has been salted and dried, remains a popular staple in many regions and is included in many preparations, as both a featured protein and as ingre-dient. Quality varies; salt cod that's been sitting around for a long time can have picked up off flavors. The best salt cod is that which you preserve your-self (packed in salt for a day, then rinsed and left to dry in the refrigerator till it's thoroughly stiff). It can be cooked whole, poached or fried, eaten with a simple sauce, shredded and mixed with cream, garlic, and potatoes for a brandade, or added to a fish stew, or eaten raw, sliced thin like pro-sciutto. All salt cod must be rehydrated and desalinated before using, one or two days in cold water that's refreshed regularly.

Salt cured: See cure (almost all curing involves salt).

Salted water: "Salted water" can mean different concentrations of salt depending on what the water will be cooking; salted water does not mean a pinch of salt has been added. For pasta, grains, and legumes, enough salt should be added so that the water tastes pleasantly seasoned, between 2 and 3 tablespoons of Morton's kosher salt (or between 1 and 1.5 ounces of any noniodized salt) per gallon; evaluate it just as you would evaluate a soup for proper seasoning level; the salt level of the water will mirror the salt concen-tration absorbed by the food. For cooking green vegetables, heavily salted water is recommended: between ¾ and 1 cup of Morton's kosher salt (or between 6 and 8 ounces) per gallon of water. The brand is important only when measuring by volume; Diamond Crystal, another common kosher salt, is just as good but is lighter than Morton's. When measuring by weight, the type of kosher salt is not significant.

Saltpeter: Saltpeter, or potassium nitrate, once used for curing meats (bacon, corned beef, dry-cured sausage, et cetera), has been replaced by sodium nitrite and sodium nitrate in the United States because the effects of sodium nitrite and nitrate are more consistent than those of saltpeter, but it's still commonly used in Europe.

Salt pork: Salt pork, usually made with chunks from the belly and the shoulder, has been preserved solely with salt and is used as a seasoning in soups, stews, and legumes. It's rarely prepared as a main dish. It's very easy to cure at home: dredge pork scraps or chunks of pork from the shoulder in salt, cover, and refrigerate for a week, redredge and cover for a second week, then rinse and pat dry. Well wrapped, these will keep for many weeks in the refrigerator and, of course, indefinitely in the freezer.

"Salt to taste": See "to taste."

Salumi: the Italian term for dry-cured meats and sausages such as prosciutto and soppressata (note that salami only refers to dry-cured sausages). (See also the French term charcuterie, a broad category that also includes cooked preparations such as pâtés and confits.) The craft of salumi is heavily indebted to the pig; its reason for being was originally food preservation, but it remains a vibrant part of Italy's culinary tradition and is enjoying something of a rebirth in American cooking as contemporary chefs have become interested in dry-curing their own meats and sausages. Salumi is often served at the beginning of a meal or as an hors d'oeuvres.

Saturated fat: See fat.

Sauce: Sauce is a fundamental component of most dishes. Any fat, acid, or liquid that adds complementary flavors, seasoning, texture, and richness functions as the sauce. While we tend to think of sauce as an identifiable and separately created component, Bolognese sauce on pasta, béarnaise sauce on steak, giblet gravy on turkey, sauce is everywhere, from the butter on a baked potato to the mayo in the tuna salad to the oil and vinegar on mixed greens to the ice cream on your pie. (See the essay Sauce, page 12.)

Saucepan, sauce pot: A saucepan is a small high-sided pan, usually one to two quarts; the high sides relative to its diameter allow for slow reduction and gentle cooking of sauces. Technically a pot has high sides and a pan has low, but in kitchens sauce pots are usually referred to as saucepans.

Saucier: The *saucier* is the member of the kitchen in charge of the sauces, often considered the most prestigious position in a traditional *brigade,* which indicates both the skill required for great sauces and also the importance of the sauce in French *haute cuisine.*

Sausage: Sausage is little more than ground meat, fat, salt, and seasonings, mixed till they're bound. Sausage can be cooked any number of ways—in patties, like ground meat, in a loaf, stuffed into casings and grilled, roasted, sautéed, or poached. If you have a grinder, sausage is very easy to make: a basic ratio includes meat and fat (fat should make up 25 to 30 percent of the total weight) and between .25 and .3 ounces of kosher salt per pound, about a half tablespoon of Morton's kosher salt. (The brand is important only when measuring by volume; Diamond Crystal, another common kosher salt, is just as good but is about 40% lighter than Morton's by volume. When measuring by weight, the type of kosher salt is not significant.) Sausage can also be thought of as a technique, one way of tenderizing a tough cut of meat or as a way of extending what you already have. Of all the methods by which we transform a tough inexpensive cut of meat into something exquisite and delicious, this is one of the best.

Sauté: a "dry-heat" cooking method, the French verb for "jump," used for tender cuts of meat and other items such as vegetables that don't require tenderizing, done in a pan using a small amount of oil. Sauté is usually accomplished with very high heat, to give flavor to the exterior of what's being cooked, but there are many levels of sauté depending on what's being cooked. A duck breast, for example, is usually sautéed over very low heat to render the fat from the skin. The proper heating of the pan before the fat or the food goes into it is an important part of sautéing as is choosing the right-sized pan (too large and the item can dry and/or burn, too small and the item or items can be crowded and steam rather than brown, and also cool down the pan and stick). Sauté technique also includes the development of fond on the bottom of the pan, browned proteins and sugars from the food that, when deglazed, can add flavor to a sauce made in the pan.

Sauté pan: A sauté pan is one with shallow sloping sides, also called a *sauteuse*.

Sauteuse, sautoire [soh-TOOZ, soh-TWAHR]: These are two types of shallow sauté pans. A *sauteuse* has sloping sides, which facilitates "jumping" food, and which are less likely to trap steam. A *sautoire* has straight sides and sometimes comes with a cover (for pan-steaming, for instance); a *sautoire* is a good pan for pan-frying as well, but because the sides don't facilitate a flow of air around the food the way sloping sides do, a *sauteuse* should be used for pan-roasting.

Savory: Savory means not sweet. The word can refer to specific dishes as well as a section of a menu, savory courses and sweet (dessert) courses, or to the kitchen itself, as distinguished from the sweet kitchen or the pastry kitchen (where desserts and sweets are made).

Scale (noun): A good digital scale is an important kitchen tool because it provides the most accurate way of measuring ingredients, which is especially critical in baking. A tablespoon of different brands of salt has different weights but an ounce of salt will have the same impact no matter the type or brand. Flour and other finely powdered ingredients measured by the dry cup can vary in weight as well. A scale is recommended for any serious kitchen.

Scale (verb): To scale means to weigh—for example, "Scale that dough into 10-ounce portions for small baguettes."

Seam: To seam, or to seam out, is to remove layers of connective tissue from between layers of muscle; the technique, for example, is used on fish so that the final dish is refined and delicate, seaming out tuna to make a tartare, or a leg of lamb to separate it into its component muscles.

Sear: To cook protein, usually meat (though some fish and shellfish as well), over very high heat to give the surface color, texture, and a more complex flavor is called searing. Searing does not "seal in juices," a common dictate debunked by McGee in the early 1980s (in fact, high heat contributes to their expulsion from the meat). When the proteins that compose meat hit very high heat, many complex flavors result. Searing also makes the item visually appealing and creates a contrasting texture to the soft interior. It's possible to sear meat in advance and chill it immediately so that it can be finished later in the oven just before serving (which you might want to do, for instance, if you needed the stovetop space for other *à la minute* preparations; be sure to allow the pre-seared meat to come up to room temperature before finishing). Searing is one of the most influential applications of heat to protein.

Season: To season means to flavor. Because we almost always use salt to enhance flavor, the verb is often used to mean salting. Seasoning can also refer to applying other seasoning or flavor enhancing ingredients whether it's a common one, such as freshly ground black pepper or vinegar, or uncommon, fennel powder or powdered orange zest.

Season (pans): Iron pans benefit from "seasoning," that is, coating its porous surface with a layer of oil, heating it, and allowing it to cool. A properly seasoned pan will have a nearly nonstick surface. To season a pan, fill it with about an inch of oil; bring the oil almost to smoking and turn off the heat. Allow the oil to cool completely, pour out the oil (if you haven't burned the oil you can reuse it), and wipe the pan clean with paper towels. To maintain this seasoning, do not wash the pan with soap, use only water; salt can be used as an abrasive for scrubbing. If for whatever reason you compromise the seasoning of the pan, scrub the pan thoroughly with a steel scouring pad so that it is perfectly clean and re-season it.

Season, seasonal (foods and dishes): While restaurant kitchens can buy just about any kind of food they want any time of year, home cooks are wise to prepare foods that are in season and also cook dishes that we associate with seasons. This means not only cooking asparagus in the spring and hard squash in the fall, it means cooking onion soup *au gratin* in January rather than in August. When you cook seasonally, you are most likely cooking what is at its peak of flavor, so the finished dishes taste better, are better for you, and have spent less time on the road getting to your store. Cooking seasonally not only makes good common sense, it also has flavor, health, and environmental advantages for the restaurant chef and the home cook alike.

Sec [*sek*]: The word *sec* means dry in French and can refer to dry cured sausages or is often used with regard to reductions, specifically to boiling almost all the liquid out of a reduction. When making a reduction of wine, shallots, and herbs to *sec,* there should be no liquid rolling around in the pan but the shallots and herbs should remain moist.

Sense, senses: Your senses are the most important tools in the kitchen. Use them all, pay attention, remember what you see, hear, taste, touch, and smell. Listen to your food, tune into the sounds of the various foods as they cook; pay attention to the ambient aroma of a kitchen and to subtle changes that indicate freshness, spoilage, degree of doneness, or burning. Pay attention to texture and resistance; how does undercooked or over-cooked meat feel? Bread dough? An underripe tomato? Is the color of the meat too pale, not seared enough? Too dark, charred and bitter? Has the sauce caramelized instead of simply reduced? How large are the bubbles in that reducing cream? A good cook engages all his or her senses in countless ways in the kitchen.

Serrated knife: Serrated knives, those with visible sawlike teeth, are good for cutting bread and a few other items with a tough crust or crumb, and so you should have one. They otherwise have limited uses because sawing food can easily damage it.

Shallot: Shallots are one of the most powerful onions in the cook's pantry because they're mild, sweet, and flavorful when cooked. This sweetness is especially valuable in sauces, in which they can be used either cooked in hot sauces or raw in vinaigrettes and mayonnaises, though raw shallot should be used judiciously. Their harsher effects can be eliminated by macerating them in vinegar; raw shallots are volatile, so they should be cut and incorporated into the food the day you're serving it (that is, don't add them to a vinaigrette that will sit for several days in the refrigerator). They are also wonderful sautéed and used as a garnish, deep-fried, roasted whole, and glazed.

Shallow poach: Shallow poach is a "moist heat" form of cooking in which the food is cooked in a small amount of liquid *a la minute*; used for natu-rally lean items such as fish. The standard method for shallow poaching is to choose a pan close to the size of the items you'll be cooking; use enough liquid—usually a stock, aromatics, and an acid—to come up about halfway on the item being cooked; often the pan is covered so that steam will cook the exposed surface. The item is removed from the pan and held while the cooking liquid, the *cuisson,* is reduced and finished with seasonings, herbs and/or aromatics, mounted with butter, and used as the sauce.

Shank: The shank is a cut just above the hoof of lamb and beef, a heavily worked muscle with lots of connective tissue that must be cooked low and slow, usually by braising.

Sharpie: This brand of permanent marker is excellent for dating and labeling food; keep one in your tool drawer along with painters' tape.

Sheet pan: A sheet pan is an important kitchen tool for baking so it's wise to spend money on good ones made of heavy-gauge aluminum that won't buckle and burn the food. A heavy sheet pan will conduct heat better, and it will stay flat and sturdy if you don't continually put it scalding hot under cold water. Sheets are available flat or with shallow sides.

Shellfish: Shellfish are divided into two categories—crustaceans and molluscs—and they share many traits. They are usually tender and so don't require much cooking, if any, and they tend to carry the flavors of where they live, what they ate.

Molluscs include abalone, mussels, clams, oysters, scallops, squid (whose shell is on the inside), all of which benefit from brief gentle cooking at most. Oysters, of course, may be the one animal we eat while it's alive and is prized for a range of unique flavors and textures. Crustaceans include lobsters, crabs, shrimp, and crayfish, and can be cooked in numerous ways—poach, roast, grill, sauté. Overcooking them will make them rubbery, so even though their shells contain a strong robust muscle, it's best to cook and season crustaceans gently.

Shock: To shock means to plunge into ice water in order to halt the cooking. Green vegetables are commonly boiled in salted water and immediately shocked.

Shoemaker: Shoemaker is kitchen slang for an untalented cook.

Shorten, shortening: Shortening is what keeps the protein in flour called gluten from forming long strands that make flour-and-water doughs elastic and, when cooked, chewy. The fat in a flour-and-water mixture *shortens* these strands so that the resulting dough will be tender and delicate (not desirable in, for instance, a baguette; a bread lacking a good chewy texture might be said to be "short"). Until recently, hydrogenated vegetable oil was the most common shortening available, but concern about trans fats has resulted in new processes for making vegetable oil solid at room temperature; if you buy vegetable shortening, choose one without trans fats. Butter is an excellent and rich shortener. Pork fat can be rendered for lard, and is an excellent shortening, especially good to use for savory crusts.

Shoulder: The shoulder is a common cut from pigs, lamb, and cows, a heavily worked muscle that must be cooked in a way that addresses its tough connective tissue (cooked low and slow or ground). Pork shoulder is often referred to as butt, Boston butt, or shoulder butt; because of its good fat content, this cut is often the one used to make sausage.

Sieve: A sieve is made of fine mesh; food is passed through it to give the food a uniform texture and remove impurities (connective tissue in a mousseline, for instance); "to sieve" means to pass food through a sieve. The word for sieve in French is tamis, and this term is often used when referring to a drum sieve; a conical sieve, used for straining sauces and stocks, is called a chinois tamis. The sieve is a tool of refinement; it's not strictly necessary to have in the kitchen but it's convenient and helpful to have and is required for some special preparations.

Skim: To remove impurities from the surface of liquids is one of the key steps in ensuring a stock or a sauce has as clean a flavor and feel as possible. It's best to skim stocks early, just after they've reached their simmer, when blood and protein has congealed and risen along with unwanted particles but while the water is still flavorless. Refined sauces should be skimmed continually throughout their cooking. The most efficient tool for skimming is a ladle, pushing fat and impurities away from the center with a circular motion so that they gather at the sides of the pot and are more easily picked up.

Skirt: Skirt is a unique cut of beef, the flavorful striated diaphragm; the skirt from the hog (and lamb) is also an excellent cut extending from the spareribs. The beef skirt is chewy but can be sautéed or grilled, or julienned and quickly stir-fried; the pork skirt is tougher and should be cooked low and slow to tenderize it (it's like eating spareribs without the bone).

Slab bacon: Slab bacon is useful to the cook in that it can be cut to the cook's specifications, chunks for stew, lardons for salad, or not at all, but rather roasted whole, then sliced.

Slicing knife: A slicing knife has a long thin blade often fluted along its length, with a rounded tip; it's used for slicing meats when very thin slices are desired, such as cured salmon. Its length allows for long strokes, helping you to make very clean cuts.

Slotted spoon: A slotted spoon is one with slots to allow liquid to drain from it. A slotted or perforated spoon is an essential cooking and serving utensil.

Slow Food: Slow Food is an international organization and movement that aims to protect the best of food—the growing, making, cooking, and eating of it—from the homogenized, corporate-driven, heavily processed food and fast food that increasingly dominates the contemporary diet. (For more information, see its site, slowfood.com.) "Slow food" has become linked to such terms as artisanal and hand-crafted and is now applied to items made this way, implying a style and attitude toward cooking.

Slurry: A slurry is a mixture of a pure starch, such as cornstarch or arrowroot, and water used to thicken sauces. It's often used in conjunction with the word lié (*jus de veau lié* is veal stock thickened with a slurry). Slurries should be mixed to the consistency of heavy cream; they should be stirred immediately before being added (the starch granules aren't soluble in cold water and will sink to the bottom), and then should be added in a thin stream to hot liquids while stirring continuously (it won't gelatinize or thicken till the water hits simmering temperatures; added too fast, it can clump). Slurries are excellent for last minute thickening, but remember that the thickening will break down after repeated or extended cooking. While it's best to mix a slurry by sight and add it to the hot liquid until you've reached the desired consistency, a basic ratio is one tablespoon of cornstarch mixed with one tablespoon of water, which will thicken to medium consistency one cup of water.

Smell: one of the most important senses in both cooking and eating. With only a few exceptions, food needs to smell good and will often be your first indication that you're cooking well.

Smoke, smoking: We smoke foods to give them additional flavor and color. As McGee notes, woodsmoke, created by heat breaking down plant tissues, is a flavoring composed of some of the same compounds found in spices. Smoking falls into a few different categories, mainly determined by the heat level. The most common form of smoking is for cured foods, such as bacon, ham, and sausages, food that is gently cooked as it's smoked in temperatures between 150° and 200°F. This is called hot smoking. Cold smoking is used for foods that you don't want to be cooked as they're smoked, such as salmon or cheese. Cold smoking means smoking food at temperatures of 90°F or below (the lower the better). Smoking above 300°F is called smoke roasting. Smoking is also done in kitchens but for briefer periods on the stovetop (stovetop smokers are widely available; it's best to have good ventilation if you intend to do any stovetop smoking). Hardwoods such as hickory and maple and fruitwoods such as apple are excellent to use for smoking (avoid pinewood or other softwoods that will give off a harsh, resinous smoke), as is tea. Smoke is a flavoring device that can be used on fish, meats, dairy, vegetables, and nuts. It can have a powerful effect, so use it judiciously.

Smoke point: The smoke point refers to the temperature at which oil begins to break down; it begins to smoke. Vegetable oils begin to smoke at around 450°F, animal fat begins to smoke at temperatures at around 375°F (see McGee).

Smoke roast: A dry-heat cooking method that combines high temperature and smoke, used to enhance the flavor of meat with smoke as it cooks. Smoke roasting is defined by a temperature of 300°F or higher inside the smoker. Smoke roasting can be done on a stovetop (using a stovetop smoker and good ventilation), in a traditional smoker, or in a barbecue grill.

Smoker: A variety of containers and cookers are used to smoke foods. They're mainly categorized by the type of smoke they offer. The most common types of smokers on the market are big kettles in which the fuel burns at the bottom and slowly cooks the food as it smokes the food. This is called smoke roasting. Smokers in which the smoke source is separate from the smoke container, or smoke box, allow for much more temperature control so that you can smoke items such as bacon and ham for many hours if you wish, or even cold smoke fish. For indoor use, there are stovetop smokers, covered pans that sit on a burner, that heat wood chips or dust, to smoke and flavor the food. Standard kettle barbecues can also be used to smoke food.

Sodium nitrate: Sodium nitrate is a curing salt used solely in dry-cured sausages to prevent botulism poisoning. It is in effect sodium nitrite with a small amount of nitrate added to it, which converts over time to nitrite, which prevents the growth of the bacteria that causes botulism in warm anaerobic conditions. (See also sodium nitrite.)

Sodium nitrite: Sodium nitrite, salt with 6.25 percent nitrite added to it, is a curing salt used to prevent botulism poisoning in sausages and smoked items, as well as to enhance flavor and color. It's what gives cured pork that distinctive hammy taste and rosy hue; it will give chicken and turkey a pink, hammy flavor as well. It's often referred to as pink salt, generically, because it's sold under various brand names. Sodium nitrite is used in the curing of bacon, ham, ham hocks, Canadian bacon, and smoked sausages. Skepticism surrounds it because it has been linked to the formation of cancer-causing nitrosamines under certain conditions. Furthermore, in large quantities it is toxic, even lethal (it's tinted pink to prevent people from accidentally ingesting it). But there has been little research that definitively suggests it's harmful in the quantities in which we eat it, far less than our ancestors ate. Nitrite and nitrate are chemicals that occur naturally in many vegetables and while there's no reason to overindulge in hot dogs and bacon that include sodium nitrite, neither should it be considered dangerous or taboo in moderation.

Soft ball stage: a term referring to a specific temperature of sugar, around 240°F, and the consistency it achieves having reached that temperature and being chilled—solid but pliable. It's used for fudge, fondant, pralines, Italian meringues, and buttercream.

Soft crack stage: a term referring to a specific temperature of sugar, around 280°F, used for taffy and other chewy candies.

Soigné [*swahn-YAY*]: the French term for elegance and excellence of execution. (See finesse.)

Soufflé: The soufflé technique takes advantage of egg white's ability to trap bubbles of air for an elegant dish that can be savory or sweet. Soufflés are less fragile and difficult than their reputation suggests and because both the *appareil,* or base (where the flavor is), and the egg whites whipped to peaks, can be readied well beforehand, or combined and frozen; they're even convenient. The common ratio is equal parts by weight egg white and *appareil.* The *appareil* should taste overseasoned because it will be mixed with unseasoned egg white. Common *appareils* are béchamel for savory soufflés and pastry cream or fruit purees for sweet ones. When you're ready to cook the soufflé, fold the whipped whites into the *appareil,* gently to avoid losing trapped air, until it's uniformly distributed. Spoon it into ramekins that have been thoroughly buttered and dusted with sugar or flour and bake in a hot oven for about 20 minutes. Serve immediately. A soufflé has achieved its height because it's filled with hot air; as this air cools the soufflé will collapse. The egg whites and the *appareil* can be made ahead of time, but they should be combined shortly before cooking; or they can be combined, portioned and frozen, then cooked. Frozen soufflés cook with good result but it's best to mix and cook them *à la minute.*

Soup: Soups can be divided into three broad categories—clear, cream, and puree—and these categories inform how we should think about soups. Clear soups are composed of stock or broth and solid ingredients and the two are kept separate and distinct (chicken noodle soup, onion soup). Cream soups are traditionally starch thickened (whether directly with a roux, or using a roux-based mother sauce, béchamel or velouté) and finished with cream (cream of broccoli, cream of mushroom). Puree soups become thick and opaque by pureeing the main ingredient (gazpacho, black bean soup). Inevitably there's crossover, especially given how few soups are thickened with starch given today's fashion (starch-thickened soups can be exquisite and should not be dismissed); many purees are finished with cream, for instance, and a cream of mushroom soup need not be thickened with starch. But when you think about cooking soup, it's useful first to imagine what type of soup you're after, rather than the ingredients that will go into it; instead of reading listings of soup recipe titles, think first, "Clear, cream, or puree?"—then move on to type of cuisine, seasonality, et cetera. The quality of clear soups is determined by the quality of the liquid used and the proper cooking of the ingredients (boiling them will cloud the soup and deteriorate delicate garnish); the quality of a cream soup is often relative to both its texture and the proper intensity of flavor of the main ingredient, which shouldn't be overpowered or washed out by by the liquid; nor should it be held at high temperatures for longer than necessary or the flavor can become stale and unpleasant. The quality of pureed soups, which typically have a coarser texture, is determined by the quality of the main ingredient, the stock used to cook the ingredient and the aromatics that flavored the stock. Secondary issues include seasoning and garnish; cream and pureed soups especially benefit from an acid seasoning, sherry vinegar for a lentil soup, for instance, white wine vinegar for a cream of cauliflower.

Sourdough: Sourdough is a technique rather than a type of bread. A sourdough bread is made using natural yeast (see starter) rather than commercial yeast, and gets some of its flavor from the acid released by the yeast. The acid generated by natural yeast is what gives the dough its name, but a sourdough bread should not be overly sour, an indication that the yeast has overfermented.

Sous chef: Literally under chef, the sous chef is second in command in the kitchen hierarchy.

Sous vide [*sue-VEED*]: Sous vide is French for under vacuum, that is vacuum sealed in a plastic pouch, and the term usually indicates that a food has been prepared or cooked within that plastic. Sous vide provides a method of cooking food at very low temperatures that results in textures that are otherwise unattainable. In busy restaurant kitchens, sous vide techniques also give a measure of convenience in that sous vide food can hit the right point of doneness and remain there for a long time without compromise. The drawbacks of cooking sous vide are that because of the low temperatures, it has no flavor from searing or caramelization, and also no crunchiness or textural contrast, factors that can be addressed in how a cook finishes a sous vide preparation, and that it can feel sterile to the cook, with no aromas, no sounds from the cooking. Cooking sous vide has become both fashionable in restaurants and controversial because of the safety issues involved with cooking at low temperatures in the anaerobic environment of the sealed pouch and because of the concern that it diminshes the craftmanship in cooking.

Spatula: There are many different types of spatulas used for purposes of turning, stirring, scraping, and spreading, and a good kitchen has a few different types and sizes. Perhaps the most useful spatula style is the offset spatula whose two angles make turning food easier than the more common spatula that has only one angle. Spatulas are always the preferred tool for turning food (rather than turning food with tongs, which can damage the food). Rubber spatulas are fundamental kitchen tools for stirring, folding, and efficiently transferring batters from one container to another.

Spices: The main issue with spices is their freshness—the fresher, the better. For optimal quality, buy spices whole rather than ground and in small quantities so that they don't linger in a cupboard or on a spice rack. Spices' volatile oils, their flavor, is drawn out by heat, so toasting them in a dry pan before grinding them greatly enhances their effect. Spices become insipid over time; smell and taste your spices to evaluate their quality before using.

Spider: A large flat mesh ladle used for retrieving fried items from hot fat is called a spider.

Sponge: 1) In bread making, a sponge indicates a method of yeast dough fermentation in which part of the flour and water and all the yeast are combined and fermented for a few hours before the rest of the ingredients are added, a technique that allows for a longer fermentation time and therefore more flavor. 2) Kitchen sponges are one of the most bacteria-ridden implements in your kitchen; they should be sterilized periodically, either with a bleach solution, or by boiling them or heating them wet in the microwave.

Sponge cake: Sponge cakes are those that use the foaming method with whole eggs—whole eggs and sugar, often heated to melt the sugar, are whipped till frothy, after which the remaining ingredients are folded in and the mixture is baked immediately to maintain as many of the trapped air bubbles as possible.

Springform pan: Springform pans have a clip that tightens and locks the pan around a separate bottom; when the clip is unlocked, it opens and the bottom (and the food cooked in the pan) is released from the sides of the pan. It's used for items that would be difficult to remove from a standard cake pan, such as cheesecake.

Stage, stagiere [*stazj, STAH-zjee-air*]: French for training period or probation, *stage* refers to a brief, unpaid period of work in a kitchen for the purpose of learning or training; the one doing the *stage* is referred to as a *stagiere*. Staging can be an essential part of an apprentice cook's training. The best kitchens can have waiting lists of people willing to work for free in order to learn.

Standard breading procedure: See breading.

Starch: 1) Starch, a polysaccharide, is composed of sugar molecules. For the cook, starch is used specifically for its thickening power, which it achieves by absorbing water, thus expanding, and throwing off smaller starch molecules (see McGee for detailed description, illustrations, and photos). Starches are divided into two categories, grain starches and root starches. While starches behave differently, the main distinction for the cook is between a pure starch and one that's not. Pure starches have been separated from protein and other molecules. Cornstarch is a pure starch; flour is not. So when thickening a sauce with flour, as in a roux (the butter separates the starch grains), the proteins (such as the insoluble gluten) and other molecules need to cook out, or rise to the top to be removed by the cook's skimming. With pure starches, neither fat nor skimming is required. 2) Starch is also kitchen vernacular for the starchy carbohydrate in a traditional meal (along with protein and vegetable).

Starter: Starter usually refers to sourdough starter, a mixture of flour, water, and a culture of natural yeasts that leaven the dough. It can also refer to any live culture added to the main ingredients to make a fermented product, such as yogurt.

Steam: a "moist-heat" cooking technique that is gentle, uniform, and typically does not impart its own flavors to what's being cooked, as higher temperature cooking can do. Steaming is usually used for fish, tender cuts of meat, and vegetables.

Steel: A steel is a kitchen tool used for honing knives, not sharpening them. A knife blade is composed of microscopic teeth, and a blade becomes dull when these teeth get out of alignment; a steel works by aligning these teeth. You can't sharpen a knife on a steel; regular use of a steel helps to maintain a sharp edge.

Stew: a moist-heat cooking method used for tougher cuts of meat. Stews are roughly distinguished from braises in that in a stew, the meat is cut into smaller pieces, there's an abundance of liquid, and it's composed of multiple ingredients all served in the cooking liquid. Otherwise all the same rules apply to stews as they do to braises: low gentle heat, optimally the cooking liquid should be about 180°F and never brought to a full boil. (See braise.) Stews, like braises, typically benefit from browning the meat for flavor before submerging it in the cooking liquid, but not always; in preparations such as *blanquette de veau,* the meat is blanched to remove some of the impurities first.

Stir-fry: Stir-fry is a "dry-heat" cooking method distinguished by very high heat and short cooking time, used for tender cuts of meat and tender vegetables. Traditional stir-fry involves a wok and a heat level beyond the reach of most home kitchens, so it's difficult to achieve at home the flavors offered by professional stir-fry equipment. But you can come close by using a very heavy-gauged pan, getting it very, very hot before adding cooking oil, and stir-frying in small batches so that the food doesn't cool down the pan.

Stock: a flavorful liquid made by gently heating vegetables, aromatics, bones, and meat to be used in the preparation of other dishes or other applications. The two fundamental factors affecting the quality of a stock are first, the quality of ingredients and second, the maintenance of gentle heat (between 160° and 180°F) for a time appropriate to the ingredients (bones require a long cooking time; vegetables cooked that long will begin to break down and compromise the flavor and yield of the stock). While you should feel comfortable measuring by sight, a common ratio for meat stock is eight pounds of bones in eight quarts of water and a pound of mirepoix will yield a gallon of stock. Using less water and/or more bone and vegetables will result in a more powerfully flavored stock. In addition to traditional mirepoix, other appropriate aromats can include leeks, tomatoes, and sachet ingredients such as parsley, thyme, bay, and peppercorns. Only use floral or sweet ingredients; don't use your stockpot like a garbage pail. (See the essay Stock, page 3.) If you're choosing store-bought stock, avoid sodium-heavy products, and remember there's a big range in quality that makes an equally big impact on the finished dish. The quality that results from stocks you make yourself is unmatched by what you can purchase. If you don't have stock, and a recipe calls for it, often water is preferable to canned broths.

Stockpot: A heavy-gauge pot that holds at least a gallon and a half is part of a well-stocked kitchen. Pots that hold more than that are helpful not only for making larger quantities of stock but for other uses as well, such as brining larger cuts of meat or whole birds.

Strainer: Of the variety of strainers available, the main consideration is the fineness of the mesh. A fine mesh strainer is often referred to as a chinois and is used to strain stocks and sauces. All-purpose kitchen strainers and China caps have a wider mesh and are used more to allow liquid to pour through it rather than to trap impurities, which is the main purpose of a chinois.

String: See butcher's string.

Subprimal: Primal cuts—the large initial breakdown of a carcass into a saddle, a hind quarter, et cetera—are broken down into smaller cuts called subprimals (the loin taken from the saddle, for instance, is a subprimal cut).

Suet: Beef fat from around the kidneys, very hard at room temperature, can be rendered and used as a cooking medium or even for larding and barding—a very flavorful, highly saturated fat.

Sugar: Sugar comes in many forms and from many sources, from sugarcane and beets to maple trees, to corn. Pure table sugar is a remarkable substance and stands with salt as one of the most valuable culinary ingredients a cook has. Dissolve it in water with some acid, heat it, and it becomes syrup to sweeten sorbet. Cook it a bit more and it becomes the material for the spokes and weavers of a spun-sugar basket. Sugar can disappear within a dish so that you don't notice its effects, or it can create a chewy texture or a brittle one. Put some vanilla beans in sugar, let it sit for a few days, and you've got a handy flavoring and sweetener for whipped cream.

The flavor of most dishes is an interplay of sweet, salty, acidic, and bitter tastes. When the sweet component is low, a pinch of sugar may be all you need to achieve the harmony your palate expects. In savory preparations, sugar is often an overlooked and underappreciated seasoning.

When you want sweetening, remember there are more options in your pantry than pure table sugar. You don't have to sweeten whipping cream with table sugar; compound sugars like brown sugar will give you a more complex sweetness. How are you serving the whipped cream? If it was with a lemon confection you might sweeten it with a fine honey. Perhaps you want the appealing bitterness of molasses in a marinade or cure to balance the salt. Table sugar is undeniably an effective and economical tool in the cook's repertoire, but remember that it's not your only option for adding sweetness to a dish.

Supreme: 1) This cut of chicken, in which the breast is taken off the bone with one joint of wing still attached (sometimes Frenched, that is, with the wing bone cleaned), provides an elegant way to serve the pedestrian breast. The word is sometimes used to apply to a fillet generally and even segmented citrus fruit. 2) Supreme is the name of a classical sauce—chicken velouté, finished with cream, mushrooms, and butter.

Sweat: To sweat means to cook vegetables or fishbones over low heat so that they begin to release their moisture without browning. We sweat vegetables, often onions, because cooking them helps to develop their flavor but sometimes we don't want either the deep color or the intense sweetness of caramelization. Meat and bones being roasted for stock will sweat if they're too crowded in the pan, and they won't brown properly.

Sweetbread: This gland, usually from calves, is prized for its richness and texture. Traditionally, sweetbreads are soaked to remove residual blood, then brought to a simmer in court bouillon, then shocked, after which their outer membrane is removed. They are then pressed beneath weights as they chill to enhance their texture. They can be finished in numerous ways, from a quick sauté to an inlay in a terrine.

T

Tablespoon: A tablespoon is ½ fluid ounce or about 15 milliliters. Three teaspoons equal one tablespoon.

Tagine: a shallow earthenware cooking vessel with a conical lid used in North African cuisine. The tagine is used for stovetop cooking (or over live coals); the unfinished interior of the lid absorbs moisture so that the food cooks covered but without a lot of steam condensing on the lid and dripping back into the food. The word can also refer to the dish made in a tagine, usually a spicy stew.

Tail: Tails that can be cooked to good effect include pigs' tails and oxtails, which must be braised or cooked low and slow. Most tails are high in collagen that will add gelatin, and therefore body, to stocks and sauces.

Tallow: Rendered beef fat is called tallow. Once used in the professional kitchen for decorative food sculpture, it's rarely used today.

Tamis [*TA-mee*]: French for sieve, a tamis is also called a drum sieve, a flat mesh through which food is pressed to remove impurities and create a fine texture. Mousselines, for instance, are often passed through a tamis before they're molded and cooked.

Tart: The tart, implying some form of shallow crust, should be thought of as a vehicle, a way to shape and focus a main ingredient or ingredients as well as to introduce contrasting flavor and texture. A tart is a vessel, and it can focus or elevate just about anything other than soup, from savory to sweet, beginning, middle, or end of the meal; the shell can be made in a mold or shaped free-form; the dough is usually flour based but it could be composed of nuts or other ingredients or it might be made from puff pastry or phyllo dough. The tart is an idea. A bunch of caramelized onions in a pan may not seem like much. But put them in a good crust, seasoned well, and you have a caramelized onion tart.

Tart pan: shallow circular pans used for shaping tarts; they come in many sizes and often feature removable bottoms and fluted sides.

Taste: The most important of our senses for cooking, one that is continuously evolving and growing throughout our cooking lives, and the most important act a cook performs. An axiom in the kitchen is: "Always be tasting." The importance of tasting your food throughout its cooking cannot be overstated.

Tea: While tea in all its varieties is a beloved beverage, it can also be used as a seasoning device, the source of additional flavor, whether liquid, gelled, or via the smoke from its leaves. True tea is made from the leaves of a specific plant, but the word tea has come to include any kind of infused liquid.

Teaspoon: A teaspoon equals ⅙ fluid ounce, or about 5 milliliters. Three teaspoons equal a tablespoon.

Temper: 1) To temper food means to avoid or prevent drastic temperature change. Most commonly we refer to tempering eggs; when eggs are combined with a hot liquid, a small amount of that hot liquid is first added to the eggs, then that egg mixture is added to the hot liquid, a procedure that prevents the eggs from curdling. But we might also remove a foie gras from the refrigerator and allow it to temper, or soften as it warms, to make removing veins easier. 2) Temper refers to a procedure worked on chocolate, gently warming and cooling it, so that when the chocolate solidifies, it will have a glossy shine and appealing snap. Failing to temper chocolate properly can result in a grainy texture and a chalky bloom. It's used in formal preparations when chocolate will be used to coat a strawberry, petit fours, candy, or as a glaze for cake.

Tempura: Tempura is a deep-fry technique in traditional Japanese cuisine, the excellence of which is defined by the lightness and crispness of the batter. Traditionally, tempura batter is composed of equal parts by volume water and flour, with an egg yolk for every two cups. It's mixed immediately before dipping and frying the food. Contemporary chefs often add a pure starch to the flour to reduce the percentage of gluten in the batter (which can make the batter tough rather than delicate), as well as baking soda and sparkling water for additional leavening. The item being battered is usually coated with flour first to ensure the batter adheres to it.

Tenderize (meat): With only a couple of exceptions, there are two ways to tenderize meat: mechanically (cutting or grinding or pounding) and by moist-heat cooking. Marinades don't tenderize meat (though enzymes in some fruits can denature some fish protein). Cutting tenderizes by breaking down long tough strands of connective tissue called collagen, and cooking with some form of water melts it and also denatures and coagulates the protein in meat.

Tenderloin: The tenderloin of land animals is a muscle that runs along the spine inside the rib cage. The slender muscle attached to the breast of poultry is also referred to as a tenderloin or tender. In all cases, it's not a heavily worked muscle and is therefore very tender.

Tendon: Tendon, which connects muscle to bone, is composed almost entirely of connective tissue, meaning it's a rich source of gelatin and so will add body to stocks. In some cuisines, notably Chinese, beef and hog tendon are a culinary treat themselves (they're cooked low and slow, served with a rich sauce and a pungent condiment as a counterpoint).

Terrine: Any dish prepared in a terrine mold can be called a terrine (pâtés, commonly cooked in terrine molds, technically are *pâtés en terrine*).

Terrine mold: Terrine molds come in all shapes and sizes, and some have specific purposes such as those for *pâtés en croute,* which have removable bottoms, but most commonly, terrine molds are rectangular and made of earthenware, porcelain or enameled cast iron (the latter often come with lids, which are convenient).

Terroir [*tair-wahr*]: French for soil, and initially used to denote specific traits of wine unique to certain soil, *terroir* has now broadened to be used in describing flavor, dishes, ingredients of a region, and even the character of the cook—any qualities that may be specific to a given locale may be said to reflect the *terroir.*

Texture: Texture is a critical factor in the success of a dish, and in some preparations, such as a custard or a creamed soup or sautéed foie gras, is as important as the taste of the food.

Thermometers: There are three important types of thermometers for the home cook. The first, which is considered an essential piece of equipment, is an instant read pocket thermometer, which can be used to determine the temperature of liquids and of the internal temperatures of meat among other things; these are available in analog and digital readouts, either of which are fine, though digital tends to be more "instant" than analog. The second type, while not essential, is convenient—a digital thermometer-timer with a cable attached allows you to monitor the internal temperature of a dish while it cooks. And the third type of thermometer is a candy thermometer, one able to read the high temperatures of oil and sugar. The once common "meat thermometers" are antiquated—as are their suggested doneness temperatures—and unnecessary. Cooking is about taking food from one temperature to another, so a good instant read thermometer is a critical, and inexpensive, piece of equipment. But having a thermometer is only the first step: using it properly is the next. A common adage in the kitchen is "A thermometer is only as good as the person using it." Pay attention to the placement of your thermometer, know what portion of the food it's measuring, check it in ice water and boiling water to make sure it's giving you accurate readings, and remember that large probes, if cold, can lower the temperature of the meat you're reading.

Thicken: See slurry and roux, the two primary mixtures we use to thicken liquids. Purees of vegetables, fruits, nuts, bread, egg, and herbs can also be used to thicken liquids as can reduction.

Thyme: Thyme is an invaluable aromatic herb and can be used throughout the cooking process from stocks to garnishing finished dishes. Fresh thyme is ubiquitous in the professional kitchen for this reason. It's a hearty perennial and easy to grow in gardens and window boxes alike.

Timbale: A timbale is a circular single-portion mold that gives shape to food, from miniature tarts to custards to the molding of vegetables.

Time: Time is something that has to be well managed in the kitchen—not only cooking times but the way we use time. We tend to use all the time we have in a kitchen, regardless what needs to be accomplished; that is, if we have an hour, we tend to take the whole hour, whether we have five things to do or twenty. We don't think of it often in these terms, but the way we use our time in the kitchen has a substantial impact on the ease and enjoyment of cooking. Generally, the more you get done well in the least time, the better you will be.

It's important to reiterate also that cooks who rely on time to know when something is done put themselves at risk. The answer to "How long should I cook this?" is almost always "It depends." Of course there are standard cooking times (a rice pilaf will be done in 20 minutes) and general orders of magnitude (we poach shrimp for minutes, not hours), but it's always best to rely on your sight, touch, and taste and the food's aroma and sound, to determine when the food is done.

Tofu: Tofu is soymilk that's curdled much like cheese and sold in solid blocks, but can come in a variety of packaging and textures depending on how it's processed. It's often used sliced or cubed in Asian cuisines where it's been a staple for centuries. Tofu has little flavor and so is used to carry other flavors, whether a hot chilli oil or the miso in a delicate broth. Its grainy, curdy texture can be a detriment and so it's often advantageous to crisp the exterior by sautéing or frying it. Tofu is a good source of protein in meatless diets, it can be smoked and added to bean dishes as you would a ham hock or bacon, or it can be blended with vegetarian sauces to give them body.

Tomalley: The soft green flavorful gland in the lobster, often called the liver, the tomalley can be eaten raw or added to sauces as a seasoning, or used to make a compound butter that will be mounted into a sauce for the lobster.

Tomato: Tomato is one of the kitchen's workhorses. Its use as garnish for a salad or sandwich is now reflexive, thoughtless. When they're at their peak, sliced, salted, and eaten with minimal adornment, few things are better. But as an all-purpose ingredient, as a cooking element, tomatoes add sweetness, acidity, and color to countless preparations. Their use in stocks—especially brown stocks, often in the form of tomato paste, which can be used raw or cooked, also called *pincé*—is critical to the finished product. They are an ever-ready sauce base that can be taken in numerous directions depending on how the tomatoes are handled, from raw to roasted to smoked. Even their abundant water, separated from the flesh, is a powerfully flavored liquid. Tomato basics are few: they very widely in quality so pay attention when you choose them (use them with abandon in the summer and fall when they're excellent, use them sparingly in the winter); plum tomatoes are available all year round and are the default choice for sauces and other general uses (find a good canned tomato you like for winter sauces); hydroponically grown tomatoes are also available year-round, uniformly red and unblemished, but these pale by comparison to those that are locally grown and stay on the vine till they're ready to eat. Don't refrigerate tomatoes because it ruins their flavor. Tomatoes to be eaten sliced or diced benefit from early salting, which enhances and intensifies their flavor.

Tomato *concassé* [*KOHN-kah-say*]: *Concassé* refers to raw chopped tomato. "*Concasser*" is French for to pound or crush, but there are levels of refinement depending on how tomato *concassé* will be used. Tomato *concassé* is traditionally made by blanching and shocking plum tomatoes to remove their skin; the tomatoes are quartered or halved, the seeds are removed, and the tomato flesh is roughly chopped. Tomatoes can also be quartered, their seeds and inner meat removed to make what are called tomato petals, which can be cut into a julienne, into diamonds for garnish or chopped into *concassé*.

Tomato petal: Peeled quartered seeded tomatoes, usually plum tomatoes, used to cut into diamonds for garnish or chopped for *concassé,* are called tomato petals.

Tongs: Tongs are a valuable kitchen tool for lifting items out of hot oil, retrieving a sauté pan out of a hot oven, turning food in a pan, but they must be used carefully. Delicate food can rip and tear or be bruised and mauled. Turning large or heavy food with tongs can also damage the food from its own weight. Tongs range in quality; buy tongs that are strong and sturdy.

Tongue: Lamb and cow tongue are valuable offal; they must cooked low and slow to tenderize the tough muscle, then peeled. Duck tongues are considered a delicacy in some Asian cuisines.

Tools: See essay Tools, page 35.

Torchon [*tor-SHOHN*]: French for dish towel, *torchon* refers to a preparation of foie gras in which the liver is rolled tightly in cloth, usually cheesecloth, and quickly poached, then chilled, unwrapped, and sliced.

Total utilization: Total utilization is a kitchen idea and practice that means, in effect, throwing nothing away, making use of all your food. An example of total utilization: you buy a chicken to roast; you use the neck and gizzard and wingtips to fortify a pan sauce; you sauté the liver and use it with the salad; the bones of the roasted chicken are reserved and used to make stock that will be the base for soup or the pan sauce for your next roast chicken. Many dishes have their origin in this idea, notably in charcuterie; rilletes, pâtés, and sausages all originated as ways of making use of "scraps."

"To taste": Many recipes instruct the maker to add an ingredient "to taste," commonly salt and pepper. This means what it says; there are many variables that go into a dish and to know an exact amount of seasoning to recommend at the end of a recipe is impractical. So it's up to the cook to taste the food and consider it and add the appropriate amount of the "to taste" ingredient. Taste and consider: does it need more salt, does it need more sweetness or acidity or additional aromatics? Does it need more depth of flavor from an umami ingredient (parmesan cheese or fish sauce)? Also, be careful of powerful ingredients like dried chillis that can vary widely in intensity of flavor and often should be added by taste. It's a valuable cooking maxim: always be tasting.

Touch: Touch is a valuable sense for the cook and a skill to be learned. Its primary use is to gauge doneness, usually in meat, by touching it and evaluating the food's resistance. But touch can also be a source of pleasure to the cook, whether running one's hand along the length of a beautiful fish or pausing to enjoy the texture of freshly rolled pasta dough.

Tourner [*TOR-nay*], **turn:** *Tourner* means to cut a vegetable into an oval shape, often described as a seven-sided football. *Tourneéing,* or turning, takes some practice and extra time, and there's more waste than with more straightforward cuts. If you peel your vegetable first, the trim can be used in numerous ways. Special curved knives called "tourné knives" are available; they won't help you turn vegetables better, only practice will do that. A turned vegetable is used in refined preparations for its elegant appearance.

Toxin: Poisonous compounds are present in a variety of foods, plants and vegetables—alkaloids in potatoes, for instance, cyanide in the pits of some stone fruits—and in some cases are produced in food by microorganisms (the muscle toxin causing botulism is generated by a bacterium). Toxins are often unstable and rendered inert by cooking, but not always.

Trans fat: Trans fats, created by the process of hydrogenation and found in margarine, vegetable shortening, and many processed foods, are believed to raise blood cholesterol. Nutritionists and chefs recommend avoiding trans fats. As a rule, it's always better to use natural fats—vegetable and olive oils, butter, lard—rather than processed fats containing trans fats and to avoid heavily processed foods, which often contains trans fats. Trans fats, because they sometimes melt at higher temperatures than other fats, can result in a greasy feel in the mouth when used in an uncooked preparation such as frosting. Because of widespread acknowledgment in the food industry that trans fats are bad, producers are required to note their presence on nutrition labels, and because more people are avoiding them, companies making food that previously contained trans fats have found alternative processes for solidifying unsaturated fat. Trans fats also occur naturally in small quanties in products such as milk and beef; these cause less concern among nutritionists and need not be avoided the way trans fats in processed food should be avoided.

Trichinosis: Trichinosis is a food-borne sickness caused by a parasitic worm in pork and wild game. The parasite today is almost unheard of in commercial pork, so it is no longer necessary to cook pork to well-done temperatures (see pork). Trichinosis is more often caused by game, such as bear.

Trim, trimmings: Always keep in mind how to put your trimmings to use, whether from vegetables (to be used in stocks) or from meat to be used for any number of purposes, adding meat to stocks or grinding it for sausage, or from fat which can be rendered. Some trim, such as silverskin, other connective tissue, vegetable peelings, is not worth saving; sometimes this trim is distinguished from what's referred to as "useable trim."

Tripe: The lining of the stomachs of the cow requires long slow cooking, optimally in a flavorful stock packed with aromatics. It's got an aroma, flavor, and bite that is its own.

Trotters: The foot of the pig is the focus of a well-known and revered bistro dish of that name; they're braised, often stuffed. The actual trotter is low in meat and high in bones. Contemporary trotter preparations tend to make use of the entire shank to compensate for the lack of meat in the trotter itself. (See pig's feet.)

Turkey: Turkey is an underused meat for eleven months of the year. The breasts when properly cooked are succulent, either roasted or grilled whole or pounded into paillards and sautéed or grilled (because smoke flavors go so well with turkey, grilling is an excellent way to cook turkey). Legs have a lot of cartilage and tendon but are very flavorful and the thighs may be the best part of the bird, meaty and flavorful, and can be roasted or grilled and eaten hot or cold. Turkey bones make an excellent stock and the carcass of a roasted turkey will make abundant quantities. Frozen commercial turkeys are insipid compared with fresh, naturally raised turkeys. Their offal, liver and gizzard, are likewise very flavorful.

U

Umami: Umami is a taste sensation defined by savoriness and depth of flavor. The word is Japanese and translates roughly as the essence of deliciousness. The effect of umami can be felt by tasting a good fresh tomato plain, followed by that same tomato salted. Many foods known to have umami are included in dishes as seasoning to enhance the umami effect, such as fish sauce, parmesan cheese, tomatoes, or mushrooms.

Unmold: To unmold means to remove a preparation from a mold. When what you are unmolding is held together by fat or gelatin, it's helpful to place the mold in hot water to warm the mold and facilitate the unmolding.

Unsalted butter: Unsalted butter is the preference of most chefs; it has a purer flavor and allows the cook to season food to his or her own taste.

Unsaturated fat: See fat.

V

Vanilla: Vanilla, one of the most popular and influential flavors in desserts (and some savory preparations), can be broken down into two categories: the vanilla bean and liquid vanilla (pure and imitation extract). There is no substitute for the vanilla bean, the fermented pod of a tropical orchid, the majority of which are grown in Madagascar. The bean is used in custards and creams, usually by splitting the pod, allowing it to steep in cream (its flavor is fat soluble), then scraping the seeds into the cream and discarding the pod. Used pods can be added to sugar to infuse the sugar with their flavor, a good secondary use for this expensive product. The effect is clean and powerful vanilla flavor. For preparations in which vanilla is a background flavor or seasoning, in cakes, in cookies, innumerable preparations, some form of liquid vanilla is used, which is easier and less expensive than the bean. Pure vanilla extract and imitation vanilla extract, synthesized from various industrial by-products, are commonly available and have a similar impact on flavor.

Vanilla sauce: See crème anglaise.

Variety meats: See offal.

Veal: Veal, male offspring of dairy cows, are slaughtered in the first months of life; the meat is prized for its delicate flavor and texture, the bones and joints for its collagen and neutral flavor. Because the young animal has abundant soft connective tissue, which melts into gelatin, its bones and joints are especially valuable for use in stock, and its tougher cuts, shoulder and shank, are excellent for braises.

Most veal available in stores comes from calves that are confined and fed a soy-formula to keep their meat pale and tender as they grow. "Bob" veal comes from calves that are not confined and are slaughtered during the first weeks of life before they would naturally begin feeding on grasses. The best veal comes from unconfined, unweaned calves. Increasingly veal that is not confined and not fed on formula is available, though this veal may be more red and less delicate.

Veal stock: Veal stock, brown and white (that is, roasted meat and bones or not roasted), is the most versatile and useful stock in the kitchen because of its abundant gelatin and neutral flavor. (See the essay on page 7.)

Vegan: A vegan, an adherent of veganism, does not eat animal products of any kind or anything produced by animals, food such as eggs, milk, and cheese.

Vegetable oil: Vegetable oil is an acceptable all-purpose cooking oil. The quality of various vegetable oils ranges from cheap cottonseed oil to utilitarian corn oil to more expensive grapeseed oil. (See cooking oils.)

Vegetables: In the kitchen vegetables are broken into a few, often overlapping categories: green vegetables (most of which need very little cooking), root vegetables (which, unless eaten raw, need thorough cooking), and aromatic vegetables (which are used to enhance stocks and sauces).

Vegetable shortening: Vegetable oil that's been hydrogenated so that it will remain solid at room temperature is used for baking and for cooking. The hydrogenation can result in trans fats, which may be as bad or worse for you than saturated fat; vegetable shortenings are now often made so that they contain no trans fats. If you use vegetable shortening, choose one with no trans fats.

Vegetarian: someone who eats no animal flesh. There are varying categories of vegetarian, from those who eat no meat but who eat fish to those called vegans, who eat no living animal or animal product.

Velouté: Velouté is a white stock—fish, chicken, or veal—thickened with roux and used as a sauce or soup base (see also mother sauces). It's used for cream soups; clam chowder is typically thickened with roux, for instance.

As a sauce base it brings body and a background flavor to a specific dominant flavor—a *sauce vin blanc,* or white wine sauce, is velouté flavored with wine and shallots; a sauce *allemande* is velouté flavored with mushrooms. Such derivative sauces, or compound sauces, are often finished with butter, cream, or a liaison. (See the essay Sauce, page 12.)

Verjus [*ver-JZOO*]: The juice of unripe grapes, *verjus* is an acidic, fruity liquid that can be used much like vinegar, from seasoning sauces to making vinaigrettes and even sorbet.

Vinaigrette: Vinaigrette should be thought of as a broad sauce category rather than as salad dressing. Some chefs say they think of it as a fifth mother sauce. Its fundamental principle, combining fat, acid, and seasonings to create an acidic sauce, is infinitely variable. The fat can be neutral (canola) or flavorful (bacon fat); the acid can range from lime juice or other citrus to vinegars to *verjus,* and combined with any variety of aromats and spices. The standard ratio for a vinaigrette is one part acid to three parts fat. But depending on the acid, or even personal taste, more or less fat may be needed (more for lime, less for *verjus,* for instance). The basic method is to combine the vinegar and seasonings, including the salt (to allow it to melt), and to whisk in the fat slowly to achieve a homogenous sauce. This will create a temporary emulsion. Using a blender can give you a stable emulsified vinaigrette, and some creamy vinaigrettes are emulsified, via egg yolk, in effect a thin, acidic mayonnaise. Mustard, which has emulsifying properties, is often included in vinaigrettes that must hold their emulsification.

Vinegar: Vinegar is one of the most important seasoning tools available to the cook. It's primary function is to add acidity, one of the fundamental qualities that help determine taste, to an ingredient or finished dish, along with a variety of aromatic notes, depending on the type of vinegar. A dish should almost always be tasted and evaluated for its proper level of acidity just as you evaluate a dish for its level of saltiness; countless dishes can be improved by a last minute addition of few drops of vinegar. Other preparations are wholly dependent on vinegar—the vinaigrette, the Spanish preparation escabeche, the French sweet-sour sauce *aigre-doux.*

Types of vinegars include those made from wine, fruit, grain (malt vinegar), and special vinegars such as balsamic and sherry. Vinegar happens because a specific type of bacteria, such as *acetobacter,* consumes alcohol and creates as a result acetic acid. Vinegar can also be made from pure alcohol to make white and distilled white vinegar, which has no additional aromatic or flavorful compounds.

White vinegar is a good cleaning fluid, and can be used in cooking but is rarely the vinegar of choice. Almost always a good wine vinegar is preferred. The quality of vinegar varies greatly—often, but not always, you get what you pay for. Taste them and evaluate and compare their flavor. When a vinegar is a main component in a dish, it's important to choose a good one. Wine vinegar is the workhorse vinegar in the kitchen, most commonly red, though white should be used when white is appropriate (in a white sauce, for instance) or desired for its flavor.

Better than buying wine vinegar is making your own. You'll need a bacteria culture, a gelatinous mass called a "mother," or "mother of vinegar," which can be bought at specialty stores or over the Internet, or, occasionally, found at the bottom of commercially sold vinegars. Wines added to these and allowed to breathe (the bacteria require oxygen) will become vinegar in two to three months.

Balsamic vinegar is made in Italy from the unfermented juice of special grapes and is aged in barrels. Again quality varies greatly; avoid cheap or generic grocery store balsamic vinegars (which are not true balsamic vinegars). (See balsamic vinegar.) Sherry vinegar, made in Spain, is another vinegar, deeply flavored by the process of aging. Again, when using sherry vinegar, choose a good one (Banyuls, from the eponymous region, is especially prized in the kitchen).

Volume: See measure.

W–Z

Walk-in: A walk-in is a refrigerated room (as distinguished from a "reach-in" cooler).

Water: Water is one of the most important ingredients and tools in the kitchen; its influence is everywhere. Paying attention to the properties and effects of water and knowing how to use them, from its boiling point (which, at sea level, is like a built-in thermostat set at 212°F), to its density, to its capacity to evaporate, to its cooling the contents of a pot, is a fundamental part of cooking.

Water bath: To cook something gently, such as an emulsified butter sauce or a custard or *pâté en terrine,* cooking vessels can be set in or over hot water. The water temperature can't rise above 212°F, ensuring the gentle temperature. (See *bain-marie.*) Ice water baths are used to chill food rapidly—whether cooling a liquid in a pot or shocking a green vegetable—or to hold food at near freezing temperatures. An ice water bath should be composed of a minimum of 50 percent ice; a water bath is not a layer of ice floating on the surface of the water but should appear to have more ice than water.

Waxed paper: Paper coated with wax is a convenient surface on which to cool sticky food, to wrap compound butter in, but for other nonstick, cool temperature uses, it's been almost completely eclipsed by parchment paper. While still preferable for cooling candy, you can't cook with it, so parchment paper is more versatile.

Weigh, weight: Weighing food or measuring solid food by weight is the most effective means of measuring (as opposed to measuring by volume). And even liquids—honey, cream, and oil, for example—in identical volumes can vary in weight. (See measure.)

Well-done: Well-done is a temperature, usually considered to be 150°F or higher, used to describe meat doneness. (It should be noted that braised meats are not finished when they're well-done—they're finished when they're tender.) (See also meat temperatures.)

Wheat: Wheat kernels are composed of the endosperm (the bulk of the kernel), the bran (the covering of the endosperm), and the germ (or embryo). The bran and germ (the latter being particularly nutritious) are what's removed from refined flour. Wheats are mainly distinguished by the quantity of protein they contain, including their gluten content, which gives doughs their elasticity. Flour made from high-gluten wheat is used for bread doughs. Durum wheat is a high-protein wheat, which is ground into semolina flour used for pasta. Whole wheat flour includes the germ and bran of the wheat kernel, which are low in protein; therefore whole wheat flour results in dough that yields a denser finished product. The germ also contains fat, so unless you use your whole wheat flour often, it's best to refrigerate or freeze it well wrapped.

Whey: This by-product of cheese making, the liquid remaining after milk has been curdled for cheese, can be cooked again to make ricotta (which means "recooked").

Whip (noun): This metal utensil used for whipping or whisking is also called a whisk. It's helpful to have at least one large whip for big jobs, egg whites and emulsified sauces (it has better aerating properties and good power), and a small one, called a sauce whip, for smaller jobs such as mounting butter into a sauce (for good control within the confines of the pan).

Whip (verb): The cook can whip food by hand or in a standing mixer with the whip attachment. Whipping is not simply for combining ingredients; it can also emulsify, aerate, and create volume.

Whipped cream: Whipped cream can be an all-purpose garnish for savory or sweet preparations depending on what it's flavored with. It's an enricher that can be salty, acidic, spicy, or sweet. (See also cream.)

Whipping cream: synonymous with heavy cream and heavy whipping cream. Try to avoid "ultra-pasteurized" cream if you intend to whip it, and remember that the colder it is, the easier it is to whip (chill the bowl as well). (See also cream.)

Whisk: See whip.

White sauce: White sauce usually refers to béchamel, but can also refer to velouté, or a béchamel- or velouté-based sauce, to distinguish it from a brown sauce, a sauce with roasted and caramel flavors.

White stock: White stock is stock made from bones that are not roasted and aromatic vegetables that have not been caramelized, to keep the stock pale and subtle. (Brown stocks have a roasted aroma and color, the complex flavors of roasting, and intense sweetness form the caramelization of the vegetables.) If the bones for white stock are not to be blanched first—and this greatly improves the clarity of the finished stock—the cook should carefully skim the stock just after it comes up to heat, removing the coagulated proteins and impurities that first rise to the surface as it does.

Wine (cooking with): Wine is both a seasoning device and a cooking medium. As a rule, don't cook with wine that you wouldn't drink; the better quality wine, the better the result. Usually the sharp, heady effect of alcohol is not desirable in food, so it needs to cook off. If you're using wine in a marinade, it's best to cook off the alcohol (and infuse the wine with aromats), then chill it before making the marinade; this prevents the alcohol from denaturing—in effect, cooking—the surface of the meat.

Wondra: Wondra is the brand name of a so-called "instant" flour, a low-protein flour that has been pre-cooked so that its granules don't clump as they hydrate, making it and other such flours good for delicate batters and pastries, as well as for thickening sauces *à la minute*.

Wood (for smoking): Use only hardwoods for smoking, such as hickory, maple, or apple or other fruitwoods; the latter are often preferred by chefs for their more subtle, nuanced flavor. Do not use softwoods, especially pine or wood from other evergreens (which produce a resinous smoke), green wood, or treated wood, which can give a harsh flavor to what's being smoked.

Wooden spoons: Wooden spoons are invaluable kitchen tools; they're gentle on your pans and gentle on the food. A wooden spoon with a flat end that can slide along the bottom and into the corners of pans is a kitchen essential.

Wrap, wrapper: Food wrappers are a strategy. Wrapping food in edible wrapers, lettuce, grape leaves, tortillas, seaweed, rice paper, wonton skins, can be a compelling and tasty way to serve food or a mechanism for framing food. Cooking food in nonedible wrappers—parchment, banana leaves—can be an effective cooking (steaming) method.

Yeast: Three kinds of commercial yeast are widely available: fresh compressed yeast, which usually comes in 2-ounce cakes, active dry yeast, and instant yeast. Instant yeast is about 25 percent stronger than active dry yeast. Most bakers have used fresh yeast, which can be frozen (though with some decrease in activity), behaves more consistently, and some feel has a better flavor, but more and more bakers are using instant because it's easier to store and lasts longer than fresh. To substitute dry yeast for fresh, use

40 percent active dry yeast, or 33 percent instant yeast by weight. Some bakers prefer wild yeast starter to commercial yeast because it produces a more complex flavor. Wild starter, which contains more than one type of yeast as well as acid-producing bacteria, is made by allowing the natural microflora in the air and the flour to grow in a flour-water mixture. Its fermenting time allows bacteria to generate acid as the yeast releases alcohol and carbon dioxide. Wild yeast can endure this acid, but commercial yeast cannot. Ultimately, the wild yeast can also be overwhelmed by the acid the quickly multiplying bacteria produce if it ferments for too long.

Yolk: Egg yolks are composed of water and a nutritious mixture of proteins and fats. They are invaluable to the cook, both as an ingredient and a tool. As an ingredient, they enrich and add flavor to countless preparations, from savory sauces to sweet desserts. As a tool they help the cook to create emulsified sauces such as the hollandaise and mayonnaise, via the molecule lecithin, and to thicken and enrich sauces such as crème anglaise. (See also egg and the essay Egg, page 22.)

Zest: The zest from citrus fruits, the colorful, oil-rich outer peel, is a powerful seasoning device. The zest can be taken off the fruit in numerous ways, with a paring knife, a vegetable peeler, a zester, or a Microplane. Zesters and Microplanes are most efficient because they separate the outer peel from the white pith, which is bitter. When using a knife or a peeler, you may need to remove the pith. Zest can have traces of bitterness also, so for refined preparations, blanching and shocking zest a few times before using can improve the flavor.

Zester: a tool that removes the zest from citrus fruits; it's convenient if you use a lot of zest, but the same result can be achieved with a knife if your needs for zest are only occasional.

ACKNOWLEDGMENTS

Michael Pardus was my first culinary instructor and my introduction to the professional kitchen. He taught me how to taste stock. He taught me how to salt food. And when I wanted to take the easy way out, he told me he was better than me, that every one of my classmates was better, and this had the desired effect.

The concise way to put it is this. He taught me everything I needed to know in order to learn the rest.

Michael Pardus continues to teach at the Culinary Institute of America, where we first met, and I am enormously grateful that he agreed to read the entire glossary and comment on it, question me, add information, and help me refine information. His help, generosity, curiosity, articulateness, the technical skill and food knowledge developed over more than a quarter century as a professional cook, chef, and teacher have been invaluable to this book.

Just months after completing *The Making of a Chef*, about Pardus and others and learning to cook at the Culinary Institute, I met Thomas Keller, who had three years earlier, in 1994, opened a restaurant in the Napa Valley called The French Laundry. It's a considerable understatement to say that this was my good fortune. If Pardus taught me what I needed to know to learn the rest, the rest began with Keller, who remains among the most respected chefs in the world. So profound was and is his example, so smart, observant, and clear-sighted was and is his approach to cooking, that to isolate what I know from what he taught me or helped me to understand is impossible. During the ten years that I have known him, and through the writing about him and with him, he taught me a lot about food and cooking, but more important by far, he taught me how to see in the kitchen. He taught me how to pay attention.

In addition to Pardus and Keller, I'd also like to thank these chefs, all of them friends, whom I called on for information or confirmation on one point or another: Brian Polcyn, Five Lakes Grill in Milford, Michigan; Dan Hugelier, Schoolcraft College in Livonia, Michigan; Grant Achatz and Curtis Duffy, Alinea in Chicago, Illinois; Michael Symon, Lola, Cleveland; in

243

Manhattan, Rory Herrmann and Jonathan Benno, Per Se, and Eric Ripert, Le Bernardin.

While slugging it out with Pardus at the CIA, I also spent time in a class called Introduction to Gastronomy taught by chef-instructor Bob del Grosso. That he is not currently teaching or cheffing is my good luck because he's had the time to read and comment on this book with the precision of a scientist and the passion of a cook.

To all of these chefs, not only for their help in this book but for their insights into this profession and into cooking, generally, as well as to so many other chefs I've learned from it's impossible to name them all, I am grateful.

Making a book is a team effort. I'm grateful to my friend and agent, Elizabeth Kaplan, my editor at Scribner, Beth Wareham, and the many others at or with Scribner who help turn a manuscript into a book, including Kate Bittman and Virginia McRae.

Finally, ultimately, I am grateful to Donna, Addison, and James, without whom nothing worth anything could happen.

BIBLIOGRAPHY

Child, Julia, Louisette Bertholle, and Simone Beck. *Mastering the Art of French Cooking*. New York: Alfred A. Knopf, 1967.

Culinary Institute of America, the. *The New Professional Chef*. New York: Van Nostrand Reinhold, 2006.

Davidson, Alan. *The Oxford Companion to Food*. Oxford: Oxford University Press, 1999.

de Temmerman, Geneviève, and Didier Chedorge. *The A-Z of French Food*. Arces: Scribo, 1988.

Editors of *Cook's Illustrated*, the. *The New Best Recipe*. Brookline: America's Test Kitchen, 2004.

Escoffier, Auguste. *Escoffier: The Complete Guide to the Art of Modern Cookery*. Translated by H. J. Cracknell and R. J. Kaufmann. New York: Van Nostrand Reinhold, 1979.

Hazan, Marcella. *Essentials of Classic of Italian Cooking*. New York: Alfred A. Knopf, 1995.

Herbst, Sharon Tyler. *The New Food Lover's Companion*. Hauppauge: Barron's Educational Series, 2001.

Keller, Thomas. *The French Laundry Cookbook*. New York: Artisan, 1999.

McGee, Harold. *On Food and Cooking: The Science and Lore of the Kitchen*. New York: Scribner, 2004.

Montagne, Prosper. *Larousse Gastronomique*. Edited by Jenifer Harvey Lang. New York: Crown Publishers, 1995.

Pepin, Jacques. *La Methode*. New York: Times Books, 1979.

———. *La Technique*. New York: Quadrangle/The New York Times Book Co., 1976.

Rodgers, Judy. *The Zuni Cafe Cookbook*. New York: W.W. Norton & Company, 2002.

Rombauer, Irma S., Marion Rombauer Becker, and Ethan Becker. *The All New All Purpose Joy of Cooking*. New York: Scribner, 1997.

Strunk, William, Jr., and E. B. White. *The Elements of Style*. New York: Macmillan, 1979.